Allied Infantry Weapons
of World War Two

ALLIED INFANTRY WEAPONS OF WORLD WAR TWO

Terry Gander

The Crowood Press

First published in 2000 by
The Crowood Press Ltd
Ramsbury, Marlborough
Wiltshire SN8 2HR

British Library Cataloguing-in-Publication Data
A catalogue record for this book is available from the British Library.

ISBN 1 86126 354 6

Typeset by Phoenix Typesetting, Ilkley, West Yorkshire

Printed and bound in Great Britain by The Bath Press

Contents

1   Introduction

It seems that no account of what occurred between 1939 and 1945 can be attempted without reference to the Great War of 1914–18 – many historians regard the Second World War as an extension of the First. This point is emphasized by the fact that in 1939 Allied soldiers went to war with many of the weapons they had last carried in earnest in 1918, but by 1945 the situation had been transformed.

Many of the weapons of 1945 would have been familiar to the soldiers of 1918, but there were a surprising number of innovations introduced during the years after 1939. It is true that in 1945 the bolt action rifle still predominated as the main infantry weapon, but that situation was already being challenged by the self-loading rifle and, to a lesser extent, by the sub-machine gun. The modern assault rifle was to be introduced on a large scale soon after 1945, its form already apparent following the introduction of the German 7.92mm MP43 series. Outside Germany, machine guns remained much as they had been in 1918, although examples such as the Bren gun demonstrated how its form could be lightened and enhanced. Infantry mortars could also throw their lethal projectiles further and at a greater rate.

Yet all these weapon types were common in 1918. Few new weapon categories had been introduced by 1945. Two exceptions were the shoulder-launched Bazooka and the PIAT that enabled the individual soldier to destroy any tank likely to be encountered and replaced the unloved anti-tank rifle. Apart from those innovations the battles of 1939–45 were fought by the Allies using weapons similar to those of 1918.

But there was a prime difference between the two wars, one imposed by the way the Second World War was fought. The Great War was one of human and *matériel* attrition accompanied by a form of static siege warfare. While the Second World War at times witnessed ferocious land battles that outweighed those of the Great War in scale and casualties (especially on the Eastern Front), its main ingredient was mechanization. Machines carried personnel in battles of movement, enabling them to operate at speeds and over distances the soldiers of 1914–18 could not have even contemplated. Within such mobile operations, which extended to airborne and amphibious warfare, the weapons of 1914–18 could survive and function, but in practice they were modified in form and effectiveness. In short, the infantry weapons of 1939–45 became extensions of mobile warfare when machines, including aircraft, assumed roles that once had to be performed by unprotected humans.

Given this situation, the operation of such machines affected the results they could attain, and machines are fallible devices that can be damaged or destroyed. Once it was realized that infantry small arms could be regarded as extensions of modern warfare their provision by industry came to be every bit as important as their employment on the battlefield. Soon after 1939 a continuing reliance on stockpiled weaponry dating from 1918 became dangerous. From 1940 onwards combat demanded and consumed weapons on an unforeseen scale that constantly grew. As the war took on a truly global scale (unlike that of 1914–18) the supply of infantry weapons to the front lines assumed an importance that came a close second to the actual use of those weapons in combat.

The Second World War was thus one of mechanical production as well as mechanized warfare. This was again a carry-over from 1914–18, but by 1939 the importance of defence production had expanded to the extent that it was on a par with military activity. Without the constant supply of weapons and all the other commodities of modern war from the factories, no combat was possible, mechanized or otherwise.

The weapons altered in design terms that made them easier to produce in a shorter time scale and at a lower cost than before, that cost being measured in raw materials, industrial capacity and craft skills as well as money and that finite resource, time. The events of the Second World War often resulted in a scarcity of raw materials for defence production through the disruption of sea and land supply routes. Manufacturing and other resources of all kinds were constantly under pressure while the demands of war imposed continuous demands on skilled personnel and their limited numbers. Weapons production had to change to accommodate such constraints. How well this was achieved is a constant feature of this account. For the Allies, the years 1939 to 1945 were fought as much in the factories as in the fields. Weapons had to be adapted accordingly.

How they were so adapted is a theme running throughout these pages. In short, the skills associated with traditional gun-making were largely abandoned. In their place came simplicity and the

A White M2 Scout Car armed with a 0.50 Browning M2 and a 0.30 Browning M1919A4 towing a 37mm M3 anti-tank gun during a training exercise in the USA.

minimal use of skilled labour, involving as few raw materials as could be devised. Functionality came to matter more than form or appearance. That fact that a weapon worked came to outweigh by far any other considerations.

Thus the Sten and the PPSh–41 sub-machine gun may now be regarded as icons of the Second World War. Apart from their crude appearance and simplicity, they could be readily manufactured by the million, and they were. They were prime examples of how production came to matter as much as combat for the Allies. Not all Allied weapons were as crude as those two examples, for weapons such as the Vickers machine gun, designed during a time when the demands of mass production were not yet a prime consideration, were not amenable to simplification or manufacturing short cuts. Yet by enabling the concentration of scarce skills and resources on these weapons the more modern, 'short-cut' manufacturing methods involved in other weapons could still play their part.

In the last resource, it has to be admitted that the Allies had one major asset that eventually sealed the fate of the Axis powers. That was the combined human, industrial and raw material resources of the United States. That nation was already a major supplier of war *matériel* of all kinds before the USA entered the war in December 1941. Thereafter the USA became the major source of Allied weaponry and war products of all kinds in extraordinary quantities, usually assuming the costs involved from the nation's own financial resources in the form of Lend-Lease.

This was just as well, for by 1941 the United Kingdom was effectively bankrupt and France was temporarily out of the running as a functioning ally. That same year the Soviet Union entered the war, not by choice but by being invaded by Germany, a power hitherto assumed to have been a 'friendly' nation. How the Soviet Union came to evict German forces from its territories and how it eventually occupied much of central Europe has often been described. Not so often recounted is the terrible suffering endured by the peoples of the USSR in not only providing the personnel to fight the invader but the weapons to arm them with . By the end of 1941 the Soviet armed forces were in poor shape, most of their armoury having been either destroyed or captured. In addition, industrial centres had been overrun; those workers and industrial resources surviving were sent east of the Urals, out of reach of the marauding Germans. Somehow the Soviet industrial workforce rose to the challenge to such an extent that by 1945 its output was on a par with, if not actually exceeding, that of the USA. American *matériel* largesse extended to the Soviet Union on a vast scale, but the bulk of Soviet weapons, especially infantry weapons, came from their own designers and factories. The Soviet contribution to the eventual defeat of Nazi Germany cannot be overemphasized and neither can the efforts made by the Soviet workforce.

The Pacific War that led to the defeat of Japan was yet another example of the American nation's industrial might. Despite many initial setbacks and difficult, island-hopping battles, it was American *matériel* superiority that finally ended the Second World War, culminating in the detonation of two weapons that by far outweighed everything that had gone before.

Yet even with the arrival of the atomic bomb it was still the foot soldier who had to occupy the defeated enemy's territory and ensure that the fighting was really over. To accomplish that in the new nuclear age infantry weapons were still needed, as they had been since warfare began. Those weapons are the ones described in these pages.

2 Bolt Action Rifles

For all the nations, Allied and Axis, that participated in the Second World War the predominant infantry weapon was the bolt action rifle. Self-loading rifles certainly made their operational debuts before 1945, but in general the bolt action rifle prevailed.

Technically, the rifle was, at best, obsolescent by 1939. Operational and tactical analysis carried out following the end of the Great War had highlighted a general need for a self-loading, semi-automatic, infantry rifle firing less powerful cartridges than had been the norm from 1914 to 1918. Yet little was done to implement the logical course of action following such findings.

The reasons why were not hard to discover. For a start, so many bolt action rifles had been produced to arm the millions of soldiers involved in the Great War that the huge stockpiles of perfectly serviceable examples left over after the war mitigated economically against the adoption of new designs. Treasuries and governments were more interested in clearing up after the worst conflict yet experienced in Europe, so there were few financial resources to spend on new weapons to repeat the process all over again. The 'war to end all wars' had been fought, the League of Nations was in the process of formation and few could see anything other than peace prevailing for years to come. All over the world, people yearned for normality and home comforts. Why rearm?

Among military establishments there was little call for change. It is an old-established maxim that military organizations tend to be conservative. Despite the lessons of the war, the decision-makers among the staff officers after 1918 and many others of their generation saw no need for any drastic alter-ations in the way their infantry were armed. Bolt action rifles had been adequate between 1914 and 1918, stockpiles were overflowing, trained soldiers knew how to use the relatively simple weapons, the capabilities and limitations of the rifles and their ammunition were well understood, and the drills so beloved by the military were well established. Why rearm?

There were other reasons why changes did not take place, but those outlined above were the main ones. They were backed by the fact that the bolt action rifle of 1914–18 was a powerful, sound and reliable weapon. As well as being well able to with-stand the rigours of service life on the battlefield, the Great War rifles could deliver their lethal, anti-personnel projectiles to ranges of 1,000m/1,100yd or so with reasonable accuracy. At closer ranges their potential firepower was more than acceptable, while, in the last resort, they could act as close-quarter pikes once bayonets had been fixed.

They were also built to last. Therein was one of the major problems faced by the inter-war planners. The rifles of 1914 to 1918 were virtually hand-made from the finest materials available and to close tolerances and high levels of craftsmanship. Yet these attributes were accepted as undesirable by 1918.

Battlefield experience had shown that few infantry encounters took place at ranges of more than 400m/440yd or so. Even at those ranges the conscript armies of the day often had difficulty in aiming and using their rifles to their full potential. The skills and troubles taken to ensure that rifles could deliver accurate fire to 1,000m or more were therefore rarely if ever required by most front-line soldiers. It was also discovered that the combat life of many rifles was short. While soldiers might have to carry and maintain them for months on end, their operational life was usually very limited – many soldiers towards the end of the Great War rarely, if ever, fired their rifles in anger. Too many rifles ended up simply as grave markers.

Many soldiers of the time noted and reported on these factors, but while the war continued there was little that could be done to alter the situation to any significant extent. What mattered was a continuous and uninterrupted flow of rifles to the armies in the field or under training. Any upheavals or modifications that might upset that supply were out of the question. All that usually happened was that some of the finer aspects of the gunsmith's craft were either relaxed or toned down; only rarely were unneeded design features omitted. The rifles of the later Great War years were therefore produced to fairly high standards and remained demanding in time, resources and skilled personnel to manufacture them, all commodities in increasingly short supply as the war imposed its own demands on the home fronts.

All these factors combined to ensure that the Great War bolt action rifles could not simply be cast aside, whatever arguments might be put forward for their replacement. Between 1918 and 1939 there were few calls upon the stockpiled rifles remaining from the Great War years. As a result, the Allied soldiers of 1939 went to war with the same rifles their fathers had known.

Yet within most Allied armies some changes had been introduced by 1939. Working within closely controlled budgetary restrictions, limited modification programmes had been implemented by many countries at least partially to update some of their stockpiled rifles. In a few cases new models were developed, nearly all of them still based on the existing and well-proven bolt action. Only the USA implemented positive steps to adopt a self-loading rifle, although the first examples did not reach the troops until well after the USA entered the Second World War in late 1941. For most other Allied nations the idea of introducing a self-loading rifle

had its attractions. Yet to produce one that would operate as reliably and efficiently as the existing bolt action models was a design and production challenge that few military and industrial establishments could take on during the 1930s.

One aspect of the bolt action rifles used between 1939 and 1945 was their variety. Every Allied nation understandably adopted its own, often home-grown designs, yet despite well-intentioned efforts to impose standardization for logistic, training and other reasons, variations among these versions were bound to arise, and they did. Yet the Allies never had to contemplate the sheer diversity of rifles, calibres and types that the German armed forces had to endure, mainly due to rushed and incomplete industrial preplanning and preparation. No matter how hard German industry attempted to supply the demands of its war machine, shortfalls always remained to be made up by the impressment of captured equipment of all types. The Allies never had to adopt such measures on any scale, other than to meet purely local crises. At times, all manner of old rifles were pressed into Allied service but they never imposed problems such as those presented by the wide array of calibres that German quarter-masters had to cater for. Allied logistic staff and armourers were much better served by having to deal with a relatively limited spectrum of rifles, but even so, the variety of types, models and variants could at times be substantial.

We commence this account with the British bolt action rifles.

LEE-ENFIELDS

For the British and Commonwealth armies of World War II the word 'rifle' meant only one thing, the 0.303 Lee-Enfield. By 1939 the armed forces of Australia, Canada, South Africa, India, New Zealand and the British-administered colonies and territories around the world had decided to abandon any other preferences they may once have had (such as the Canadian selection of the Ross rifle during the Great War) to adopt the Lee-Enfield.

A 0.303 No.1 Mark III rifle.

The name Lee-Enfield was liberally applied. During World War II three distinct models of this rifle were to be encountered: the No.1 Mk III, the No.4 Mk 1 and the No.5 Mk 1. Their differences will be outlined below but it is sufficient to say they all owed their basic outline to a series of rifles with origins in the Lee-Metford rifles of the 1880s. Innovations, such as a revised system of rifling, resulted in a change of designation to Magazine Lee-Enfield in 1895. By the Second Boer War (1899–1902) this was in production for the British Army, replacing all the rifles then in use.

Both the Lee-Metford and the Magazine Lee-Enfield rifle fired a rimmed, bottle-necked 0.303in/7.7mm cartridge. Early bullets had rounded noses, later changed to more pointed and stream-lined 'spitzer' bullets, providing better external ballistics but which meant that revised sighting arrangements had to be introduced. Nearly all the standard issue anti-personnel Ball bullets were lead, covered by a cupro-nickel jacket. The brass cartridge cases were rimmed at the base and filled with cordite for the propellant (early cartridges for the Lee-Metfords contained black powder). Cases were a nominal 56mm long so the metric designation for the 0.303 cartridge is 7.7 × 56R (bullet calibre: 7.7mm, cartridge case length: 56mm, R: rimmed). Over the years numerous projectiles other than Ball were introduced, from tracer to incendiary and armour-piercing but in numerical terms the ordinary Ball cartridge predominated as far as rifle users were concerned.

The Magazine Lee-Enfield rifles had an overall length of just over 1.25m/49.2in. Cavalry units considered this was too long for their requirements so they asked for a shorter carbine version. Other arms of the service, such as the artillery and combat engineers, also requested carbines because they would be handier to carry and use as adjuncts to their normal combat activities. Experience in South Africa also demonstrated that the Magazine Lee-Enfield was really too long and awkward for comfortable carrying and handling. For once, staff planners listened to the soldiers in the field. In 1902 a series of trials took place with the intention of providing one model of rifle acceptable to all.

The result was the Short Magazine Lee-Enfield Mk 1, or SMLE. Adopted in late 1902, the SMLE had an overall length of 1.133m/44.6in, not much shorter than the original (which became the Long Magazine Lee-Enfield) but enough to satisfy all users, including the cavalry, the Royal Navy and the Royal Marines, while bringing the benefits of standardization to all. The SMLE also introduced several features thought necessary as the result of experience in South Africa. These included a charger guide to assist in rapid-loading the five-round chargers used to fill the ten-round box magazine and wooden hand-guards that completely enshrouded the barrel. The 0.303 cartridge was carried over.

Modifications imposed by service experience were gradually introduced to the extent that the SMLE Mk III emerged in 1907. It was this rifle, to

Royal Engineers searching for the edge of a minefield while carrying 0.303 No.1 Mark III rifles.

be renamed the No.1 Mk III in 1926 as part of a paperwork tidying-up exercise, that became the basis of the rifles that were to serve British and Commonwealth armies for over fifty years.

The Mk III handled well. Not only was it handy to carry but the bolt action was smooth to operate and functioned well even under the worst conditions of the Western Front. By 1914 a trained soldier could fire at least fifteen aimed shots a minute – experts could squeeze off many more. A long bayonet (about 17in/432mm long) was issued with every rifle, as was a small oil bottle and a cord pull-through for cleaning the inside of the barrel; these latter items were stowed behind a small trap in the

buttplate. The rifle was carried on a webbing or leather sling.

The Mk III featured a sliding closure device known as the cut-off. This acted as a loading table across the top of the magazine to seal it off after it had been fully loaded. Single rounds were then hand-loaded on to the cut-off to be chambered as the bolt was closed for each shot without disturbing the magazine's contents. The intention was that fire could be kept under strict control to prevent ammunition wastage, while the loaded magazine could be conserved until the tactical situation demanded its full potential. The cut-off was not considered essential so that late production SMLE variants dispensed with the cut-off altogether, although provision continued to be made for one even on some No.4 rifles.

In retrospect, the sighting arrangements seemed rather optimistic. The rearsights were calibrated up to 2,000yd/1,830m, with another device known as a long-range sight (or dial sight) located on the left-hand side of the handguard. This was a short, open, sight arm swivelling on a range scale calibrated up to 2,800yd/2,560m. It was not intended for accurate individual use but was meant to be used by several soldiers firing together, each using his long-range sight to direct controlled volleys at a general area.

The intention was to cover the target area with suppressive fire rather than actually to hit a specific target. This was another idea emanating from the so-called 'Bisley School' of marksmanship, a group of officers and target-match riflemen who became highly influential in service rifle matters during the early 1900s. They called for soldiers to be trained to deliver long-range rifle fire, believing that much of their fighting would be carried out at extreme ranges. Once close-range trench warfare became established during the Great War there was little or no call for such niceties so the long-range sight was no longer provided. (Rifles with cut-offs and

Soldiers practising house-searching drills carrying No.1 Mark III rifles. From the camouflaged helmets this could have been on Malta.

long-range sights were still being issued for cadet training during the early 1950s, as the author can testify.)

Rifles with extras such as the cut-off and the long-range sight omitted, along with some other details, to hasten and assist manufacture were designated the No.1 Mk III*. This entered production during 1915 at a time when the demand for rifles to arm the rapidly expanding British Army was reaching crisis level. Any production short cuts were therefore valuable yet the No.1 Mk III* was still almost entirely hand-made and finished, down to small details.

The No.1 Mk III* became the most numerous of all the SMLE rifles by far. It was produced not only at the Royal Small Arms Factory at Enfield Lock, just to the north of London (hence the name Enfield) but at numerous other factories and sub-contractors. British production lines were also established by BSA at Sparkbrook, Birmingham and LSA at Old Ford, London. Numerous other firms became involved as sub-contractors for components and production tools. By the end of 1918 British production of the SMLE had reached 3,854,106, Enfield Lock alone supplying just over two million.

Planning for further production of the No.1 Mk III* began again during the late 1930s to anticipate the likely demands of the coming war. BSA established a SMLE production line at their Small Heath facility, the line remaining active until late 1943. This facility also reconditioned many old SMLEs, as well as assembling complete rifles from old or cannibalized spare parts. Even after 1943 the manu-facture of spare SMLE components continued for some time at several BSA factories around Birmingham.

The same model was also adopted by Australia and India. These two nations introduced the No.1 Mk III* to their own production lines, both of which continued to produce the rifle for many years after British-based production initially tailed off during 1919. Australian manufacture of the No.1 Mk III* centred around Lithgow, New South Wales, until 1955; their final production total between 1939 and 1955 was 415,800. Part of the early Australian output was diverted to the United Kingdom during the Great War, the same happening again following the Dunkirk evacuation of 1940.

Australian production methods and materials meant that small differences from the 'British' rifles were inevitably introduced. The same happened with the Indian SMLEs. Their main production centre was the Rifle Factory at Ishapore, where SMLEs in several forms remained in production until the end of the 1950s at least; the production total between 1939 and 1945 was about 700,000, including some reconditioned examples. As late as 1963 about 250,000 of these old 0.303 rifles were re-engineered to accommodate the more powerful 7.62×51mm NATO cartridge; that programme continued until 1970. These remain in Indian service to this day, usually with police, border guards or internal security forces. A sporting rifle based on the SMLE is still available commercially from Indian Ordnance Factories, although these are likely to be rebuilt examples.

The earlier mention of Dunkirk prompts comment on the loss of over 300,000 rifles, plus stocks of 0.303 ammunition, when the British Expeditionary Force (BEF) left France in May and June 1940. This total was more than enough to equip several German infantry divisions based in France; they knew the SMLE as the 7.7mm *Gewehr* 281(e), the (e) denoting *englisch*.

For the Allies, the SMLE (No.1 Mks III and III*) was still in widespread service in 1945, although by then it was largely relegated to training, home defence and garrison duties. Also likely to be

---

Rifle No.1 Mk III*

Calibre	7.7mm; 0.303in
Length	1.133m; 44.6in
Length of barrel	640mm; 25.2in
Weight	3.93kg; 8.656lb
Muzzle velocity	634m/s; 2,080ft/s
Feed	10-round box magazine

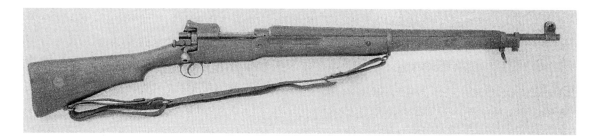

The handsome lines of the 0.303 P14 rifle.

encountered was the old Long Magazine Lee-Enfield. After Dunkirk rifles were in such short supply that even those veterans from the Boer War era were withdrawn from dusty storerooms and issued to the Home Guard or to units guarding airfields, factories and other important buildings and localities. Canadian Ross rifles from the Great War also found their way across the Atlantic for such duties.

The No.1 Mk III* proved to be an excellent all-round service rifle, but it was not renowned for pin-point accuracy, even if trained marksmen could produce startling results. When special sniper weapons were called for during the Great War selected rifles were equipped with telescopic sights and proved to be satisfactory enough but they never managed to attain the standards of accuracy that some others could attain, especially those provided with Mauser-based bolt actions and heavy barrels. The nearest the No.1 Mk III series came to such standards were the special rifles provided with heavy barrels by the Australians towards the end of World War 2.

P14 INTERLUDE

At this point a diversion must be made to cover the rifle that became known to the British as the Rifle No.3 Mk 1. This was a complete departure from the Lee-Enfield family as it was designed in response to a stream of complaints relating to the SMLE from

the Bisley School of rifle enthusiasts. This vocal group found many faults with the No.1 Mk III, ranging from poor accuracy to many matters of detail, but accuracy was always its prime complaint. The No.1 Mk III, as has been mentioned, was not a specialist marksman's rifle but a sound, all-round service weapon. This cut no ice with the Bisley School which pressed for an alternative more to its liking.

Such was its influence that a design based on a modified form of the Mauser front-locking lug bolt action (the Lee-Enfield used a single rear-locking lug which was considered as too variable in operation for consistent accuracy) appeared in 1913. Known as the Pattern 13, or P13, the new rifle fired a powerful 0.276in/7mm cartridge that did away with the rim of the 0.303 round, another factor the Bisley School did not favour. The P13 promised to be everything its protagonists had called for. It was accurate (it had the adjustable aperture backsights deemed essential by the Bisley School), handled well and the bullet retained its excellent ballistics at extreme ranges.

In 1914 the P14 appeared, embodying modifications found necessary during a series of trials. Matters were on course for the P14 to be adopted to replace the Lee-Enfield altogether, but the events following August 1914 changed all that. The very idea of a switch to a new service rifle during a major war was enough to ensure that further P14 development was shelved.

It was not relegated for very long. By 1915 the

need for service rifles to arm the expanding ranks of Kitchener's Army had reached crisis level. Alternatives had to be considered and the P14 was one option. With a change of calibre to 0.303 the P14 was accepted; it later became the Rifle No.3 Mk 1, but was usually known as the P14. By the time it had been accepted production proved to be a further obstacle. All British factories capable of making rifles were already working at full stretch and so American firms were asked to help out. Winchester and Remington responded to the extent that P14s were soon pouring off three dedicated assembly lines.

There were problems however. The P14 had never been as fully developed as it should have been and thus some features of the design proved to be awkward, the overall length of 1.175m/46.25in being one drawback as far as front-line soldiers were concerned. The rush to production in the US also brought problems with the interchangeability of spare parts in its wake. At the time such inconveniences had to be accepted, but the P14s, named by the Americans as the Enfield to differentiate it from their own Springfield (of which more later), never did gain the same level of British acceptance as the Lee-Enfield series. However, the inherent accuracy of the P14 proved invaluable once the British Army had accepted a need for snipers. Equipped with telescopic sights, the P14 became the 'British' preferred weapon for the role. Few non-sniper P14s were seen on the Western Front, the bulk of the output being diverted to training and guard duties in Britain. By the time the first examples had been shipped over the British rifle production demand and supply situation was easing somewhat.

At this point the P14 story becomes more international. By 1917 the British P14 contracts were being run down in the US just as the Americans became aware they were about to become involved in the Great War. Production capacity for the American Springfield rifle was way below what would be required to equip the new US Army divisions so another twist in the P14 story occurred. It was decided to adopt the P14 as an expedient service

rifle, but to adopt it unchanged from the British standard was not even considered. For a start, the drawback of the interchangeability of spare parts was considered unacceptable for the US Army, as was the 0.303 cartridge. Despite the many calls for rifles, some time was taken to eradicate the interchangeability problem and the calibre was altered so that the new rifle, known as the M1917, could fire the standard US 0.30-06 cartridge.

An indication of the capabilities of the US small arms industry of 1917–18 was that in about a year a production total of 2,202,429 M1917s had been reached. They saw service on the Western Front, but as soon as the Great War ended the majority were immediately directed to storage. Relatively small batches were sold or passed to Belgium (where they were provided with 7.92mm barrels) and the new Baltic states.

In 1940 US M1917s were still stacked in armouries. It was just as well, for in that same year the British Army was faced with the danger of a German invasion at a time when the bulk of their available weapon stocks had been left in France. The USA sent over about 615,000 M1917s from their stockpiles to provide rifles for the Home Guard at a knock-down cost of $7.50 each; a further 119,000 M1917s followed during 1941. To ensure that enough ammunition was available to be fired from these weapons (and the other rifle-calibre weapons sent over at the same time), the American government also delivered over 138 million 0.30-06 rounds.

These rifles considerably relieved the British

A Home Guard training with a 0.30 M1917 rifle.

armed forces' shortage, for it meant that all available Lee-Enfields could be released for front-line duties. M1917s ended up on many merchant ships, including fishing boats, while others were carried by Royal Navy minesweepers. Once again, many M1917s were converted for the sniping role. As the British rifle supply position eased, M1917s were released from holdings to be para-dropped into occupied Europe to arm resistance groups.

US largesse was also extended to China. From 1941 onwards a precise total of 152,241 M1917s were sent there while a further 40,000 went to other countries in the Far East and elsewhere.

THE No.4

To return to the Lee-Enfield saga: from 1941 onwards the preferred front-line model was the No.4 Mk 1, although it never completely supplanted the old No.1 Mk III rifle before 1945. The No.4 had its origins in the rifle production difficulties of the Great War years. No.1 rifles, even when manufacturing short cuts had been introduced, were expensive in materials, resources and, most important of all, in the skilled hand-finishing of almost every component. Some method of easing manufacture had to be found. The only answer was a complete redesign.

Comparison between a No.1 Mark III (left) and a No.4 Mark 1 (right); the No.4 sports a weatherproof cover for the bolt action.

The process commenced as early as 1924 with a series of trial rifles known initially as the No.1 Mk V. Although this was still identifiable as a Lee-Enfield, numerous modifications were introduced, most of them intended to assist their anticipated mass production. Troop trials with the No.1 Mk VI, introduced in 1926, continued until the early 1930s. In 1931 the design was accepted for service as the No.4 Mk 1.

Changes from the No.1 Mk III and III* included a strengthened bolt action and receiver, a heavier barrel that protruded from the forward handguard, a relocation of the backsights to a position over the receiver, plus numerous changes of detail to speed production. One oddity was that the cut-out was reintroduced, only to be omitted later. Even the former knife-pattern bayonet was replaced by a short 8in/203mm cruciform blade, later reduced to a simple spike.

The end result, apart from easier manufacture, was a great improvement over the earlier models. Although the total length remained about the same as before, the combination of a heavier barrel and an increased sight radius meant that the potential accuracy was much enhanced at ranges up to about 800yd/875m. After that, the old No.1 Mk III series had the accuracy edge. Once again, the venerable 0.303 cartridge was carried over.

Although the design of the No.4 Mk 1 had been established by the end of 1933, mass production did not start until late 1940. Before then some short production runs had been established for 'educational' purposes at a number of manufacturing centres, including Enfield Lock, but the numbers involved were small as the necessary funds for large-scale production were not yet available.

When mass production did begin in late 1940, Enfield Lock, the traditional home of the Lee-Enfield, was destined never to manufacture the No.4 Mk 1. Production became centred at the Royal Ordnance Factories at Fazakerley (near Liverpool) and Maltby (near Sheffield). Another line was established by BSA at Shirley. Numerous sub-contractors were involved in components manufacture to the extent that the controlling of the flow of components to the main manufacturing centres became a major management achievement in itself. Total British production of the No.4 had reached just over two million by the time the war ended. Production at Fazakerley did not cease until 1956.

Despite the establishment of the three main production centres in Britain it became apparent that yet more rifles would be needed. Once again,

the United States were asked to help out and, as before, they did so with a will. Not content with manufacturing No.4 rifles in the USA, the American government also paid for them in the form of Lend-Lease. US production was centred around the Savage Arms Corporation facility at Chicopee Falls, Massachusetts, while another line was created in Canada by Small Arms Ltd at Long Branch, Ontario. The number of No.4 rifles from

The No.4 Mark 1in action with Canadian troops in Italy.

An unusual illustration of a No.4 Mark 1 in action alongside a German 9mm MP40 sub-machine gun.

these two factories between 1941 and 1945 reached 1,236,706. All but 40,000 of this total (which went to China) were destined for the British and Commonwealth armies. Two thirds of the Long Branch output was retained for the Canadian armed forces. Out of the Long Branch output of 952,000,

Rifle No.4 Mk 1

Calibre	7.7mm; 0.303in
Length	1.13m; 44.43in
Length of barrel	640mm; 25.2in
Weight	4.14kg; 9.125lb
Muzzle velocity	751m/s; 2,465ft/s
Feed	10-round box magazine

some 330,000 were despatched to Britain.

The North American rifles featured extra production short cuts, some of which were also adopted in Britain. For instance, the original precision leaf sights calibrated up to 1,300yd/1,120m were replaced by a simple, hinged battle-sight intended for combat conditions at 300 and 600yd (275 and 550m). Although the sight would be frowned upon by most marksmen, the simple device proved to be perfectly satisfactory during most combat encounters. Another short cut was the provision of only two rifling grooves in place of the original six. Once again, this measure proved perfectly satisfactory once in service. Wherever possible, machined components, such as the foresight guards, were replaced by stampings. One item noticeable to any soldier was a revised and simpler method of removing the bolt for cleaning. North American

The sniper's weapon, the 0.303 No.1 Mark 4(T).

rifles with these short cuts embodied were known as the No.4 Mk 1*.

Even with the combined British and North American production, it was late 1942 before the No.4 could be issued on any significant front-line scale, and even then only to special formations such as the airborne brigades. The North African and most of the Italian campaigns were conducted using the old No.1 rifles, but by the end of the war the No.4 was well established and the No.1 had been relegated to second-line duties. The Australian and Indian armies continued to utilize their local facilities to manufacture the No.1. India never adopted the No.4, while Australia accepted a batch in 1942 only as a stopgap measure to ease the local supply situation.

The main combat variant of the No.4 Mk 1 was the No.4 Mk 1(T). This was a converted No.4 Mk 1 or 1* with a No.32 telescopic sight (although other sight models were involved) and a cheek piece. Selected rifles were sent to Enfield Lock or Holland & Holland to be stripped and restocked before the sight mountings were carefully installed. After careful alignment, the sight and the rifle were then permanently 'paired'. The result remained the standard British sniper rifle for many years after 1945.

After 1945 the No.4 Mk 1 continued to be manufactured in a variety of different forms, the most drastic being its conversion to fire the 7.62×51mm NATO cartridge. But it was not until 1992 that the last of the Lee-Enfield rifles based on the No.4 was phased out of service. That was the 7.62mm L42A1 sniper rifle. By then Lee-Enfield rifles had served with the British armed forces for over a hundred years. Some still remain in British armouries for target shooting.

JUNGLY No.5

There was one other Lee-Enfield rifle introduced before the end of the fighting in 1945, the Rifle No.5 Mk 1, a cut-down version of the No.4 intended for use in the jungles of the Far Eastern theatre. It retained most of the features of the No.4, but the length was reduced to just over 1m by cutting back the barrel, adding a conical flash hider to the muzzle, removing weight where possible and modifying the forestock accordingly. The muzzle attachment was highly necessary, since firing the powerful 0.303 cartridge from a shortened barrel resulted in considerable muzzle flash, plus a sharp recoil that necessitated the provision of a rubber butt pad to partially reduce the effects on the firer's shoulder. An 8in/203mm knife-pattern bayonet was reintroduced for the No.5.

The No.5 rifle was originally an offshoot from a programme intended to lighten the No.4. Cutting back the barrel was but one measure investigated from 1942 onwards. The resultant flash and recoil drawbacks were acknowledged as such, but

Side view of the attenuated 0.303 No.5 Mark 1.

accuracy seemed to be reasonable up to about 500yd/460m so trials continued until an initial batch of rifles was manufactured at Fazakerley during mid-1944; BSA later became involved in No.5 production. By the end of 1944 No.5 Mk 1 rifles were in use in the Far East, where their handiness and reduced weight proved to be highly acceptable, leading to its name of 'Jungle Carbine'. About 50,000 were issued.

Yet the No.5 never became a popular weapon. The excessive flash and recoil were never eliminated, while it soon became noticeable that accuracy started to suffer after only a limited amount of service use – 'wandering zero'. This was eventually traced to a weakened interface between the receiver and the barrel, a side effect of attempts to reduce the weight as much as possible. The 'wandering zero' was finally laid to rest with the revised No.5 Mk II but this model was never accepted for service. In addition to the accuracy problem, barrel wear was

deemed excessive to the extent that barrels had to be changed too frequently for logistic and maintenance acceptability.

After 1945 there were times when it seemed likely that the handier No.5 would eventually replace the No.4 as the British service rifle, but it never happened. The troubles inherent in the No.5 were eventually deemed to be too many to be overcome while the prospects of a self-loading rifle were regarded as more promising than had once been thought possible. The type was therefore officially declared obsolete in July 1947, making the No.5 the shortest-lived of all the service Lee-Enfields. Even after that date some production continued so the No.5 served on with the British Army in Malaya and elsewhere and with several Commonwealth armed forces.

Attempts to produce shortened No.1 rifles were made in India and Australia between 1942 and 1945; the Australian design would have been the Rifle No.6. None got past the troop-trial stage. Canada developed a carbine based on the No.4 but only about fifty were ever manufactured.

One footnote to the No.5 story was that, once its production had ceased at Fazakerley, the lines reverted to the No.4, but this time with a revised trigger mechanism that resulted in the No.4 Mk II. In addition, the No.4 Mk 1* went back into production at the Canadian Long Branch facility in 1949 and 1950 to meet the demands of the Korean War, just under 50,000 examples being manufactured.

Rifle No.5 Mk 1	
Calibre	7.7mm; 0.303in
Length	1.003m; 39.5in
Length of barrel	476mm; 18.75in
Weight	3.25kg; 7.15lb
Muzzle velocity	731m/s; 2,400ft/s
Feed	10-round box magazine

DE LISLE

Before leaving the Lee-Enfield saga, mention must be made of an odd diversion of the Lee-Enfield family into the field of suppressed weapons. The advantages for special forces (and others) of a firearm with a reduced firing signature are self-evident, but as most of such weapons are specifically designed for special forces they do not often intrude into the usual histories of firearms. The weapon known as the De Lisle Carbine did, for it was based on the Lee-Enfield No.1 Mk III.

The De Lisle Carbine started life as a silenced 0.22 sporting rifle devised to allow a Berkshire-based engineer named William De Lisle to augment his family's meat intake with rabbits taken without his disturbing the neighbours. His home-made conversion came to the attention of the authorities dealing with weapons for possible covert military use so it became more 'official'. A silencer test-bed chambered for 9 × 19mm Parabellum ammunition was devised, but the supersonic bullet proved troublesome. A change to subsonic 0.45 ACP ammunition proved more successful and so it was decided to adapt old Lee-Enfield rifles to accommodate this pistol round and a De Lisle pattern silencer, more accurately described as a suppressor.

A batch of surplus Lee-Enfield No.1 Mk III rifles was sent to the Ford Motor Company at Dagenham where seventeen conversions were eventually

De Lisle Carbine	
Calibre	11.43mm; 0.45in
Length	908mm; 35.75in
Length of barrel	184mm; 7.25in
Weight	3.7kg; 8.25lb
Muzzle velocity	N/A
Feed	7-round box magazine

made. These proved that the 0.45 De Lisle Carbine could operate as required, although it was never completely silent on firing. As far as the target was concerned, at 50m/55yd some noise could be heard but it was difficult to recognize it as a rifle shot. Beyond that distance nothing could be heard. As a bonus there was no muzzle flash.

Converting the Lee-Enfields to 0.45 calibre was no straightforward task. It took time and a great deal of skill on the part of the gunsmiths involved and, as far as they were concerned, they already had enough to do. A production contract for an initial 500 carbines was therefore moved to the Sterling Engineering Company, just down the road from Fords. The Sterling De Lisle carbines differed in several respects from the Ford batch, one instance being the introduction of modified Thompson sub-machine gun barrels. They were modified by inserting gas vents along the bore to allow firing

The De Lisle carbine; note the suppressor housing around the barrel and the small magazine for the 0.45 ACP ammunition.

gases to enter a series of sound baffles before the bullet left the muzzle, reducing the firing signature in the process. The barrel and baffles were surrounded by a light alloy sleeve (originally drawn steel).

Mating 0.45 Thompson barrels to 0.303 Lee-Enfield bolt actions was no easy matter, especially as many of the actions were well worn. Interchangeability of the associated parts between carbines proved impossible as almost every component had to be hand-finished to fit one particular carbine, the only 'original' Lee-Enfield component left over being the wooden butt. Even the 0.45 M1911 pistol seven-round magazine involved had to be altered. The conversions therefore took time and were expensive.

Almost as soon as they left the Sterling factory, finished Carbines were whisked off to occupied Europe or issued to Commando units. In the event only about 125 De Lisle carbines were finished

before the contract was cancelled, one of them being intended for airborne use by having a folding butt. Almost all the completed De Lisle carbines were destroyed after 1945 to prevent them falling into hands considered dangerous.

Operational records regarding the De Lisle carbine are sparse although they were certainly fired in anger during many clandestine missions. Their virtual silence at ranges up to an intended 400m/440yd made them valuable weapons on occasion, even though to fire pistol ammunition from a relatively short barrel (only 184mm/7.25in) resulted in poor accuracy at longer ranges.

SPRINGFIELDS

The US Army has always been exacting about its service firearms, to the extent that any change of rifle policy has always been met with close scrutiny

Cheerful-looking US troops posing for the camera during training in Australia; the rifles are Springfields.

The clean lines of the classic M1903 rifle with its Model 1905 bayonet.

from a wide audience. Yet in 1903, when a new rifle was adopted to replace the old Krag-Jorgensen, there appear to have been few complaints. The new rifle was the Model 1903 (M1903), a design based on the German Mauser 98, but with numerous changes introduced to suit American requirements, coupled with a new 0.30 (7.62mm) cartridge. The designers of the M1903 followed the same lines as the British SMLE in that one model of slightly less than the then-usual length was available for the infantry, the cavalry and all other users.

The M1903, named the Springfield after the Springfield Armory where it was first made, turned out to be a remarkable rifle. Not only was it accurate and reliable but it had excellent handling qualities and was made with good materials finished to a high degree (it remains a collectors' classic). Yet, despite all its virtues, the M1903 did not last long in its original form.

The main reason for this was the cartridge, the 0.30-03. This had a rounded bullet, replaced in 1906 by a pointed 'spitzer' bullet. This, allied to a slight reduction in case length, resulted in the 0.30-06, the 06 denoting the year-of-type classification. The adoption of this 7.62 × 63mm cartridge meant that all M1903 rifles produced up to 1906 had to be virtually rebuilt to accommodate all the necessary changes.

The 0.30-06 round proved to excellent for its role. It remains in production to this day, although now mainly for target shooters and hunters. The main nature used between 1940 and 1945 was the Ball M2, although many other types were developed and issued. The total American production of 0.30-06 ammunition from 1940 until 1945 reached 25,065,834,000 rounds (not all of them destined for rifles).

The USA entered the Great War in 1917 with an inventory of about 600,000 M1903 rifles. This soon proved to be insufficient to arm the expanding US Army, even with an additional production facility established at the Rock Island Arsenal, and so recourse was made to the expedient M1917 rifle mentioned earlier. The procurement of the M1917 was made doubly necessary by government cutbacks in defence spending introduced as late as 1917. These meant that skilled workers laid off at both Springfield and Rock Island were being dispersed just as the USA entered the war. Getting the two government establishments back into full production was not easy at a time when skilled personnel were needed for every aspect of defence production. Consequently the production of M1903s before 1919 was a modest 312,878. By any normal yardstick this was a significant total but it was small compared with the output of the M1917 during the same period (over two million).

Production was not assisted by the design of the M1903. This involved hand operations at every stage of manufacture. The reward for this came in the excellent accuracy and ease of handling already mentioned, yet by the early 1940s the manufacturing demands imposed by the original M1903 were considered unacceptable. Thus in May 1942, even though the M1 Garand had already been adopted (*see* Chapter 3), the M1903A3 was type classified with numerous measures introduced to reduce the necessary number of manufacturing processes. The introduction of the M1903A3 emphasized the unwelcome fact that the M1 Garand was not yet being manufactured on the scale necessary to equip the once again expanding number of Americans in uniform. As the Springfield Armory was tooling up for the M1 Garand, Remington became involved in M1903A3 production, as did the Smith-Corona Typewriter Corporation. (The interim M1903A1, introduced in late 1929, featured a butt stock with an integral pistol grip but with few other significant changes. The M1903A2 was not an infantry rifle but a sub-calibre device used during artillery training.)

Many American servicemen never did encounter the M1 before the war ended in 1945. Among the first waves of soldiers landing in Normandy in June 1944 were units still equipped with M1903 series rifles. Even as the war ended many second-line units still carried Springfields. Few US Navy personnel ever saw an M1 Garand.

Most World War Two servicemen not provided with the M1 were increasingly issued with the M1903A3 Springfield. This model outwardly resembled the earlier models, apart from the less involved finish, but closer examination revealed several components produced by stamping or other

M1903A3	
Calibre	7.62mm; 0.30in
Length	1.105m; 43.5in
Length of barrel	601mm; 24in
Weight	3.63kg; 8lb
Muzzle velocity	858m/s; 2,805ft/s
Feed	5-round box magazine

production short cuts. The sights were rearranged and simplified while barrels with six or even two rifling grooves were introduced in place of the usual four. These alterations did little to reduce the handling and serviceability of the Springfield and the overall dimensions remained much the same as before. One bonus was that the weight was reduced slightly, from the 3.94kg/8.7lb of the base M1903 to 3.63kg/8lb for the M1903A3. In general, the M1903A3 was a good service rifle, even if it lacked the refinements of the earlier models. It is still sought after by competition shooters.

As more and more M1s were issued the numbers of Springfields in US service declined in proportion and so did the production flows. Production of the M1903A3 finally ceased in February 1944. By then

The mass-production model, the M1903A3 Springfield rifle.

Remington and Smith-Corona had manufactured 1,318,951 between them (including M1903A4 sniper rifles). Even after February 1944 Remington continued to make spare parts for the M1903A3.

As they were withdrawn from US service, Springfields were handed out to numerous forces, regular and irregular. This process had started as early as 1940, for, among the rifles sent over to the Britain after Dunkirk, were 64,003 Springfields for the Home Guard, further depleting the stocks that would later be required by the American armed forces. The British government went so far as to place contracts for new Springfields, but, in the event, they were taken over by the US government and no new Springfields ever reached the British armed forces.

As during the Great War, the United States acted as the arsenal for the Allies, the Springfield being but one item among many handed out freely and in abundance. For example, Chinese forces received 107,470 Springfields. It became the service rifle of many post-1945 armies in Europe and elsewhere, a typical example being France. Before 1945 11,015 Springfields were issued to the Free French forces; more were issued to French resistance units.

As mentioned earlier, there was one further variant of the M1903 series, the M1903A4, which was produced from late 1942 onwards. This was a dedicated sniper's rifle for it completely lacked the usual iron sights; they were replaced by a M73B1 × 2.5 telescopic sight. Other changes included a pistol grip stock and a revised bolt handle. During 1943 and 1944 28,365 were produced, some of which survived into the Korean War period. The US Marine Corps had its own variant, the Model 1942.

This was a M1903A1 with the addition of a x10 telescopic sight.

THE SOVIET UNION

For the Soviet armed forces there was only one service rifle, the Mosin-Nagant. Self-loaders and sub-machine guns may have become part of the Soviet armoury by 1945, but the Mosin-Nagant outnumbered them all and was issued to every branch of the Soviet armed forces. The Mosin-Nagant also had the distinction of being the oldest design of all the Allied rifles still in use in 1945, for it was adopted as far back as 1891.

The Mosin-Nagant rifles were originally designed by one Sergey Ivanovich Mosin. He adapted a rather complicated bolt action devised by the Belgian Nagant brothers (Emile and Leon) for a rather long (1.3 m/51.2in) magazine rifle that became known as the *3-lineya vintovka obr 1891g* (3-line rifle Model 1891). The 3-line feature of this designation refers to an old Russian system of measurement indicating a calibre of 0.30 in/7.62mm (1 line equalled 0.1in almost exactly).

This Model 1891 remained the basis of the weapon still in service in 1945. The bolt action may have been complicated but it proved reliable enough and remained virtually unchanged until the end. Initially there were three variants, one for the infantry, a so-called dragoon model and another for Cossack cavalry. There was also a Model 1907 carbine.

As happened with other rifles of the period, the cartridge was changed after 1908 when a new

Soviet classic – the Mosin-Nagant 7.62mm Model 1891/30.

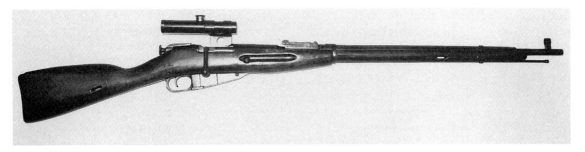

The sniper version of the Model 1891/30, seen here with a PU optical sight.

pointed 'spitzer' bullet was introduced, resulting in the replacement of the rear sights. The rimmed cartridge, the 7.62 × 54R, is still in widespread use with the former Eastern Bloc and other nations to this day, with no signs of its slipping from favour. This therefore is the longest surviving of any of the current service rifle cartridges, although these days it is usually fired from machine guns.

One feature of the Mosin-Nagant rifles was a long cruciform-pattern bayonet that seems to have been carried as an almost permanent fixture on the rifle. This made the rifle/bayonet combination a lengthy weapon to carry and use (1.66m/65.4in), especially in confined spaces, but that never seems to have bothered the Tsarist forces or their Soviet successors. The integral box magazine held five rounds. Models from Tsarist times were still around to be brought out of armouries in 1941 following Operation *Barbarossa* (the German invasion of the Soviet Union), but by then they had been

largely superseded by a later Mosin-Nagant rifle.

After the Russian Revolution, the newly established Red Army decided to adopt the dragoon model as their standard issue rifle and so the other variants were no longer manufactured. It was appreciated that many aspects of the Model 1891 could be simplified, but, due to the numerous upheavals and other difficulties that followed the Civil War, it was not until 1930 that anything could be introduced on any scale. The result was the Model 1891/30.

Following other design trends elsewhere, the Model 1891/30 was intended for mass production. At the same time everything was 'metricated' to modern standards. For instance, the old Model 1891 rifles had their sights calibrated in *arshins*, an archaic Russian measurement equivalent to about 0.71m/28in. On the Model 1891/30 the sights were calibrated in metres and were otherwise altered in several respects, the foresight being protected by a sight hood. Numerous parts were simplified or omitted altogether. As one example, the receiver on the Model 1891/30 became cylindrical in outline, in place of the earlier hexagonal contours. The revised model worked just as well as before.

Once the production of the modified rifle was established, attention was turned to two further variants. One was to emerge as the Model 1938 carbine, reflecting the changes introduced on the Model 1891/30 rifle. The other was what was termed a sniper rifle with telescopic sights, introduced in 1937–38, but it has to be explained that the

Model 1891/30

Calibre	7.62mm; 0.30in
Length	1.232m; 48.5in
Length of barrel	729mm; 28.7in
Weight	4kg; 8.7lb
Muzzle velocity	811m/s; 2,660ft/s
Feed	5-round box magazine

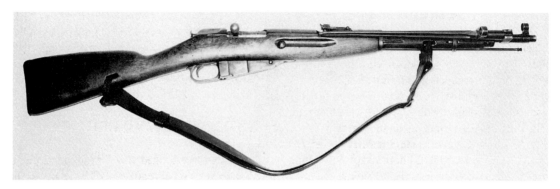

The 7.62mm Model 1944 carbine, the longest-lived of all the Mosin-Nagant bolt action rifles.

Red Army used the term 'sniper' rather loosely. The Soviet practice was to issue rifles fitted with telescopic sights to users many would term skilled marksmen, trained to search for and eliminate enemy officers and other prime personnel targets. At all other times the marksmen undertook routine infantry duties. Although Soviet marksmen were highly skilled and exacted a terrible toll in German lives, they remained an integral part of the infantry and other formations and were not as highly trained or closely controlled as most Western snipers were (and still are). Even so, many Soviet soldiers, male and female, produced prodigious 'scores'. An example was Nikolay Ilyin who achieved a tally of 496 before perishing in, of all things, a bayonet attack.

Several models of telescopic sight were issued for these Model 1891/30 sniper rifles, the most common during the Great Patriotic War years being the PU with a magnification of ×3.5. A later alternative was the ×4 PE with dual mounts for the telescope. Rifles fitted with telescopic sights had their bolt handles turned down to avoid hitting the sight bodies as the bolts were opened.

A late production variant was the Model 1944 carbine, originally intended as a much handier and lighter weapon to arm support personnel and specialists such as signallers and combat engineers; its length was 1.02m/40in with the fixed bayonet folded back. Despite exhibiting the usual carbine drawbacks of muzzle flash and pronounced recoil, the Model 1944 soon came to be preferred to the Model 1891/30 rifle, to the extent that production of the long rifle ceased in early 1944. Post-war, the Model 1944 carbine replaced the old rifles but it, in its turn, was soon ousted by the post-war generation of self-loading rifles. The Model 1944 may still be encountered in some parts of the world.

One striking fact regarding Mosin-Nagant rifles between 1941 and 1945 was the sheer number involved. Although it cannot be confirmed precisely, it is estimated that between those years more than 12 million Mosin-Nagant rifles and carbines were produced, often under dreadful conditions in relocated, makeshift factories following the deep German armoured thrusts of 1941. Factories at Izhevsk manufactured 11,145,000 units just by themselves.

Model 1944 Carbine	
Calibre	7.62mm; 0.30in
Length	1.02m; 40in
Length of barrel	518mm; 20.4in
Weight	4.03kg; 8.9lb
Muzzle velocity	766m/s; 2,514ft/s
Feed	5-round box magazine

These totals mask the fact that production of the Model 1891/30 had been planned to cease altogether as early as July 1940 in favour of self-loading rifles. A formal announcement was made to this end. Although production did indeed tail off for a while, it was rapidly reinstated when it became apparent that troubles with Germany were looming. Following the German invasion the fact that it took only 13 hours to manufacture a Model 1891/30 while a self-loader took 20 hours kept bolt action rifles pouring from the factories to replace the huge losses inflicted by the Germans. The output in 1940 ended up as 1,375,822 rifles. During 1942 the total number of rifles was a remarkable 3,026,765, to which could be added 687,426 carbines.

By 1944 the tide had turned. Enough rifles had been produced to meet any possible future demands while at the same time the production of sub-machine guns and self-loading rifles was increasing to reflect the highly mobile, close-quarter tactics then being adopted. The long Mosin-Nagant rifles were awkward and unhandy to carry on vehicles, while their long bayonet 'reach' was needed less and less. What was needed was firepower, plus ease of aiming and carrying. The newer types of weapon suited these requirements more readily. Only the Model 1944 carbine could go any way to do so, which partially explains its post-war retention.

During 1941 and 1942 huge numbers of Mosin-Nagant rifles and carbines fell into German hands, so many so that the Model 1891/30 (the type most readily absorbed into German service) became a virtual standard issue to many garrison and second-line units throughout occupied Europe. The official German designation was the 7.62mm Gewehr 254(r). Sniper models, also adopted in significant numbers, became the 7.62mm Zielfernrohrgewehr 256(r).

Another Mosin-Nagant user was Finland, but here the model involved was the base Model 1891. Numbers of these were obtained after Finland gained its independence in 1917. The Finns fitted new heavy barrels and altered the furniture to produce a number of models known collectively as the *Pystykorva*. All the Finnish Mosin-Nagants were very accurate. Another user of the Model 1891 between the wars was the new state of Yugoslavia, while Poland also used the same model, usually with Mauser-pattern fittings to match their Mauser Model 1898 rifles.

THE FRENCH COLLECTION

It is often overlooked that during the Great War France suffered dreadfully. Russia might have endured more casualties in numerical terms but French casualties bore more heavily on the nation's post-war capabilities as they formed a greater percentage of the population. After 1918 France was therefore much reduced in the energy, morale and productivity that motivates any nation. The French military establishment mirrored this general malaise by their determination never to fight another war that might replicate the terrible experiences of 1914–18. Their military stance became defensive to the extent that innovation was almost totally excluded from French military philosophy. What had proved good enough to save France in the war had to be good enough for the future.

This situation had its effect on the French small-arms holdings of 1939, especially with rifles. The *poilus* of 1939 carried the same rifles as their fathers did in 1914 but with the added touch that even in 1914 many of the French rifles were already antiques. After 1918 there was little incentive to do anything about the holdings of service rifles, even though the number of elderly models still in existence was too large for comfort, by any measure.

An indication of the age of many of the rifles still in service in 1939 is the fact that the Gras modèle 1874 was still being carried by some troops. This single-shot veteran (there was no magazine) was the first French rifle to utilize a metallic cartridge, originally with a calibre of 11mm, later altered to 8mm. There was also a carbine version. Both should have been replaced well before 1914 but, since about 2.5 million had been manufactured, getting rid of them was a major undertaking no treasury would contemplate. The *modèle* (mle) 1874 was therefore still to be found in 1918 and the inter-war stagnation of the French armed forces ensured that this was so in 1939. By then it had been relegated to the use of colonial troops and units such as airfield guards; but the very fact that it was still in service at all provides an example of how the French military outlook of that period was entrenched in the past.

After 1918 the French distributed some mle 1874s to some of the post-1918 emergent nations. Poland and Yugoslavia received batches, as did Greece.

The single-shot feature of the mle 1874 was seen as a shortcoming early in its long career and so the bolt action of the mle 1874 was allied with a tubular magazine holding eight 8 × 50R cartridges containing smokeless propellant. The result was the 8mm mle 1886, popularly known as the Lebel.

When first introduced, the Lebel was a thoroughly modern service rifle, although some flaws were soon discovered. As a result the mle 1886/93 appeared in 1893 with a strengthened receiver, changes to the furniture and alterations to the sights. It was this model that went to war in 1914 and again in 1939. In 1939 the French armed forces still had an inventory of about 3 million Lebels issued to many front-line units as well as second-line and garrison troops.

Whoever had to use the Lebel found it a cumbersome and unwieldy weapon. It was 1.303m (51.3in) long and an *épeé* bayonet added to the overall length. As would be expected, the Lebel was manufactured to high standards with good materials, so its longevity was assured – examples were still being encountered during the Algerian campaigns of the 1950s and the 1960s. By any standard the

mle 1886 Lebel	
Calibre	8mm; 0.315in
Length	1.303m; 51.3in
Length of barrel	798mm; 31.4in
Weight	4.245kg; 9.35lb
Muzzle velocity	725m/s; 2,380ft/s
Feed	8-round tubular magazine

Lebel was an anachronism in 1939, but one attempt had been made to update a proportion of the existing stockpiles. This began in 1935, the main measure being to cut back the barrel, reducing the total length to 959mm (37.75in). Other changes were introduced to the sights and the furniture. One result of these modifications was that the tubular magazine capacity was limited to only three rounds. Once modified, the rifle became the mle 86/93 R 35. The actual number of conversions appears to have been small.

So many Lebels were captured by the Germans in 1940 that the type became almost a standard issue for German units based in France; they knew it as the 8mm Gewehr 301(f). Lebels were also distributed to the armies of Greece and Yugoslavia, thus many ended in the hands of Balkan partisan units.

The Lebel may have been a success in French Army hands before 1914, but it was considered to be unsuitable for units stationed in the colonies and too complicated for use by colonial troops. They were issued with a series of rifles and carbines based on a design known as the Berthier, after its chief

The famous Lebel rifle – the mle 1886/93.

The mle 86-R-35, a belated attempt to modernize the Lebel.

designer André Berthier. The first Berthier design adopted by the French was the 8mm mle 1892 with sub-variants intended for the cavalry, heavy cavalry and the gendarmerie. These were followed by the mle 1892 intended for the artillery. This multiplicity of sub-variants, all essentially the same apart from minor fixtures and fittings, was a typical practice of the time.

The Berthier carbines featured a box-type magazine loaded from a three-round charger. The same loading method later appeared on a rifle intended for units in the French colonies, and primarily Indo-China. This was the 8mm Fusil mle 1907 dit Colonial, based on an earlier design trialled in Indo-China, the mle 1902. This rifle took no note of the gradual reduction in the length of service rifles taking place in the Britain and USA, having an overall length of just over 1.321m/52in. At the time this seemed to matter little. Gradually the Berthier mle 1907 started to supplement the Lebel in mainland French Army service, especially after 1914. Once trench warfare became established the Berthier rifles demonstrated that they were far more suited to these conditions than the Lebel. Loading was easier and the *poilu* preferred the handling of the Berthier to that of the old Lebel.

As a result, the Berthier mle 1907 was rushed into mass production with changes made to the bolt mechanism and the sights. It became the mle 1907/15 and was so favoured that by 1918 some 2,500,000 had been manufactured; production of at least one contract was completed in the USA by Remington. The result was that in 1939 the mle 1907/15 was in service in significant numbers, not only with the French forces but also in Greece, Poland, Romania and Yugoslavia (these nations also procured the original mle 1907). The type was still in service in the French colonies after 1940 and so it ended by serving with both the Free French and the Vichy armed forces.

One Great War innovation was the Berthier mle 1916. The original three-round magazine capacity was seen as a disadvantage when compared with other rifles of the time so the capacity was increased

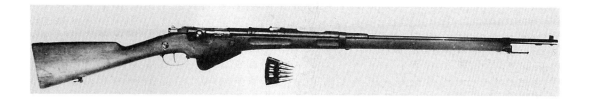

The Berthier mle 1916 with a five-round magazine capacity.

The MAS 1936, the last new European bolt action rifle to enter service

to five rounds on the mle 1916. After 1918 the mle 1916 was distributed to the usual French-influenced nations such as Greece, Poland, Romania and Yugoslavia. More went to Turkey.

There was also a mle 1916 carbine, again with a five-round magazine. This model was still issued to French internal security forces as late as 1980.

Some small arms development did take place between the wars in France, but on a scale limited by indifference as much as financial restrictions. One exception was a new rifle cartridge, the 7.5 × 58mm mle 1924. For several reasons this cartridge was not satisfactory and therefore after five years it was replaced by the shorter 7.5 × 54mm mle 1929C, still in service in France and its dependencies to this day.

The 7.5mm cartridge was intended to be fired from all future French rifles and machine guns, the first rifle being the Fusil MAS 1936, of which more later. By the early 1930s it was appreciated

that it would take time to get the new rifle into production and so as an interim or fail-safe measure it was decided to transform the mle 1907/15 to accept the new cartridge. The full title for the modified rifle was the rather cumbersome Fusil d'Infantrie modèle 1907, transformé 1915 et modifié 1934. Thankfully, the term mle 1934 was more widely applied. As well as replacing the barrel, the opportunity was taken to shorten it slightly, resulting in a total length of 1.08m/42.5in; the five-round magazine was standard. The mle 1934 was a serviceable enough rifle but only about 40,000 had been converted by the time the Germans invaded France. This model, along with the other Berthier rifles, then entered the German inventory. The mle 1934 became the 7.5mm Gewehr 241(f) while the earlier mle 1907/15 became the 8mm Gewehr 302(f); the mle 1916 became the 8mm Gewehr 304(f).

As mentioned above, the 7.5 × 54mm mle 1929C cartridge was intended for use with a new rifle that would finally emerge as the Fusil MAS 1936. A prototype of this was produced as early as 1932 but development was unhurried, even though by 1932 the design was somewhat anachronistic. This time the selection was a modified Mauser bolt system, with the locking lugs to the rear of the bolt instead of at the bolt head. This feature resulted in an awkward, forward-facing bolt angle. The magazine capacity remained at five rounds. As with all previous French service rifles, there was no safety catch. Overall, the MAS 1936 was an awkward

mle 1907	
Calibre	8mm; 0.315in
Length	1.321m; 52in
Length of barrel	797mm; 31.4in
Weight	3.9kg; 8.6lb
Muzzle velocity	725m/s; 2,380ft/s
Feed	3-round box magazine

MAS 1936

Calibre 7.5mm; 0.295in
Length 1.019m; 40.13in
Length of barrel 574mm; 22.6in
Weight 3.67kg; 8.29lb
Muzzle velocity 823m/s; 2,700ft/s
Feed 5-round box magazine

design with few items of note other than that it was the only modern rifle the French had in 1939. It was the last newly designed, European, bolt-action service rifle to enter service before the self-loaders took over.

By 1939 the 7.5mm MAS 1936 was in full-scale production at the Manufacture d'Armes de Saint-Etienne (hence MAS), with most of the output going to the French Army's new mechanized divisions.

The number manufactured before the Germans marched in was about 250,000, more than enough to equip several German infantry divisions stationed in France; they knew it as the 7.5mm Gewehr 242(f).

There was one sub-variant of the MAS 1936, the MAS 1936 CR39. Intended for alpine and airborne units, this model was slightly shorter (889mm/35in, compared with the 1.002m/39.45in of the MAS 1936) and the total carry length could be reduced still further (to 625mm/24.6in) by the provision of a folding aluminium butt stock. None reached the troops because full production had yet to start before the war ended for France in 1940.

There the story of the French rifles finished as far as World War 2 was concerned. Many of the rifles mentioned above were still to be encountered as late as 1945 (many in the hands of the hapless German *Volkssturm*), but well before then most French rifles were of more use as museum pieces than service weapons.

3   Self-loading Rifles

The term 'self-loading rifle' denotes a rifle that fires a single shot every time the trigger is actuated. The associated automatic rifle fires when the trigger is pulled and continues to do so for as long as the trigger is pressed or the ammunition supply lasts. Long before they became a practical reality, both types of rifle had attracted the attention of firearms designers, but it was not until the introduction of smokeless propellant in a metallic cartridge case that the idea could pass from wishful thinking to practical hardware. Before then the old black powder-based propellants combined a lack of the energy needed to make moving parts operate effectively with a startling propensity to introduce fouling that ensured that moving parts could not move at all.

Automatic fire from small arms came with the machine gun. Translating machine-gun operating techniques to shoulder-fired rifles took more time and attention than the first generation of self-loading rifle designers at first appreciated. Even before the Great War self-loading rifle designs had appeared in some numbers, the US Army alone testing no fewer than twenty-five between 1901 and 1917, from as far afield as China and Denmark. All were rejected.

The propensity of designers to provide their progeny with a fully automatic fire mode usually rendered them so delicate and unreliable that they were unsuitable for military service. In addition, firing full-power cartridges on fully automatic from a weapon as light as a rifle meant that the excessive recoil soon drove the muzzle away from the intended target, wasting ammunition while making firing very uncomfortable. The one notable Great War exception to these drawbacks, the Browning Automatic Rifle (BAR; *see* Chapter 5) was actually a form of light machine gun.

Only when an automatic fire mode was omitted did the first practical self-loaders appear during the 1930s. Since most armed forces insisted that self-loading rifles had to use the full-power rifle cartridges of the day (for ammunition supply reasons), the technical challenges imposed were difficult to overcome. The power generated by standard rifle cartridges could indeed provide the recoil or gas power for self-loading mechanisms, but the stresses and strains created by high-energy propellant loads meant that the resulting rifles had to be cumbersome as well as heavier than their bolt action counterparts.

The early self-loaders also tended to be far more complicated and time consuming (and therefore costlier) to manufacture than bolt action rifles. As a general rule, their complexity also made them far more difficult for the average soldier to master, look after and use. These unfortunate qualities meant that soldier-proof, self-loading rifles took longer to reach the troops than was at first foreseen.

When the troops did get them the advantages of self-loaders became evident, for the firepower of the individual soldier was multiplied by a significant factor. Not only could shots be squeezed off more rapidly but the point of aim remained on or close to the target during the self-loading cycle. Manipulating a bolt action always took time, no matter how experienced the firer, while the process of operating the bolt tended to take the sights off the target for an instant, thus needing more time to realign the sights and the target. For these reasons, self-loading rifles soon became readily accepted by front-line soldiers, especially snipers for whom the advantages of self-loading were amplified.

The Second World War was the first occasion when the self-loading rifle was employed on any scale. Some designs were fielded during the Great War but they were not a success – there were still too many design and operating challenges to be overcome. Yet by the early 1940s viable designs were not just in the offing but in front-line service.

Most Western observers tend to assume that the American M1 Garand was the first such rifle to see active service. It was not, for other countries preceded it. We shall start with one of them, the Soviet Union.

RUSSIAN LEADERS

Although Russian designers had already produced design studies some years before, the father of the Soviet self-loading rifle is generally regarded as Vladimir Fedorov. He was experimenting with a selective-fire automatic rifle as early as 1907, but his efforts met with little support from the Tsarist military hierarchy. They viewed technical developments such as automatic rifles with suspicion, as they tended to with any innovation.

Fedorov's rifle also suffered from another drawback as far as they were concerned. By 1912 he had come to appreciate that the Russian standard 7.62 × 54R cartridge was too powerful for the mechanisms he was devising; to accommodate the stresses involved would result in the rifle being too heavy. In its place he adopted the medium-power Japanese Arisaka 6.5 × 51mm semi-rimmed cartridge to inflict less strain on his mechanism, one based around the barrel's recoiling a short distance to actuate the spent case, ejection and self-loading cycles. The result was the first Russian self-loader, the so-called Avtomat, or, in full, Avtomaticheskaya Vintovka Fedorova obr 1916g (AVF-16), which displayed several futuristic features. Apart from the reduced-power cartridge, the Avtomat had a detachable box magazine

holding twenty-five rounds and the ability to fire on fully automatic at a cyclic rate of 600 to 650rpm.

Despite a general lack of enthusiasm for the project and the limitations of the Russian defence infrastructure before 1917, to which could be added the need to provide non-standard calibre ammunition, the Avtomat was manufactured in limited numbers from 1916 onwards at the Sestroretsk Weapons Factory. Work was interrupted by the 1917 Revolution, only for limited production to start again in 1919 as a measure to equip the new Red Army. By 1925 all production work on the Avtomat had ceased, although experiments and trials with light machine guns using the Fedorov principles continued until the late 1920s. The total number of Avtomats produced was no more than 3,200.

The Avtomat was ahead of its time. Many small arms specialists regard it as the forerunner of the modern assault rifle. Although it saw only limited use, it demonstrated that it was serviceable and reliable. Its main shortcoming was that it was very demanding in production resources at a time when the new Soviet Union had more pressing priorities.

Avtomats were taken from storage and issued for front-line use during the 1940 Russo-Finnish War, a period when it seems that anything that could fire was pressed into service. Thereafter Fedorev's Avtomat faded from the scene.

Tokarev and Simonov

During the 1920s Soviet military planners were already advocating the replacement of Mosin-Nagant bolt action rifles with self-loaders. By 1930 the outlines for such a rifle had been prepared. The weight was to be limited to a maximum of 4kg/8.8lb, selective fire was required and details such as the provision of a knife bayonet were included in the specifications. Perhaps the most important requirement as far as the designers were concerned was that the standard 7.62 × 54R cartridge had to be involved.

The specifications led to a number of design bureaux entering rifles for a series of competitive

The Simonov AVS-36, the first of the World War Two self-loading rifles to enter service.

trials leading to acceptance by the Red Army. The bureaux were led by highly respected men such as Fedor Tokarev and Vasily Degtyarev, while an entry was submitted by a team led by Fedorov. Of the early entrants none were considered worthy of final selection. All the entrants emerged as too heavy while none displayed the reliability levels that were expected.

However, of the submissions made, a design from Tokarev showed promise. Tokarev, a contemporary of Fedorev, had devised a recoil-operated, self-loading rifle mechanism as early as 1907, but a lack of opportunity to carry out the necessary development work during the following years meant that it was 1925 before his ideas were translated into a firing prototype. The prototype worked but was too heavy and unreliable. He indicated that his design could meet the specifications only if a reduced calibre, less powerful cartridge was adopted. This was duly noted but as it would take some time to develop a suitable cartridge (a calibre of 5.35mm/0.21in was suggested, as was a futuristic 5.45mm/0.215in). Tokarev decided to devise a gas-operated system for his rifle. He considered that such an approach would be more productive, especially as the military asked for the capability to launch rifle grenades from the muzzle, something not possible with his original recoiling barrel mechanism.

Development progress was slow throughout the early 1930s. There were many technical challenges

to overcome and the authorities grew weary of the programme's taking so long. At this stage another contestant appeared on the scene with an alternative offering. This was Sergey Simonov, a talented designer who had first devised a self-loading rifle in 1926. Observing the results of the competitive trials, he determined to produce something better.

Simonov also adopted a gas-operated mechanism. It seemed to work so well that in 1934 it was accepted in place of all the other submissions, although Tokarev continued to work on his rifles. Full acceptance took place in 1936, so the new rifle was named the Avtomaticheskaya vintovka Simonova obr 1936g, or AVS-36. By 1938 it was in service and was combat-tested during the 1939–40 Russo-Finnish Winter War. It was found wanting.

The AVS-36 carried over many of the problems encountered in all the self-loading designs of the period. The AVS-36 proved to be heavy and complicated, too much so for many soldiers issued with it. It required frequent cleaning and maintenance, for the bolt reciprocated in an open slot though which dirt and debris could enter to cause malfunctions. A muzzle brake had to be added to reduce the recoil forces and the muzzle blast, both of which were significant to the point of user discomfort. In short, the AVS-36 was not fully soldier-proof.

Although the AVS-36 was just being issued for service, it was decided to run yet another series of

The interim SVT-38, out of production by 1940.

trials. This time a revised Simonov rifle was pitted direct against the latest form of Tokarev rifle, although an entry from Nikolay Rukavishnikov was also included (it eventually fell by the wayside). The results were inconclusive as neither rifle displayed any clear superiority, while reliability problems continued to be evident. It was at this stage that politics entered the fray. Simonov was a Communist Party member with enough standing to influence opinions at high level. Another round of trials therefore began, this time backed by the findings of an appointed commission that indicated that the Simonov rifle was the better of the two, especially by being lighter, easier to manufacture and requiring smaller quantities of raw materials.

It was to no avail. Further prolonged testing demonstrated that the Tokarev rifle had the durability edge over the Simonov. To finish the matter once and for all, Stalin himself decided to give the Tokarev design his personal blessing. The result was that AVS-36 production ceased and plans were

made to mass produce the Tokarev product at Izhevsk, the long-term intention being to replace the Mosin-Nagant 1891/30 rifle.

Tokarev's rifle became the SVT-38. First issued in July 1939, it displayed some shortcomings. Despite weighing 3.95kg/8.7lb, it was prone to an alarming number of breakdowns caused by the inevitable knocks of service life, extreme cold and the ingress of dirt. A design revision, mainly centred around the strengthening of the mechanism while paring away weight elsewhere, resulted in the SVT-40, which then became the main production variant from July 1940 onwards. Over 1,326,000 SVT-40 rifles were made before the end of 1942, plus a further 51,000 SVT-40s fitted with telescopic sights for snipers (a matching variant of the AVS-36 was also produced before it went out of production). The final production total when the SVT-40 production run ended in 1945 has not been discovered but has been estimated as just under two million.

The SVT-40 was never perfected. At 3.89kg/8.56lb it was still considered too heavy and, despite a muzzle brake, its recoil was considered as too uncomfortable, but it emerged as a much better combat weapon than all the other contemporary Soviet models. The unreliability problems were never entirely eliminated and were amplified when an AVT-40 variant was introduced with a fully automatic fire mode. Few AVT-40s were made; a carbine variant suffered the same fate.

Despite its shortcomings, the SVT-40 was also better than its German counterparts, the 7.92mm

SVT-40	
Calibre	7.62mm; 0.30in
Length	1.222m; 48.1in
Length of barrel	625mm; 24.6in
Weight	3.89kg; 8.56lb
Muzzle velocity	830m/s; 2,723ft/s
Feed	10-round box magazine

Comparison between the SVT-40 (top) and the AVS-36 (bottom).

Gewehr 41(W) and the 41(M). Those two models displayed so many problems in service that when examples of the SVT-40 fell into German hands they integrated the Tokarev gas-operated mechanism into their 7.92mm Gewehr 43, the best of the German self-loaders firing a full power rifle cartridge. Captured SVT-40s were usually pressed into German service; they became the 7.62mm SlGew 259(r).

Cartridges

As mentioned above, it was appreciated that the attempt to develop self-loading rifles firing full-power rifle cartridges was bound to result in technical, weight and reliability problems, to say nothing of excessive recoil. Full-power cartridges were designed to be effective at extended combat ranges, a need rarely encountered during actual combat. Soviet designers were aware that one solution was to develop smaller-calibre cartridges with reduced propellant loads. Lower-powered cartridges would be adequate at most real-life combat ranges while offering the prospect of shoulder-aimed, automatic-burst fire. Senior military planners were not enthusiastic about such an approach, but their conservatism had been gradually overcome by 1940, only for work on all such developments to be shelved once war began. It should be

noted that these pre-war developments were conducted without any reference or consideration to the German 7.92mm *kurz* cartridge programme.

By 1943 matters had improved to the point when ammunition of lower power could be considered once again. Many possibilities were investigated before consideration was given to a 7.62 × 39mm rimless cartridge, the calibre apparently being selected to utilize as many existing manufacturing facilities as possible. This round, the M1943, became the most widely manufactured rifle cartridge of all time, both in numerical and geographical terms. It was still in widespread production when the new century began, as it is the round fired from the 7.62mm AK-47 series, the famous Kalashnikovs.

The Kalashnikov was not the first weapon to use the M1943 cartridge. That distinction went to the SKS-45, another self-loader based on a Simonov carbine first shown during 1941. The 1941 model suffered from two factors, one being the retention of the full power 7.62 × 54R cartridge and the second the outbreak of the Great Patriotic War in the same year. It was 1944 before attention could be directed back to the design and by then it could be revised to accommodate the new M1943 cartridge with all its handling and other advantages. The war was over by the time the resulting SKS-45 was ready so that it strictly falls outside the scope of this work.

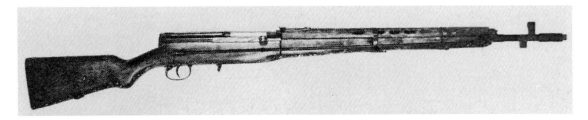

An early production example of a SVT-40.

THE GARAND

In the previous chapter it was mentioned that any change of policy regarding American service small arms was closely scrutinized by a wide audience. This factor came to the fore during the selection process for the rifle that was to become the standard service model for the US Army in the years from 1936 onwards. The reasons why were many and various but they tended to centre around the fact that the M1903 series Springfield was then considered (by Americans) as one of the finest service rifles available anywhere. Anything that followed it had to be even better.

Set against this, the Army had always been open to technical innovation and was no stranger to the self-loading concept. Official interest could be traced to 1900 (the Army's rejection of twenty-five self-loader designs before 1917 has already been described). Balanced against this were two factors: a perennial lack of defence funding during times of peace and an inherent and well-entrenched conservatism at all command levels. These combined to make the development saga of the M1 Garand long and controversial.

The experiences of 1917 and 1918 prompted the US Army to investigate the self-loading rifle further than just to test existing designs. Their efforts were assisted by the recruitment of John C. Garand to the design and development staff of the Springfield Armory during 1919. Garand had by then already designed a light machine gun. Its operation relied on the cartridge primer's igniting the propellant while at the same time blowing outwards to the rear to provide the initial impetus to the breech. The light machine gun was eventually dropped as its functioning required non-standard ammunition, and so Garand concentrated his attentions on self-loading rifles.

With the limitations of his light machine gun principle accepted, he turned to a mechanism whereby gas was tapped off from the barrel close to

The handsome lines of the 0.30 M1 Garand rifle.

the muzzle and directed via a piston rod to actuate a rotating bolt-locking mechanism and to load another round. Similar systems were also utilized by many other designers, although they usually differed in detail. To get such a rifle from the drawing board to production took a great deal of time and technical resource. Garand was starved of the latter, his work being constantly supervised while specifications were repeatedly altered or amended by a top-heavy Armory bureaucracy. Overall, the programme was notable for its complete lack of urgency.

One major amendment arose in 1924 when

another respected American small arms designer based at Springfield, John D. Pedersen (responsible for the short-lived Pedersen device that converted the Springfield rifle into an automatic weapon during 1918), was also called upon to develop a self-loading rifle. The first thing he proposed was a change in the ammunition calibre from 0.30in (7.62 × 63mm) to 0.276in (7 × 51mm). By 1927 this proposal had been accepted and thus Garand was forced to alter his rifle, originally chambered for the standard 0.30-06 cartridge, to accept the 0.276 calibre (this was the T3E2).

From 1925 onwards a series of trials involving

Winter training with a M1 Garand.

both rifles took place. As usual, they were followed closely by a huge audience both within and without the military community. It soon became apparent that the change of calibre to 0.276 was not popular with the Army, for a variety of reasons that included replacement costs, doubts about accuracy and a lack of understanding of the need for any change at all. Nevertheless, by 1932 it had been decided by the Ordnance Board (who ran the Springfield Armory) that they would procure the Pedersen rifle, the T1E2. It seemed that approval was forthcoming from almost everywhere apart from the intended end-user, the Army, or, more particularly, the Chief of Staff, General MacArthur.

He rejected the Pedersen 0.276 rifle outright, quoting the stockpiles of 0.30 rifles and ammunition already on hand, backed by a dearth of any funding for their replacement. Any changeover during the cash-starved 1930s would have heralded a lengthy period of logistic, training and other confusions. It was back to the standard 0.30 cartridge and the Garand rifle.

Fortunately for all concerned, all this time Garand had been perfecting his 0.30 rifle. Anticipating the objections that were bound to arise when his design was subjected to acceptance testing, his careful work resulted not only in a sound design but one that could be mass-produced. Despite being constantly beset by financial restrictions and a general lack of support, Garand also developed the machine tools and gauges that would be necessary to manufacture his rifle.

In January 1936 and following extended troop and other trials, Garand's years of steady work were rewarded by acceptance of his rifle by the US Army as the Rifle, Semiautomatic, Caliber 0.30, M1. It soon became apparent that acceptance would not be followed by mass production as American defence funding was still at a low ebb, while many production engineers within the Armory considered that the M1 was too complicated for them to fabricate. At that time the Springfield Armory was short of skilled personnel and modern machine tools. Much of the Armory's tooling was decades old and incapable of producing the tolerances the M1 rifle

required, so that it was not until late1937, and following a re-equipment programme, that low-level series production could begin. By 1939 it had been decided that private industry should be involved in M1 production to widen the manufacturing base; the Winchester Repeating Arms Company of New Haven, Connecticut, was awarded a contract.

It was late 1939 before the first production M1s were demonstrated to the American public and troubles then began in earnest, especially from the most prominent civilian organization with an interest in small arms, the National Rifle Association (NRA). The NRA did not like what it saw, criticizing many aspects of the weapon, from its accuracy to its reliability. It was true that the early production examples displayed teething troubles, most being traced to a major bane of the small arms designer's life – the manufacturer's making slight alterations to the specification to suit his production methods or perceptions. These difficulties were soon eradicated but another controversy then arose to add fuel to the NRA arguments.

It came in the form of the Johnson Model MR-2 rifle. This was a recoil-operated self-loader with several unusual features, such as a 10-round rotary magazine and a detachable barrel. It had been developed by Melvin M. Johnson, a Marine Reserve officer. Johnson's rifle had been examined by the US Army during 1938 and, while it was willing to admit that it worked well enough as presented, the Army considered that it displayed few advantages over the M1. By 1938 the M1 had been extensively and successfully tested and was about to go into mass production. The Johnson had yet to experience this process and so it was not recommended for further consideration.

The influential NRA was at that time on a par with the British Bisley School mentioned in the previous chapter. The NRA too expected great things from any new rifle. It had been allowed to fire M1s during a series of rifle matches held in late 1939, during which the M1s were adversely compared with the finely tuned M1903 Springfields then used by the NRA for long-range

The one that caused all the selection fuss, the Johnson semi-automatic rifle, clearly showing its rotary magazine.

target shooting. Not surprisingly, the M1s, intended to be service rifles not match rifles, did not fare as well as the trusted Springfields. Yet within the rarefied atmosphere of the NRA this comparison did the reputation of the M1 no good at all. Once the non-acceptance of the Johnson rifle became known, controversy flourished, from newspaper exposés to Congressional investigations. There seemed to be no end of 'experts' ready to testify that the Johnson rifle was more accurate, contained fewer parts and was easier to maintain. Congress, to its credit, withstood all such entreaties, insisting that as the M1 was already in production it should stay that way.

But even then the furore did not fade. The US Marines postponed their acceptance of the M1 until a series of trials, also involving yet another self-loader from Winchester, had been exhaustively performed. The M1 emerged as a clear leader (the Marines adopted the M1 during 1941); so thereafter

---

M1 Garand

Calibre 7.72mm; 0.30in
Length 1.107m; 43.6in
Length of barrel 609mm; 24in
Weight 4.313kg; 9.5lb
Muzzle velocity 855m/s; 2,805ft/s
Feed 8-round box magazine

---

the Johnson rifle gradually disappeared from the scene.

A number of Johnson rifles were, however, manufactured by the Cranston Arms Company of Providence, Rhode Island, for the Dutch East Indies and Chile. The US Marine Corps also procured a batch in 1941–42 when rifles were in short supply; they were issued to special forces only and even then not for long.

With the Johnson rifle episode out of the way the US Army could concentrate on the M1. It liked what it found. The M1 was a handsome, well-made rifle that handled well, despite its weight of 4.313kg/9.5lb; the weight was slightly offset by the well-balanced handling. Ammunition was fed into the magazine in an eight-round clip which was ejected as the last round was fired. One often-mentioned shortcoming of the ammunition-feed system was that single rounds could not be loaded; it was all eight rounds or nothing.

The one major drawback of the M1 was that it was expensive to produce and the initial production was slow. Despite Garand's development of the tooling, it took time to establish production lines and to train workers to the necessary standards. The M1 contained over seventy components that required nearly one thousand machining operations. The result was a good, sturdy service rifle, considered by many as the best of all the Second World War self-loaders. By 1945 it was the standard American service rifle, the first self-loader to be issued on such a large scale (although bolt-action

Springfields still remained in service as the war ended).

By mid 1941 about a thousand M1s were turned out at Springfield every day; to which Winchester added another hundred. (By the time the US entered the war in 1941 the M1 inventory stood at nearly 350,000.) In the period after Pearl Harbor this was raised to 3,000 and 725, respectively, but, even with the introduction of production short cuts, this was still not enough. As mentioned in the previous chapter, the M1903A3 bolt action rifle had to be kept in production to make up the shortfall between demand and supply. It was 1943 before the situation eased.

Using a M1 Garand rifle to launch a M9 anti-tank grenade.

By the end of the war in 1945 the production total for the M1 had reached 4,007,731; production still continued after 1945. To this could be added 6,896 M1C and M1D sniper rifles equipped with optical sights, leather cheek pads and other aids to accuracy. Apart from those two sniper variants, the M1 remained unchanged before 1945, although experimental and test models were produced in profusion to enhance features of the design, some of which were introduced after the war ended. The main postwar modification to the Garand action was the addition of a selective-fire facility.

Almost as soon as M1 production started a proportion was already earmarked for Lend-Lease. The forecast total was one million, but due to the constant demands from the American armed forces the final total was limited to just 104,137. Of these the largest total went to the Free French (58,114) while 38,001 went to 'British Empire' forces. Exactly who the latter were is uncertain but Canada received a further 8,014. China and the USSR received just one M1 each, those singletons being carefully recorded in post-war accounts.

During 1944 some M1s inevitably ended up in German hands as the 7.62mm SlGew 251(a); they were fielded by German special forces during the Battle of the Bulge at the end of 1944. There was also a Japanese copy, the 7.7mm Rifle Type 5. By the time the Japanese had mastered the tooling necessary for production the war was almost over and only prototypes were made.

THE BABY

There is one weapon that has yet to be mentioned here, even though it cannot be regarded as a self-loading combat rifle. It was a firearm now categorized as a personal defence weapon (PDW). The PDW may be described as an self-defence weapon between a pistol and a rifle, intended for use by personnel who either operated in the second-line echelons or had to devote much of their combat-equipment-carrying capability to items such as mortars, machine guns or radios. The PDW was intended for use at relatively short combat ranges and had to be light enough for general handiness and portability, while being lethally effective when called upon in earnest.

By 1938 the infantry branch of the US Army had decided that for such personnel the pistol was too short-range and inaccurate for combat effectiveness at anything longer than arm's reach. By contrast, the rifle was too cumbersome and heavy to add to existing loads. The sub-machine gun was deemed as too limited in range and, in any case, in 1938 the sub-machine gun was not in the US inventory on any significant scale. What the infantry wanted was a self-loading, light rifle or carbine, with a facility for fully automatic fire, weighing no more than 5lb/2.27kg, and with a maximum combat range of 300yd/274m. The magazine capacity was to be anything from five to fifty rounds, later revised to fifteen or thirty rounds.

The Ordnance Board originally objected to the infantry's request. Not only had they enough to do already but it was apparent that to meet the infantry's specification a new type of low-power ammunition would have to be developed. The infantry tried again in 1940 and this time they were luckier. Before long matters assumed their own momentum, something that came to mark the entire subsequent programme.

Within a few months Winchester was able to propose a suitable cartridge developed from an existing product. This new cartridge became the 0.30 carbine, or 0.30 M1 (7.62 × 33mm). It is undeniable that this cartridge lacked muzzle energy and striking power, but it was considered effective enough at the short ranges intended. Anything more powerful would have been too much for the type of light automatic weapon for which it was designed.

The new cartridge was accepted in October 1941 with low-rate production commencing soon after. What was then needed was a weapon to fire it from. Once again, matters proceeded at speed, for the Ordnance Board decided to issue the requirement to industry. Seven manufacturers eventually took part in what was to be a competitive test programme, the preliminaries indicating that the proposed weight

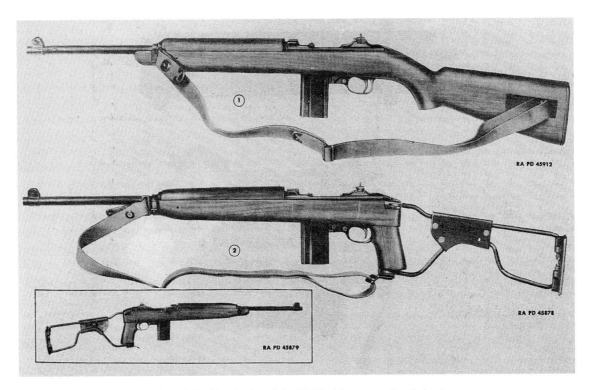

Service manual illustrations of a M1 Carbine (top) and the M1A1 airborne version (below).

limitation of 5lb/2.27kg was too optimistic. This limitation was relaxed, along with the need for a fully automatic fire mode. Of the original seven entrants only four were considered worthy of further consideration, although none were completely satisfactory.

At this point the Winchester Repeating Arms Company re-entered the story, for they had privately developed a full-power 0.30 experimental rifle. Reduced in scale, it was proposed that the ideas inherent in this design could meet the infantry's requirements. Winchester had left it rather late to make a submission but a hastily prepared prototype performed so well that the test officers requested Winchester to make the modifications needed in such a hasty venture. Within just over a month six examples were ready for final testing. In October 1941 the Winchester product was selected for type classification as the Carbine,

Caliber 0.30, M1, soon (incorrectly) nicknamed the 'Baby Garand', or simply the 'Baby'.

The entire process from the Ordnance Board's original approach to industry had taken just over a year. Only two months elapsed from Winchester starting work on their entry to full acceptance. It was a remarkable example of American 'can do', contrasting sharply with the protracted M1 Garand saga.

The general sense of urgency now seemingly inherent in the M1 Carbine programme continued to drive it onward. An initial call for 886,698 Carbines was made, but Winchester, already extended by M1 Garand production, could not meet such a demand by themselves. GMC's Inland Division became a contractor, with the intention that both Winchester and Inland would turn out 1,000 Carbines a day. After Pearl Harbor the original production requirement was raised to one million by the end of 1942, a vastly over-optimistic request when it was apparent that it would take months to prepare production lines and tooling. (The actual 1942 total was 115,000.) Yet the M1 Carbine programme continued to expand under its own impetus with a further five contractors establishing production lines. Few of the five had any experience of gunmaking, being manufacturers of items such as domestic hardware and typewriters, but they more than coped.

Demand for the Carbine continued to expand until four million were requested to be delivered by the end of 1943. Two more contractors were added to the list, by which stage special arrangements had to be made to try to integrate all the work being carried out at so many locations, to say nothing of the allocation of the necessary raw materials. By the

---

M1 Carbine

Calibre	7.62mm; 0.30in
Length	904mm; 35.6in
Length of barrel	457mm; 18in
Weight	2.36kg; 5.2lb
Muzzle velocity	600m/s; 1,970ft/s
Feed	15- or 30-round box magazine

---

end of 1943 M1 Carbine production was running at 500,000 every month and the supply was at last meeting demand. Soon after, the seven production centres were cut back to the original two, Winchester and Inland, who continued to manufac-

Training the hard way, a US soldier toting a M1 Carbine.

ture Carbines until after the war ended. The final M1 Carbine production total was 6,117,827. This was by far the largest output of any American small arm between 1939 and 1945, a total paralleled only by the Soviet small arms industry.

This concentration on Carbine production, one of the more remarkable of all American gunmaking achievements, has meant that the gun itself has not yet been described. It was a gas-operated mechanism with gas tapped off from the barrel to drive an ingenious breech mechanism that achieved much within the confines of a restricted volume. The original mechanism allowed for self-loading only to keep things simple and speed development, but there seem to have been few complaints on this point.

The M1 Carbine was readily accepted as a handy little weapon weighing just 5.2lb/2.36kg. There were complaints that the cartridge lacked power, but that had to be accepted for it was designed as such. Many soldiers came to prefer to carry the Carbine rather than the bulkier M1 Garand, even in the front line, so gradually its issue expanded away from the original target population to infantry officers and NCOs.

The M1 Carbine series followed the same lines as the M1 Garand as far as Lend-Lease was concerned. The need to get Carbines into the hands of the American armed forces meant that few were available for issue elsewhere, but 122,824 were handed on to others. The largest number by far went to the Free French (96,983) with most of the rest going to the 'British Empire' (25,362).

The M1 Carbine was the base model with wooden furniture and a fifteen-round magazine. The M1A1 was intended for issue to airborne forces and other specialists as it had a folding frame butt stock which reduced the total length from 35.5in (901mm) to 25.4in (645mm) when folded.

On the M2 the originally specified fully automatic fire mode was added by the introduction of a fire-selection mechanism and lever. The usual fifteen-round box magazine was replaced by a curved item with a capacity for thirty rounds. Many M2s were factory-converted M1s. The M3 was

produced in the smallest numbers of all the Carbines as it had provision for an infra-red night sight; just over 2,000 were made.

Many soldiers considered the introduction of the fully automatic fire mode on the M2 as a retrograde step. The mechanism became more prone to jams while low temperatures or dirt could cause the mechanism to operate at less than the planned cyclic rate of 750–755rpm. Many soldiers also thought that the use of the automatic fire mode generally wasted ammunition while doing little to enhance total firepower. This, coupled with the low striking power of the cartridge, gradually signalled the end of the Carbine in American service after 1945. Although it served on throughout the Korean War period and beyond it was gradually replaced by other weapons and is now rarely employed by any military organization.

It does retain a place within some police and paramilitary forces where an 'overkill' capability would be a disadvantage; the ammunition continues to be manufactured widely. Recently an Israeli company (Israel Arms International) has even chosen to manufacture an M1 Carbine clone known as the M888, still firing the same 0.30 Carbine ammunition. This product, apparently aimed at the American sporting and police markets, is the latest in a line of M1 Carbine clones produced since 1945.

FRENCH ODDITIES

Other than the Soviet Union and the USA, no Allied nation fielded self-loading rifles before 1945; after that date they proliferated, but that is another story. Yet there was one nation that has to be mentioned, namely France, even if its contribution between 1939 and 1945 was somewhat muted.

French designers had been experimenting with self-loading rifles since about 1888, when the Clair brothers commenced work on a series of designs which were tested until 1911 by the military authorities in such great secrecy that little information regarding them now exists. In 1910 an

mle 1917

Calibre 8mm; 0.315in
Length 1.33m; 52.4in
Length of barrel 798mm; 31.4in
Weight 5.26kg; 11.6lb
Muzzle velocity 725m/s; 2,380ft/s
Feed 5-round box magazine

alternative was proposed in the form of the STA8 (or A6), designed by an artillery officer named Meunier. The Clair and the Meunier rifle passed into history with no practical results. But their concepts did not die with them, for once the Great War began the need for some form of self-loading rifle became apparent. At first it seemed that the self-loader's tactical slot was to be filled by the infamous CSRG mle 1915 light machine gun (the Chauchat; *see* Chapter 5), but that weapon exhibited so many problems that attention turned to a self-loading rifle designed by a team containing Ribeyrolle, Sutter and Chauchat. They produced the 8mm RSC (after their initials), adopted by the French Army as the 8mm mle 1917.

This was rushed into production in April 1917, apparently without thorough testing, although the name Chauchat might have given some pause for thought after the experience involving his CSRG light machine gun. As it was, the mle 1917 was no better nor worse than any other self-loader of its generation. Despite its being issued to selected marksmen, the gas-operated mechanism was a constant cause of trouble due to component breakage. In addition it was cumbersome (the overall length was 52.4in/1.33m) and it was heavy

(11.6lb/5.26kg). It also jammed frequently. An attempt to overcome at least some of these problems was attempted with the shorter and lighter mle 1918, but none were manufactured before the armistice. Limited production (about 4,000) of the mle 1918 was carried out thereafter.

The mle 1917 fired the standard 8 × 50R Lebel cartridge fed into the fixed magazine in five-round clips. A total of 86,333 mle 1917s were assembled at the Manufacture d'Armes de Saint-Etienne, using components produced at several other facilities. After 1918 both models were used operationally during a number of north African campaigns against insurgents but the bulk of the weapons were assigned to storage. In 1935 their self-loading limitations were demonstrated by a programme to modify them into manually operated, bolt action rifles. Few were apparently so converted and those few were classified as reserve weapons.

By 1940 the mle 1917 and the 1918 were obsolete and virtually forgotten, but one oddity was that after 1940 the German Army listed both types in their lists of captured equipment. There are unconfirmed reports of numbers of these rifles seeing action in their hands on the Eastern Front. This seems unlikely, yet the mle 1918 appeared in German ordnance returns as the 8mm SlGew 310(f).

Contrary to general belief, the French ordnance authorities did carry out some experimentation regarding self-loaders from 1924 onwards at Saint-Etienne, but only at a low priority level. This resulted in the acceptance of a 7.5mm mle 1940 MAS, but when the Germans invaded in 1940 only prototypes existed. Development of this model began again after the Germans withdrew in 1944 but it was 1949 before the type was adopted by the post-war French Army.

4   Sub-machine Guns

As with so many military innovations, the sub-machine gun was a German invention from the Great War years. It is often stated that the Italian 9mm Villar Perosa of 1915 was the first sub-machine gun to be fielded. Although technically that weapon qualified as a sub-machine gun, it was not deployed as such and ended up as more of a light machine gun for mountain warfare rather than any other category of firearm. It has to be accepted that the Villar Perosa was a wrong turning, soon overtaken by the true sub-machine gun.

The German Great War sub-machine gun was the 9mm Maschinenpistole 18/1 (MP18/1) from the Bergmann company. The designer was Hugo Schmeisser, a name soon synonymous (often inaccurately) with many German sub-machine gun developments. The MP18/1 embodied all the features that subsequent sub-machine guns were to possess.

British soldiers demonstrating three of the first M1928 Thompson 0.45 sub-machine guns to reach the UK in mid-1940.

Perhaps the most important feature of the MP18/1 was that it fired pistol ammunition on fully automatic (there was no single-shot mode). It was developed from about 1916 onwards as a source of portable, short-range firepower to clear the enemy from the close confines of trenches. The use of relatively low-powered pistol ammunition (in the case of the MP18/1 it was the 9×19mm Parabellum cartridge) permitted automatic fire from a handy, shoulder-aimed light weapon. Ammunition was fed from a detachable, side-mounted snail magazine, soon replaced by a simpler box magazine holding thirty-two rounds.

Weapon operation was simple since the low-powered cartridge was kept locked in the chamber at the instant of firing purely by the forward-moving impetus produced by the mass of the heavy bolt. Only when the impetus had been overcome by the rearward-acting forces produced by the cartridge propellant could the bolt move to the rear. By that time the chamber pressure had fallen to safe levels. The rearwards-travelling bolt ejected the spent case and compressed a return spring. If the trigger was held depressed, the bolt could then move forward again under return-spring pressure to repeat the cycle. This simple operating system, known as blowback, became an inherent feature of the sub-machine gun.

If these characteristics were replaced by something seemingly more attractive on any other design, troubles always seemed to follow. There were plenty of hopeful inter-war designs to demonstrate this basic truth as the sub-machine gun gradually became more widely adopted. It provided the individual soldier with a source of firepower that could be devastating at short ranges. But at short ranges only. The use of pistol ammunition meant that effective ranges were limited to about 200m/219yd at best. Beyond that the sub-machine gun could be effective in highly trained hands, but accuracy and striking power became a matter of chance. That did not prevent many inter-war designers from providing all manner of embellishments such as sights calibrated to many hundreds of metres, the capability to be mounted on complex tripods and oversize magazines to permit prolonged burst fire. Experience was to show that these enhancements were unnecessary. By 1939 many of them had already vanished.

The sub-machine gun also had another attraction overlooked during the inter-war years when designs began to proliferate. Being inherently simple weapons they could be produced quite cheaply using the most basic of metal-working tools while remaining highly effective ammunition-delivery systems. Yet, no doubt to produce more 'added value' to their products and to maintain the high standards inherent in traditional gunmaking, most inter-war sub-machine guns were manufactured to high standards using the finest materials. The resulting weapons worked superbly, but what was to become evident was that many labour-intensive features of the guns could be either omitted or simplified to an alarming degree when the situation demanded. Many of the guns mass-produced under desperate circumstances between 1939 and 1945 horrified many end users for, thanks to their apparent crudity and lack of finish, they looked quite unlike any firearm encountered before. But they worked, within their design and ammunition performance limitations.

Once again, the Germans were to the fore in the field of simplified gun production with their MP38 and MP40 but they remain beyond our account. The Germans did indeed influence much sub-machine gun design between 1939 and 1945, but to begin with the British experience indicated the main trends.

THE LANCHESTER

Before 1939 the British Army had little time for the sub-machine gun. Despite having suffered from the impact of the weapon during 1918, its tactical role was either misunderstood or ignored. Direct comparisons with the performance of rifles or light machine guns seemed to place the sub-machine gun in the unwanted category, while the oft-employed term 'gangster weapon' did little to enhance the

Lanchesters at work – Canadian sailors escorting blindfolded U-boat personnel at a port in southern England.

reputation of the type. The various sub-machine guns tested by the Army between the wars did not result in any change of heart.

By the end of 1939 that attitude had undergone a complete reversal. Although contact with the German forces in France had been limited to little more than patrolling, British soldiers accepted that the sub-machine gun, or machine carbine as it was officially referred to, was indeed a valuable

weapon. To save time Thompson sub-machine guns (*see* below) were ordered from the USA at great expense, while the need for a home-produced weapon was accepted as a high priority. By January 1940 an example of a German MP28/II was under test in Britain. The 9mm MP28/II was a selective-fire version of the original MP18/1 produced by Haenel during the late 1920s as an export model.

With the Army's requirements apparently met for

Lanchester Mk 1*

Calibre	9mm; 0.354in
Length	851mm; 33.5in
Length of barrel	200mm; 7.9in
Weight	4.343kg; 9.65lb
Muzzle velocity	366m/s; 1,200ft/s
Feed	50-round box magazine
Cyclic rate of fire	600rpm

the time being by the purchase of Thompsons, the needs of the Royal Air Force and the Royal Navy remained to be met. Again, to save time it was decided to adopt the 9mm MP 28/II virtually unchanged, the production contract being awarded to the Sterling Armament Company of Dagenham where George Lanchester was the chief designer. His name was therefore applied to the 'new' gun.

The Lanchester machine carbine was a typical example of the high production standards applied to sub-machines gun during the inter-war period. It was also heavy, expensive and slow to produce. It was soundly and solidly made with, for some reason, a heavy brass magazine housing; the unwieldy, side-mounted magazine held fifty rounds of 9 × 19mm Parabellum ammunition. There was provision to fix a bayonet to the muzzle while the

wooden stock was the same as that for the No.1 Mk III* rifle. The original selective fire mechanism was later removed to produce the automatic-only Lanchester Mk 1*.

In the event, the entire output of about 75,000 Lanchesters went to the Royal Navy and some Commonwealth navies, where its strength and handiness were of great value to, for instance, boarding parties. (The Royal Air Force adopted the Sten.) Although production ended in October 1943, Lanchesters served on for many years after 1945, a fine example of the traditional gunmaker's art, later regarded as dated and outmoded almost from the time it was introduced.

STENS

German influence was also apparent on the next stage of British sub-machine gun development. It was initiated by the appearance of the 9mm MP38, on which all previous conventions of gun design and manufacture were set aside. Instead of a fine finish and craftsmanship, the MP38 exhibited plastics in place of wood and pure functionality in all aspects of its operation and handling. With the MP40 this approach was taken one stage further by the introduction of stampings, rivets and other manufacturing short cuts intended to churn out the MP40 even more rapidly and cheaply. Gunmakers

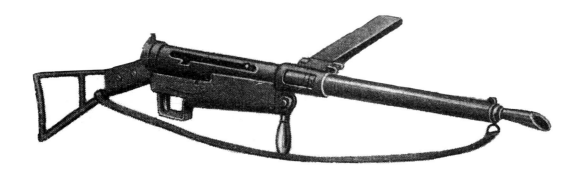

This retouched illustration of a Sten Mark 1 came from a German recognition manual. For some reason the retouched illustration makes the barrel look much longer than it actually was.

of the old school regarded the MP40 with distaste, but even they were forced to admit that it worked as well as any more refined weapon.

The MP40 approach was not lost on the British. Following the Dunkirk evacuation, the British were short of all categories of weapon and military equipment, to the point of desperation. Once again, the German MP28/II was taken as a starting point, simply because it was on hand and worked, while the manufacturing techniques employed on the MP40 were also examined. A simplified and lightened Lanchester prototype emerged, but what also emerged was that the prototype could be distilled still further in design terms to an absolute minimum, while still functioning as an effective weapon.

This 'minimal' weapon was developed under the auspices of the Royal Small Arms Factory at Enfield Lock. Major Shepherd was in charge of the department responsible while the designer was H.J. Turpin. Their surname initials plus the first two letters from Enfield resulted in the name Sten.

In essence the Sten retained all the operating features of the MP28/II reduced to the absolute limit to lessen weight and cost, but most of all to simplify and speed mass production. The result was the Sten Mk 1 on which simplicity and manufacturing short cuts prevailed; 9×19mm Parabellum ammunition was selected because of its lethal performance at close ranges, while, as a long-term bonus, any captured stocks of it could be employed. The Mk 1

Sten Mk 2	
Calibre	9mm; 0.354in
Length	762mm; 30in
Length of barrel	197mm; 7.75in
Weight	3kg; 6.625lb
Muzzle velocity	366m/s; 1,200ft/s
Feed	32-round box magazine
Cyclic rate of fire	540rpm

retained some wood in the form of a short forestock and a folding foregrip but even these were omitted on the first production variant, the Mk 1*.

The first Sten displayed everything that was to follow. The basis of the weapon was a steel tube containing the one-piece bolt and acting as a shroud for the barrel. The butt stock was constructed by using tubular steel welded together at the final stages of manufacture. Sub-assemblies and components were supplied from a host of sub-contractors, most of which had never been involved in any form of gun manufacture. Machining operations were reduced to a minimum while extensive use was made of stampings.

Simple as the Sten Mk 1* was, after about 100,000 had been made it gave way to the Mk 2 which was even simpler. It was also shorter, the

The austere Sten Mark 2, the most numerous of the Stens.

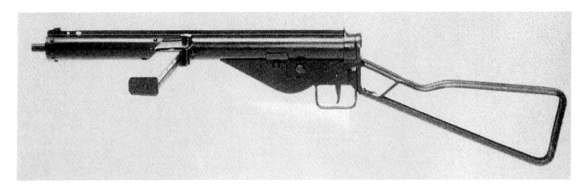

The Sten Mark 3, designed for ease of production with no frills.

A Sten Mark 2 in the hands of a French combatant.

An airborne soldier demonstrating his Sten Mark 5 to an audience of Home Guards and cadets.

original barrel being replaced by a reduced-length, screw-on assembly, while the butt became a single tubular strut with a welded butt plate. The barrel had only two rifling grooves, while the rudimentary sights were fixed at 100yd/91m. The 32-round box magazine protruded to the left, although the magazine housing could be swivelled downwards to the vertical position to close the ejection port against the ingress of dirt and debris when not in use.

The magazine was the weakest aspect of the whole design. While the gun performed even better than expected, the magazine, copied from that of the MP40, proved to be a constant source of troubles that were never eradicated. Since the magazine was basically a stamped steel box, it was hardly a precision product and so in use it became

prone to malfunctions. The feed lips were easily distorted, while any dirt finding its way into the magazine interior soon jammed up the rounds. These faults remained with the Sten throughout its service career, the only remedy being a ready supply of spare magazines. To overcome at least some potential failures, magazines were normally filled with thirty rounds instead of the intended thirty-two.

At the time the Sten was first issued during 1941 the weapons supply situation was so desperate that the British Army had to live with the magazine's shortcomings. Initial reaction from users of the gun was hardly favourable for the Sten looked more like a collection of steel tubes than a weapon. Yet soldiers soon learned to accept that it worked and was every bit as lethal as more elaborate weapons.

The suppressed Sten Mark 2(S) used by special forces.

It was also light and compact, being far more amenable to the mobile operations that became more widespread as the war continued. The first test in combat came at Dieppe in August 1942.

The Sten Mk 2 became the workhorse of the Sten family with over two million manufactured by the Royal Ordnance Factories at Fazakerley and Theale. More came from BSA and Long Branch, Canada. Sub-contractors were legion. The cost of a Sten Mk 2 was about £3 – later marks cost £5. (A Lanchester cost £14.)

The Sten Mk 2 was widely issued, not only to the British armed forces but to many resistance organizations within occupied Europe. It proved to be invaluable for the latter for the Mk II was easily stripped down without tools into a few component groups for concealment or clandestine transport. Some resistance organizations even took to manufacturing their own copies, Denmark being a prime example.

The Sten's ease of manufacture also impressed the Germans to the extent that they produced their own version, the 9mm MP3008, during the latter stages of the war in Europe. The MP3008 could be identified as a Sten derivative, but the magazine was underneath instead on the left-hand side. The German Mauser-Werke also copied the Sten direct as the Gerät Potsdam, even reproducing British markings, although for what purpose has yet to be discovered.

As the Sten Mk 2 fired low-velocity pistol ammunition it could be readily converted to accommodate a sound suppressor for special operations units – this was the Sten 2S. There was also a Sten Mk 6 with a sound suppressor.

The Sten Mk 3 was designed by the toy manufacturers Lines Bros, and featured a fixed barrel and

Sten Mk 5	
Calibre	9mm; 0.354in
Length	762mm; 30in
Length of barrel	198mm; 7.8in
Weight	3.9kg; 8.6lb
Muzzle velocity	366m/s; 1,200ft/s
Feed	32-round box magazine
Cyclic rate of fire	540rpm

A most unusual illustration of a Sten Mark 6(S) in combination with an early form of infra-red night sight.

other measures to speed production yet further; 876,886 were manufactured by them.

The Sten Mk 4 was intended for use by airborne forces and had a folding butt. It was not adopted because the Mk 5 was considered more promising. By the time the Mk 5 appeared in 1944 the need for rapid production was easing and so more attention could be directed towards making the Sten more end-user acceptable. It therefore had a wooden stock plus wooden pistol and forward grips, although the forward grip was not a success and was later removed. There was provision for a bayonet and even an acceptable foresight assembly from the No.4 rifle. Some alterations were also made to the trigger mechanism. Overall, the construction and finish of the Mk 5 were much better than of the earlier, rushed models. Some observers have stated that the Sten Mk 5 was the best of all the 1939–45

sub-machine guns, but it has to be remembered that the old magazine problems remained unsolved.

Total production of all the Sten variants came to 4,184,237. The last of them were not withdrawn from service until the 1980s although by then none were serving with the regular British forces. The Sten design may still be detected in many of the crude sub-machine guns produced in back-street workshops wherever prolonged guerrilla or revolutionary warfare takes place. The Sten is with us still.

Despite the huge numbers of Stens produced between 1941 and 1945, there were numerous other British guns offered for consideration. None were accepted, most now surviving in memory only, but one came closer than the others. This was the Patchett 9mm sub-machine gun, another product of the Sterling Engineering Company, first put forward in 1942. Favourable troop trials took place during 1944 and the type was later ordered for the British Army. However, the first deliveries were made only after the war ended and thus the Patchett and the subsequent Sterling sub-machine guns fall outside the scope of this work.

OWEN AND AUSTEN

The outbreak of the Second World War found the Australian Army in much the same position as the British regarding sub-machine guns, with the happy difference that, as the war was taking place on the other side of the world, there seemed to be no immediate urgency to obtain any. The Australian Army was content to await whatever happened back in the mother country while ordering about 20,000 0.45 Thompson sub-machine guns from the USA in the interim.

During 1940 the Army became aware that Evelyn Owen from Wollongong had devised a 0.22 sub-machine gun with a drum-pattern magazine. At that point the Army was not very interested, but by some

Owen	
Calibre	9mm; 0.354in
Length	813mm; 32in
Length of barrel	250mm; 9.85in
Weight	4kg; 8.8lb
Muzzle velocity	419m/s; 1,375ft/s
Feed	33-round box magazine
Cyclic rate of fire	680–700rpm

path the manager of Lysaght's Works at Port Kembla heard of Owen's gun and decided to recommend that it should be used as the basis for the development of an Australian sub-machine gun. Once they had examined the Owen prototype more closely the Army decided that perhaps there was promise in the design.

From that point on the Owen gun became more of a team effort than a personal crusade, with Lysaght engineers introducing their own ideas. Gradually the gun progressed through a series of

The overhead magazine denotes this as one of the Australian Owen 9mm sub-machine guns.

Austen	
Calibre	9mm; 0.354in
Length	884.5mm; 33.25in
Length of barrel	198mm; 7.8in
Weight	3.97kg; 8.75lb
Muzzle velocity	366m/s; 1,200ft/s
Feed	28-round box magazine
Cyclic rate of fire	500rpm

test models in various pistol calibres before its final form emerged. By then the original drum magazine had been replaced by a box magazine positioned so that it pointed directly upwards. The ammunition was settled as 9 × 19mm Parabellum.

By that time the Japanese had entered the war and thus the need for sub-machine guns was more pressing. The Sten had also entered the picture, along with another Australian design named the Austen. This outwardly resembled the Sten in its general layout, down to the side-mounted magazine, but much of the internal mechanism was taken from the German MP38; the folding butt was copied direct from the MP38 as was the shrouded bolt. The Austen Mk II had a cast aluminium frame.

A period of wrangling followed. Both the Owen and the Austen gun had their proponents, with the general mood at first seeming to favour the adoption of the Austen. Shoot-offs between the two guns were conducted with inconclusive results, for each gun worked as well as the other. It became apparent that the Owen gun was the more durable of the two, being largely constructed of steel while the Austen involved some diecast alloy parts. The result was something of a compromise, with production orders being placed for both weapons. By the time the production of both had ceased the Austen total was 19,914 and that for the Owen was 45,433.

The preponderance of the Owen was due to its becoming the preferred Australian gun, gradually replacing the Thompsons in service. Although heavier and bulkier than the Austen, the Owen was far more rugged and better suited to the rigours of service in operational theatres such as New Guinea, a consequence assisted by the provision of design measures to keep dirt out of the bolt area. The outstanding feature of the Owen, the vertical thirty-three-round magazine, proved to be no problem in action, the simple sights being offset to the left of the tubular receiver. Other features of the Owen included a removable barrel – not for cooling purposes (early models had finned barrels to assist in that regard) but as an aid to cleaning. Once in service, many Owen and Austen guns were painted in camouflage colours to blend with the local foliage.

At one stage it was suggested that a batch of 60,000 Owen guns would be procured for the US Army in 0.45 calibre. Nothing came of that but it does indicate a measure of the high regard in which the Owen gun was held. After 1945 the Owen gun served on with the Australian armed forces until at least the mid 1960s.

THOMPSONS

The Thompson sub-machine gun has already been mentioned for, as far as the British and the Australians were concerned, it was the only weapon of its type on the open market when they first decided to adopt sub-machine guns in 1939–40. By then the design of the Thompson was nearly twenty years old since it had been developed as a 'trench broom' to sweep the Great War trenches clear of the enemy.

The designer was John T. Thompson, a director of the Auto Ordnance Corporation of New York, together with John Bliss and Thomas Ryan. The first prototype was belt-fed, although the outlines of the 0.45 Thompson gun became apparent only with the Model 1919. This had a box magazine and the twin grips that became a characteristic of the inter-war models. By then the Great War was over and so sales of the new weapon were few, apart from a few to police forces and diversions to the Irish Republican Army and criminals. Demonstrations in

Instruction on the 0.45 Thompson M1928.

1920 to the American military aroused interest to the extent that Auto Ordnance decided to place a contract with Colt's to manufacture 15,000 examples of what became the Model 1921. Auto Ordnance then had no manufacturing capacity of their own but they did supply the necessary jigs, tools and gauges. Unfortunately, that military interest soon waned and thus Auto Ordnance were left with stocks of guns and parts that remained with them for nearly twenty years.

The Model 1921 was a well-made and rather heavy weapon with a cyclic rate of fire of about 800rpm. The locking mechanism was complicated, with a hesitation lock system engaging a small locking component in friction-locking slots at the instant of firing. The machining of this locking piece (the H piece from its shape) had to be very

precise, and the same applied to many other components; the gun was therefore costly. Further cost was added by providing the barrel with cooling fins. A box magazine held twenty rounds but drum magazines were also available. One of these could hold as many as 100 rounds, although this proved to be too many for weight and reliability purposes. The other drum magazine, the one so prominently displayed in numerous Hollywood gangster movies, held fifty 0.45 ACP rounds.

The first significant military sales came in 1928 when the US Marine Corps acquired a small batch. On this Model 1928 the foregrip was replaced by a straight wooden fore-end, while the muzzle was fitted with a slotted device to reduce muzzle climb when firing bursts. The cyclic fire rate was reduced to 700rpm by adding a stronger return spring.

Thompson Model 1928

Calibre	11.43mm; 0.45in
Length	857mm; 33.75in
Length of barrel	267mm; 10.52in
Weight	4.88kg; 10.75lb
Muzzle velocity	280m/s; 920ft/s
Feed	30-round box magazine
	or 50-round drum
Cyclic rate of fire	600–725rpm

Even with the Marine Corps order, sales remained slow throughout the 1930s until war began in Europe. The French government then placed an order for 3,000 Thompson guns, soon followed by another for a further 3,000. In February 1940 the British asked for as many Thompsons as could be supplied. The initial order was for 450 guns, soon rising to 107,500, plus 249 million rounds of 0.45 ammunition. By that time the Thompson had been accepted for US Army service as the M1928A1.

Although Auto Ordnance established its own production facility at Bridgeport, Connecticut, they could not supply such demands within the required time scale and so the Savage Arms Corporation of Utica, New York, was contracted to produce the Thompson gun. Orders then began to flow in at such a rate that it became obvious that the gun was too complicated to manufacture in time to meet the pressing demands, especially from Britain where invasion seemed imminent. By August 1941 318,900 guns were on order, including 20,450 for

Thompson M1928A1 on a custom-built motor cycle mounting.

Sub-machine gun, Caliber 0.45, M1.

the American armed forces. By 1942 the American government had assumed responsibility for all outstanding orders, thereafter supplying Britain under Lend-Lease arrangements. By then British orders stood at 514,000.

Auto Ordnance and Savage initiated a programme to determine how the Thompson could be rendered simpler to manufacture. The first result was the M1928A2, where components such as the muzzle device, barrel fins and the complicated sights were all eliminated, while some minor ones became pressings instead of machined parts. It was still not enough and so the government redesigned the Thompson completely.

The result was the M1 on which the original Thompson locking system was replaced by a

---

Thompson M1

Calibre	11.43mm; 0.45in
Length	813mm; 32in
Length of barrel	267mm; 10.52in
Weight	4.74kg; 10.45lb
Muzzle velocity	280m/s; 920ft/s
Feed	30-round box magazine
Cyclic rate of fire	700rpm

---

straightforward blowback using a heavier breech block. There was no provision for drum magazines and the standard of finish was much reduced. Even so, the M1 was still heavier, more difficult to manufacture and demanding in raw materials than other contemporary weapons such as the Sten, even after the M1A1 was introduced with a fixed firing pin rather than the hammer-operated equivalent on the M1. By then the cost of a single gun had been reduced from the $209 of 1939 to $45.

Production of Thompsons ceased in 1944 after 1,387,134 had been made. Not all of those ordered by Britain reached their intended users, for well over 100,000 were sent to the bottom of the Atlantic during the U-boat campaign. Those that did were sorely needed. During 1941 and 1942 the Home Guard were given priority over the Regular Army as invasion still seemed near. Gradually, Thompsons were issued throughout the British armed forces and some were diverted to the Indian Army.

Other Thompson gun users included the Free French and China. After 1945 Thompsons were passed on to other nations to such an extent that it would be foolish to state that the type has entirely passed from service; Thompsons were still being carried by Turkish soldiers during the early 1990s.

Throughout its life the Thompson was a popular weapon even if it was heavy and bulky. It did at least

Recognition manual comparison of M2 (Hyde) sub-machine gun (top) and Thompson M1A1 (below).

resemble what users recognized as a gun, something that could not be said for weapons such as the Sten or the US M3. Like the Sten, the M3 was another expedient.

THE M2 AND THE M3

Before beginning the M3 story, mention must be made of one weapon that did not succeed, the 0.45 M2 sub-machine gun. This was designed by George Hyde, a highly productive designer, who was at that time working with the Inland Division of General Motors, hence the name Hyde-Inland bestowed on the prototype. This gun was one of many submitted to the US Army for tests during a period when it seemed that any form of weapon resembling a sub-

machine gun had to be considered for possible adoption. Needless to say, many of the hopefuls were soon rejected for good reasons, but the Hyde-Inland performed well and was considered worthy of type-classification as the M2, although on a substitute standard basis.

The US Army tested every possibility as the Thompson gun was expensive and complicated to manufacture in quantity. What was needed was something simpler and cheaper, and the Hyde-Inland M2 seemed to qualify at least partly. Capacity was earmarked at the Marlin Firearms Corporation of New Haven, Connecticut, but production difficulties soon became apparent, especially from sub-contractors not used to firearms manufacture. The first production M2 was not delivered for acceptance testing until March 1943, some months after the M3 had been declared as standard. Production of the M2 therefore never did get under way and the design passed into small arms history.

The M2 had been overtaken by the M3, another weapon designed by George Hyde with inputs from Inland Division engineers. The US Army, acknowledging the trends set by weapons such as the MP38/MP40 and the Sten, had called for an all-metal construction sub-machine gun with manufacturing, cost and performance characteristics similar to those of the Sten. One oddity of the detailed specification was that the weapon had to be capable of firing either the US 0.45 ACP or the 9×19mm Parabellum pistol ammunition, with a minimum of part changing.

The result became the M3 in December 1942. Soon nicknamed the 'Grease Gun' because of its appearance, the M3 was a compact blowback, all-

Hyde M2	
Calibre	11.43mm; 0.45in
Length	815mm; 32.1in
Length of barrel	307mm; 12.1in
Weight	4.2kg; 9.25lb
Muzzle velocity	293m/s; 960ft/s
Feed	20- or 30-round box magazine
Cyclic rate of fire	500rpm

metal weapon with a telescopic wire stock and a minimum of finish. The main receiver body was two pressed steel components welded together. Owing to the heavy bolt involved, the cyclic rate of fire was about 400rpm, making it comfortable to use. An ejection port cover acted as a safety catch when closed. To change from 0.45 to 9mm ammunition required a change of barrel, bolt and magazine housing adapter as the usual 0.45 magazine holding thirty rounds was replaced by one of the Sten pattern. As with the Sten, M3 magazines were a constant source of trouble. Another longer-term problem was the charging device on the right-hand side of the receiver. Actuating this rather flimsy-looking lever cocked the weapon, but once in service it was found that this component was prone to wear and breakage. The immediate solution was a change to a better grade of steel, but while this was being investigated it was found that the lever and its

This illustration of an M2 in action clearly shows why it was dubbed the 'Grease Gun'.

M3	
Calibre	11.43mm; 0.45in
Length	757mm; 29.8in
Length of barrel	203mm; 8in
Weight	3.7kg; 8.15lb
Muzzle velocity	274m/s; 900ft/s
Feed	30-round box magazine
Cyclic rate of fire	350–450rpm

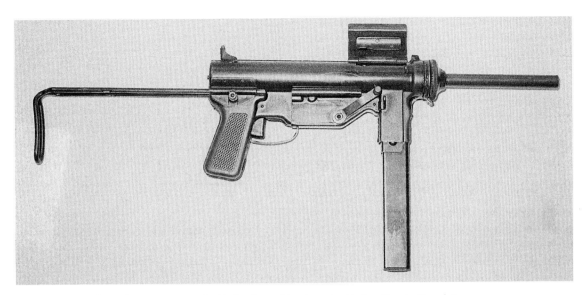

This is the M3 sub-machine gun, recognizable by the cocking lever just below the ejection slot

internal linkages could be omitted altogether. In their place a recess was drilled into the bolt to accommodate a forefinger to pull back the bolt for cocking. With this change the M3A1 was type-classified in December 1944.

Production orders for 300,000 examples of the original M3 were awarded to the Guide Lamp Division of General Motors at Detroit as they had considerable experience of steel stampings from their normal activity manufacturing car headlamps. Bolts were manufactured by the Buffalo Arms Corporation. The path to full production was not smooth for problems arose when the fabrication methods had to be altered slightly to suit the

This illustration of the 0.45 M3A1 sub-machine gun clearly shows the holes into which a finger could be inserted for cocking; the flash hider was an optional extra.

available tooling and welding processes. Supply of the M3 gradually lagged to the point where M1A1 Thompson production had to be maintained past the time when it had been planned to be phased out.

M3 production did not begin in earnest until 1943. By 1945 621,133 had been manufactured. A few were fitted with sound suppressors for special operations. Another optional muzzle attachment was a flash hider cone.

The M3/M3A1 was not greatly liked by the US forces. Soldiers were forced to admit that it worked but the gun's nickname did little to improve its acceptance, many soldiers preferring the bulkier and heavier Thompson. Even so, the M3 and the M3A1 remained in the US inventory for many years; there were plans to restart production during the Korean War but nothing came of that. The type was still available for issue to US Army tank crews during the 1990s and many other nations still retain the type. The M3/M3A1 is one weapon that continues to appear in odd places because large numbers were parachuted into occupied Europe (chambered for 9mm ammunition) and were widely distributed throughout the Far East.

OTHER AMERICANS

It has already been mentioned that the US Army tested many sub-machine guns before opting for the

Reising Model 50	
Calibre	11.43mm; 0.45in
Length	908mm; 35.75in
Length of barrel	279mm; 11in
Weight	3.06kg; 6.75lb
Muzzle velocity	280m/s; 920ft/s
Feed	20-round box magazine
Cyclic rate of fire	550rpm

M2 and then the M3. Most submissions were rejected, usually on the grounds of unreliability or complexity, but such was the need to get sub-machine guns into service during 1941 that three types, the already-mentioned M2, the M'42 and the Reising, did get through the test procedures and into production.

The Reising was named after its designer, Eugene C. Reising, and was manufactured by Harrington and Richardson during 1941. Although it was never fully type-classified, the Reising was produced in limited numbers (about 10,000), the majority of them going to the Marine Corps where they proved to be troublesome. The main production model, the 0.45 Reising Model 50, was a blowback weapon firing from a closed bolt using a complicated hammer mechanism. Other elaborations were a

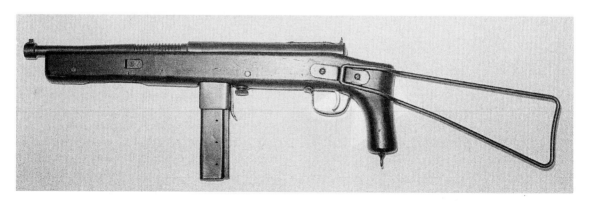

The unfortunate 0.45 Reising Model 55 intended for airborne forces; the Model 50 had a wooden butt stock.

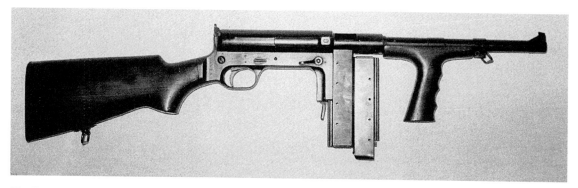

The United Defense Corporation Model 1942, known as the UD M'42 or, to British special forces, the Marlin.

muzzle compensator, a finned barrel and a finger-cocking latch under the forestock. These features made the Model 50 expensive and difficult to manufacture.

It fact, the Reising was altogether complicated, to the extent that little consideration was given to making the weapon work under adverse conditions. It proved to be highly prone to jamming. After employing them in combat on Guadalcanal, the Marines demonstrated their opinion of the Reising by dumping the survivors in a river. The Reising Model 50 is therefore a collector's piece today, as is the Model 55, modified for airborne troops by having a folding wire butt, a pistol grip and no muzzle compensator.

The second American sub-machine gun that got to the production stage was the United Defense

Corporation Model 1942, or M'42. As with the Reising, the M'42 was never officially accepted for service but ended by being so in any case. Compared with the Reising, the M'42 was a much more serviceable design, originally chambered for the 0.45 ACP pistol cartridge but capable of conversion to 9 × 19mm Parabellum ammunition. It was very well made, resulting in good reliability.

The M'42's designer was the highly versatile Carl Swebilius, with the production being carried out by the Marlin Firearms Company at New Haven. The guns, in 9×19mm calibre, were originally intended for the Dutch East Indies, but once that part of the world had been overrun by the Japanese there were undelivered guns available for whoever might want them. The US Office of Strategic Services (OSS) stepped into the breach. As a result the M'42 ended by being involved in numerous cloak and dagger activities in the Second World War, an undetermined number of the guns being passed to British special forces operating in the Mediterranean area; the British knew the M'42 as the Marlin.

One perceived drawback of the M'42 was its magazine capacity of only twenty rounds. Swebilius overcame this by connecting two magazines in opposition so that an empty one could be rapidly removed and inverted to insert the other. This is now a common procedure, although most practitioners simply tape two magazines together.

M'42	
Calibre	9mm; 0.354in
Length	820mm; 32.3in
Length of barrel	279mm; 11in
Weight	4.14kg; 9.12lb
Muzzle velocity	400m/s; 1,312ft/s
Feed	20-round box magazine
Cyclic rate of fire	700rpm

Although only about 15,000 M'42s were manufactured they provide an interesting study; their operational careers would make an equally interesting topic for research.

SOVIET BEGINNINGS

If Hollywood was to be believed, the most ardent users of sub-machine guns between 1939 and 1945 were the German armed forces, for every World War 2 film epic seems to display the photogenic MP38 or MP40 in almost every appropriate frame. The truth is that within most German formations the issue of sub-machine guns evened out at about one per infantry section. This allotment was rarely exceeded. By contrast, the Soviet Army distributed sub-machine guns on a lavish scale. Some infantry formations, especially the 'tank descent' units carried into battle on the backs of tanks, were issued with little else.

As with most other sub-machine gun users, the acceptance of the type into the Soviet ranks was by no means a smooth operation. It had been decided

PPD-40	
Calibre	7.62mm; 0.30in
Length	787mm; 31in
Length of barrel	267mm; 10.5in
Weight	3.63kg; 8lb
Muzzle velocity	488m/s; 1,600ft/s
Feed	71-round drum
Cyclic rate of fire	800rpm

as early as 1925 that sub-machine guns would form part of armament of the Red Army, yet development was slow and at one juncture virtually ceased.

The Soviet sub-machine guns of the 1920s and the early 1930s were uninspired derivatives of the German MP18/1 chambered for the 7.62 × 25mm Type P pistol cartridge, the cartridge later adopted for the sub-machine guns of the Great Patriotic War. It was 1934 before a model was standardized, the Pistolet-Pulemet Degtyarev obr 1934g (PPD-34). Production of this appears to have been limited to

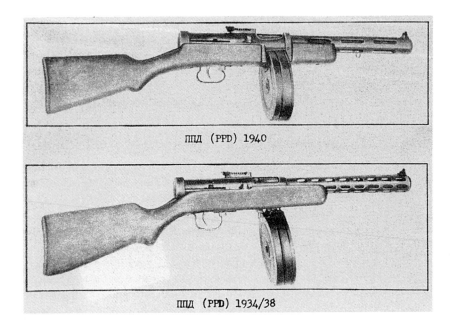

ППД (PPD) 1940

ППД (PPD) 1934/38

Early Soviet sub-machine gun models: (bottom) the 7.62mm PPD-34/38 and (top) the 7.62mm PPD-40.

little more than trial batches and even then only for possible issue to higher ranking officers. At that time the Red Army had other priorities and Stalin's purges were about to begin, limiting the initiative for acceptance on any scale. It was 1938, still during the purges, that a modified PPD-34/38 appeared, but that also failed to meet with general approval, most officers regarding it as a somewhat dangerous weapon for some reason, although it appears to have been a sound enough design.

One criticism of the PPD-34 was that the twenty-five-round, curved box magazine contained too few rounds for combat. A drum magazine was therefore substituted on the PPD-34/38. The magazine for the PPD-34/38 held seventy-three rounds, but it proved troublesome and a revised design appeared on the next model, the PPD-40. This was approved for production, although by later Soviet standards the output was little more than desultory. The combined total for the whole of 1940 was just over 81,000.

This was due to several factors, one being that many surviving Red Army officers, cowed by the purges, were reluctant to say or do anything that might upset Stalin, especially as he retained matters such as small-arms procurement and production under his personal control. As many officers lacked knowledge or guidance regarding the role of the sub-machine gun during infantry operations, the PPD series were hardly issued on any significant scale, most remaining stockpiled in depots. Few dared to issue such a misunderstood weapon since mistakes could lead to serious trouble for the miscreants. In the meantime, further sub-machine gun development lapsed into a state of torpor.

That outlook changed during the Winter War of 1939–40 against Finland, when the Finns demonstrated to the Soviet soldiers exactly what sub-machine guns could achieve in determined and well-trained hands. The Finns had the 9mm Konepistooli m/31, a drum-fed design almost universally known as the *Suomi* (Finland). Although the Soviet high command emerged from the campaign with their objectives achieved (albeit also sustaining heavy losses), they learned many hard lessons along the way, one of which was the devastating impact of sub-machine guns during close-quarter combat. Some PPD-40s had been carried by the Soviets during the Winter War, but the general lack of understanding of their role limited their effectiveness.

Once the lesson had been grasped, demand for sub-machine guns grew dramatically. At that point the second reason for the low production of the PPD-40 became apparent. The PPD series, from the PPD-34 onwards, were manufactured by using the old, time-honoured methods and materials, with numerous machining and time-absorbing processes, all requiring skilled labour and the finest raw materials. A rapid expansion in production rates would therefore take time before anything significant could emerge, and the Soviet Union was running out of time. In June 1941 the Germans invaded.

'Pah-Pah-Sha'

Within a few months what few sub-machine guns the Red Army had once owned were mostly lost as the German Army cut huge swathes into Soviet territory. By the time the Germans were approaching Moscow at the end of 1941, the total Soviet sub-machine gun inventory stood at only a few hundred.

It was desperation time in almost every aspect of Soviet military activity, but as far as sub-machine gun designs were concerned the solution was at hand. The PPD series had been devised at a time when gun-making techniques were still highly skilled. By 1941 ways had been devised to simplify and speed many manufacturing processes without any loss of subsequent operational performance. Weapons such as the German MP40 and the British Sten demonstrated the lengths to which such simplifications could be stretched.

The Soviets were thinking along the same lines quite independently of developments elsewhere. During 1940 Georgiy Shpagin produced the prototype of a weapon that was to become a symbol of the eventual Soviet victory over the aggressors.

By the end of 1940, Shpagin's sub-machine gun had been adopted to replace the PPD series. As

PPSh-41, the classic Soviet sub-machine gun of the Great Patriotic War years, seen here with both its 35-round box or 71-round drum magazine.

always, it took time to prepare production lines for the new model that became the PPSh-41, known to the Soviet Army as the 'Pah-Pah-Sha'. In essence, Shpagin took the basic outlines of the PPD series and made everything much simpler to manufacture, to the extent that threaded unions between components and sub-assemblies were virtually eliminated. In their place came spot weldings, securing pins, pressings and a minimum of machining processes. The only component receiving particular care was the barrel, produced by cutting a standard Mosin-Nagant rifle barrel into three lengths. This, in common with other Soviet sub-machine guns, was

chromed to prolong its life while requiring a minimum of maintenance. This point was important because Shpagin knew that procedures such as cleaning and routine maintenance would be virtually non-existent once front-line Soviet soldiers got their hands on any weapon.

Despite its rough finish and hasty manufacture, the PPSh-41 soon proved to be a rugged and reliable weapon, capable of operating under all conditions and in all weathers. Ammunition was fed from a seventy-one-round drum magazine, providing the individual soldier with a sound firepower base, but, in practice, despite having great visual and photogenic impact, the drum proved to be slow to reload while being problematic to manufacture. At one point it took as long to manufacture a drum as the rest of the PPSh-41. Consequently the complicated drum was phased out and replaced by a thirty-five-round box magazine, although the drum was still in widespread use when the war ended. When it was first issued, from February 1942 onwards, the box magazines proved to be somewhat flimsy and were easily distorted or otherwise damaged. The immediate solution was to double the thickness of the steel sheet involved to 1mm. No problems arose after that modification.

Initially, the only problem regarding the PPSh-41

PPSh-41	
Calibre	7.62mm; 0.30in
Length	840mm; 33.07in
Length of barrel	269mm; 10.6in
Weight	3.5kg; 7.7lb
Muzzle velocity	488m/s; 1,600ft/s
Feed	35-round box magazine or 71-round drum
Cyclic rate of fire	900–1,000rpm

was that there were not enough of them. Almost as soon as production facilities had been established they had to be dismantled and moved east of the Urals, out of reach of the advancing Germans. It was late 1941 before the new factories, established in haste and under dreadful conditions, could even start to meet the huge demands being imposed on them. The design of the PPSh-41 meant that unskilled operatives could manufacture most of the gun and so once production did start it became possible to turn out thousands.

By the end of 1941 the PPSh-41 production total had already reached 55,147. The 1942 figure was 1,499,269. Such quantities were badly needed since by mid-1942 all basic combat commodities were at a premium. Gradually, one platoon in every Soviet infantry company received PPSh-41s in place of rifles, while many battalions had an entire company armed with the gun. Within many formations this

allotment was exceeded, especially among shock attack units such as the tank descent troops. This widespread issue of sub-machine guns meant that their users had to come to very close quarters with their enemy to be fully effective, but such basic and brutal tactics came to be the norm on the Eastern Front.

These close-range tactics had their effect on the PPSh-41. Early models had tangent sights calibrated to 500m/547yd. The sights proved to be not only unnecessary but difficult to manufacture. They were therefore replaced by a simple flip-over sight for 100 and 200m (109 and 219yd) without problems or complaint from the field. Another production short cut arose with the recoil buffer inside the receiver, something made necessary by the rather high cyclic rate of fire of about 900rpm. The buffer was originally a fibrous material difficult to supply in the quantities required. As an interim

Every one of the ski soldiers shown in this 1943 photograph is carrying a PPSh-41 sub-machine gun.

Polish soldiers fighting with the Soviets turning their PPSh-41 sub-machine guns against the German occupiers of Prague.

the fibre was changed to rubber. Rubber was not entirely satisfactory, so another change was made to leather washers. The leather buffers not only worked, they proved to be cheaper and easier to manufacture.

Yet another production saving introduced when demand was still outstripping supply was to cut down old rifle barrels in place of new ones. Such barrels proved adequate but they were still chromed before issue.

The final production total for the PPSh-41 has not been found but it has been estimated at over five million. Even today the PPSh-41 may still be encountered in places such as Albania and Vietnam, many of those in Vietnam being post-war Chinese copies, the Type 50. Other post-war manufacturers were Hungary, Iran and North Korea.

By 1945 the PPSh-41 had also been adopted by the Germans. They captured so many that the PPSh-41 became almost a standard German weapon as the 7.62mm MP717(r). By 1945 the Germans were converting captured PPSh-41s to fire 9 × 19mm Parabellum ammunition feeding from MP40 magazines – the magazine housings were modified accordingly. Exactly how many were so converted is not known but it appears to have been programmed to equip the Waffen SS.

The PPS

The success of the PPSh-41 was such that several other Soviet sub-machine guns appearing between 1941 and 1945 were never adopted. Despite their attractions and technical innovations, none offered

The sub-machine gun at its most basic, the 7.62mm PPS-43 manufactured in Leningrad during the siege.

any significant advantages over the PPSh-41 at a time when it was in full production. Among such guns was the first weapon designed by Mikhail Kalashnikov of post-war assault-rifle fame. His design, like so many others of the period, did not progress past prototypes.

There was one major and important exception, the guns designed by I.K. Bezruchko-Vysotsky and adapted for production by Aleksey Sudaev. Unlike many of his contemporaries working on small arms, Sudaev was primarily an engineer who became involved in small arms only as a result of adverse circumstances, namely the siege of Leningrad. During those epic 900 days, any provision of fresh weapons and combat stores was drastically curtailed or, at times, impossible, so the besieged had to produce what they could using their limited local resources.

Bezruchko-Vysotsky and Sudaev had already prepared the outlines of a simple sub-machine gun before Sudaev was sent to Leningrad to organize the production of it locally. The result, the PPS-42, was even more austere than the PPSh-41; but, despite being reduced to the point of crudity, the PPS-42 was highly successful. It proved to be rugged, reliable and easy to handle, having a cyclic rate of fire limited to 600 to 700rpm, while requiring a minimum of machine-tool resources or skilled labour to assemble.

The PPS-42 was constructed by using heavy gauge steel pressings only, apart from the barrel. Wood was limited to the pistol grip side plates, although this was later changed to hard rubber. Everything on the gun was at its most fundamental, an example being the muzzle attachment. This doubled as a muzzle brake and muzzle-climb compensator although it was only a simple strip of steel curved to shape and riveted and spot-welded in position; a drilled hole enabled the bullet to travel on its way. It was simple to make and cost little – but it worked. The same could be said of the all-metal butt that folded up and over the receiver, and there were many other design details that could be quoted, such as the thirty-five-round box magazine unique to the model – there was never any provision

PPS-43	
Calibre	7.62mm; 0.30in
Length	820mm; 32.3in
Length of barrel	254mm; 10in
Weight	3.04kg; 6.7lb
Muzzle velocity	488m/s; 1,600ft/s
Feed	35-round box magazine
Cyclic rate of fire	700rpm

for a drum magazine. Fire was automatic only, although a trained user could squeeze off single shots.

Such a weapon, rushed into production using barely trained labour, was bound to have faults and they duly appeared. The difference between the PPS-42 and many other weapons of the time was that the former was field-tested in action only just outside the factory where it was assembled. Any problems revealed could therefore be transmitted direct to the production line for modifications to be immediately incorporated. By mid-1943 such modifications reached the point where a new designation became necessary, that of PPS-43. The differences between the two models were mostly of detail, although the folding butt was shortened and changes were made to the ejector and the magazine housing.

Many observers have since commented, with hindsight, that the PPS-43 was better in many respects than the PPSh-41. The PPS-43 was lighter, more compact, easier to handle while remaining highly reliable and capable of absorbing hard knocks. It was easy to field-strip and required little training prior to use. In addition the PPS-43 was also cheaper.

The PPS-43 remained in production after the siege was lifted and was issued to units away from the Leningrad front. However, the numbers involved never approached those of the PPSh-41, the total final production figure being about one million. Several reasons have been put forward for this, one being that the PPSh-41 was too well established to be dislodged from its prime position during time of war. Another more sinister reason relates to Stalin's suspicions regarding the defenders of Leningrad. They frequently operated without his direct control or permission and were thus suspected of being politically unreliable. The PPS-43, being an instance of Leningrad's independence from Stalin, was therefore never accorded the recognition it deserved.

The latter point remains undetermined, even now. It did not prevent the PPS-43 from having a long career after 1945, being widely copied or manufactured in countries as diverse as China and Poland. One post-war copy, the 9mm DUX 53, was adopted by the West German Border Guard, but the PPS-43 had already gained German approval before the end in 1945. Early in that year serious consideration was given to copying the PPS-43 to equip the German armed forces but the war ended before that could happen. Captured PPS-43s were adopted by the German Army as the 7.62mm MP709(r).

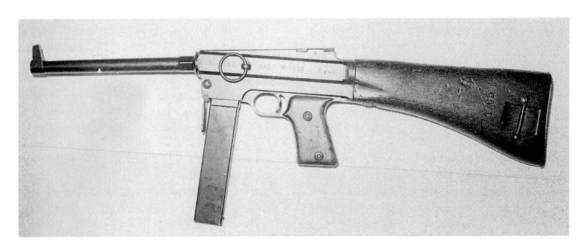

The French 7.65mm MAS mle 38, kept in production after 1940 for the Germans.

FRENCH EFFORTS

The French Army experimented with sub-machine guns as early as 1918 but during the inter-war years their enthusiasm waned as budgets for new weapons shrank. A 1925 effort to develop a copy of the German 9mm MP18/1, the STA, languished after about a thousand examples had been manufactured for troop trials in Morocco. It was 1935 before the sub-machine gun was considered again, by the state-owned Manufacture d'Armes de Saint-Etienne (MAS). Their efforts were to have an unfortunate outcome.

Development of the sub-machine gun finally adopted in 1938 as the 7.65mm mle 1938 MAS was carried out at a leisurely pace with numerous trial and development models being made before a decision was reached. It was based on the production methods of the past, for it was a well-made gun with most of its components machined from solid metal. As a result, the compact mle 1938 MAS was extremely durable and reliable, but it was complex and expensive, having refinements such as a non-reciprocating cocking handle combined with a cover that kept dirt out of the interior. The fixed wooden butt housed the recoil spring.

For some reason the French Army decided to chamber the mle 1938 MAS for the 7.65mm Longue (7.65 × 19.5mm) pistol cartridge, a cartridge rarely encountered outside France and one considered, even at that time, as rather low-powered.

Preparations to manufacture the mle 1938 MAS also proceeded at a leisurely pace to the extent that when the Army decided during 1939 that they urgently needed sub-machine guns, they were still awaiting the first delivery from Saint-Etienne. As a stopgap it was therefore decided to purchase 3,000 Thompsons from the USA. Another stopgap involved about 3,250 9mm MP Erma sub-machine guns taken from Republican soldiers interned in France following the end of the Spanish Civil War. These had been stockpiled against their possible use at a depot at Clermont-Ferrand; few of them were actually issued to field units.

mle 1938 MAS	
Calibre	7.65mm; 0.301in
Length	623mm; 24.9in
Length of barrel	224mm; 8.8in
Weight	2.87kg; 6.38lb
Muzzle velocity	350m/s; 1,150ft/s
Feed	32-round box magazine
Cyclic rate of fire	600–700rpm

By the time the Germans invaded France in 1940 deliveries of the mle 1938 MAS from Saint-Etienne came to only 1,958 examples. Few, if any, reached the front line since the first issues went to the Garde Mobile, an internal security force. Following the fall of France, the occupying Germans discovered that the Saint-Etienne production line remained intact and so they simply took it over. Production continued for them until the Liberation of 1944 – they knew the weapon as the 7.65mm MP722(f). They would no doubt have preferred to modify the design to accommodate their own 9 × 19mm Parabellum ammunition but, as this would have taken time and resources, the 7.65mm Longue cartridge was tolerated. The bulk of the Saint-Etienne output went to German garrison units and their paramilitary offshoots based within France.

Once the Germans left in 1944 production of the mle 1938 MAS continued until 1950 for the reformed French Army and police force.

There were two other French sub-machine guns of the 1940 period, the ETVS and the Petter. The ETVS was quite an advanced design, complicated by having a side-folding butt and folding magazine housing to save space when carried. The ETVS, like the Petter, did not reach anything like mass production status before the German take-over but small field-trial batches did reach the troops, only to vanish into the chaos after the collapse of France. Neither was resurrected later.

5 Light Machine Guns

The Allies never adopted the general purpose machine gun concept so avidly embraced by the German armed forces before 1939. After 1945 the concept of using a single model of machine gun capable of being adapted for a wide array of tactical roles and applications was accepted almost universally, but the Allied nations did not make such a drastic switch while they were still at war. Instead, they continued to manufacture and categorize machine guns as either *light machine guns*, portable enough to be carried and handled by a single soldier, or *heavy machine guns*. The latter were served and carried by a team and mounted on a tripod, or some other type of static mounting, to deliver prolonged bursts of fire to extreme ranges. By 1945 the term heavy machine gun had been redirected to machine guns having calibres of about 0.50in/12.7mm, so the alternative term of *medium machine gun* became applied to tripod-mounted machine guns with rifle calibres. This chapter will deal with the light machine guns employed by the Allies.

As with so many other types of weapon, the light machine gun came to prominence during the Great War. Although heavy machine guns dominated the Western Front battlefields they were all too often organized separately from the units they were meant to support and were slow to respond or adapt to a tactical situation. They were also difficult to move. The introduction of light, portable machine guns provided the infantry of both sides with their own means of delivering automatic fire where and when it was needed.

For once, the Great War Allies were in advance of the Germans in the development and application of the light weapon. The American Lewis Gun was available in 1914, as was the French Hotchkiss mle 1909. Both were followed by the infamous French Chauchat. Before those the Danish Madsen was first marketed in 1904. By contrast, the best the German designers could do was belatedly convert their standard heavy Maxim into the 7.92mm leMG 08/15, a weapon that was just about portable but otherwise generally unsatisfactory. Between them, the Lewis and the Chauchat started a process that revolutionized infantry tactics, providing the infantry with their own means of suppressing enemy manoeuvre both in attack and defence. By 1918 these two weapons had been joined by the American Browning Automatic Rifle (the BAR), a hybrid regarded by some as an automatic rifle, while to others it was a rather light light machine gun.

The Lewis, the Hotchkiss, the Chauchat and the BAR were still to be found in 1939, although by 1945 only the BAR remained in widespread service. Between the wars they had been joined by several new light machine gun models and more appeared during the war years. By 1945 the light machine gun had settled down into a more or less established form. It was fired from a folding bipod to take the weight of about 9 kg/20lb or slightly more. Ammunition was usually fed from a box or drum magazine although some designs retained belt feed – the latter was usually an awkward feature on a portable weapon. Although one soldier could usually carry and use the weapon in action, within many armies it was usual to allot a team of two to each gun. One carried and fired the gun while the other carried ready-use ammunition and items such as spare barrels, where applicable.

EARLY LIGHTS

The first true light machine gun has usually been regarded as the Fusil Mitrailleur Hotchkiss mle 1909, although the Danish Madsen predated it. The Madsen went on to have a long and varied history, appearing in many guises and chambered for many ammunition calibres. It was a sound and reliable light weapon that was sold widely (one of the earliest customers was Tsarist Russia), but as the rising block locking mechanism was complicated in the extreme, the construction methods involved meant that to purchase any Madsen gun was an expensive proposition. Despite this, the Madsen was distributed widely and many were still in service throughout Europe in 1939, as well as South America and China. As well as bipod- and tripod-

mounted examples for infantry use, Madsens were also mounted in tanks and aircraft.

Somehow, the Madsen light machine gun remained on the periphery of the story of small arms, having little influence on the development of other weapons other than heralding light machine gun tactics at a time when all machine guns were still in their tactical infancy. The Madsen was still being marketed during the late 1950s, but by then there were few takers.

To return to the Hotchkiss mle 1909: it was developed in 6.5mm calibre as a lightened version of the heavier Hotchkiss machine gun series (*see* Chapter 6). The mle 1909 carried over a finned barrel, the gas-operated mechanism of the heavier models and the method of feeding rounds into the gun on thirty-round metal strips. One feature of

A forerunner, the Hotchkiss mle 1909, seen here mounted on a tripod for some reason.

> **Hotchkiss mle 1909 (UK)**
>
> Calibre   7.7mm; 0.303in
> Length   1.19m; 46.85in
> Length of barrel   600mm; 23.6in
> Weight   11.7kg; 25.8lb
> Muzzle velocity   ca 740m/s; ca 2,430ft/s
> Feed   30-round metal strip
> Cyclic rate of fire   500rpm

the mle 1909 was that cocking was accomplished by actuating a bolt handle in much the same manner as on a bolt action rifle. A small tripod bore the weight of 11.7kg/25.8lb.

This gun, adopted by the French and the British Army as well as the American (as the 'Benét-Mercié'), was intended to be a cavalry weapon although by 1914 its issue had spread to other arms. Experience soon demonstrated that the mle 1909 was totally unsuited to trench warfare conditions. It was therefore discarded by most users, only to become the machine gun carried by the first British tanks. These tank guns were chambered for British 0.303 ammunition and as such were retained by British cavalry units until the late 1930s. Any weapons still in French service were withdrawn soon after 1918, apart from a few examples in fortifications.

By 1940, whatever 0.303 Hotchkiss light machine guns remained in British armouries had been withdrawn to training establishments, the Home Guard and to provide makeshift air-defence weapons for airfields, merchant shipping and fishing boats. They were retained only until something better became available. Examples remained in service in Greece in 1940, although many of these were enhanced models such as the lighter mle 1922 and the mle 1926; the latter were delivered chambered for either 6.5 or 7.92mm ammunition.

While the Hotchkiss mle 1909 may not have been of much practical use after 1914, it did provide the

French Army with an indication of the potential of the light machine gun. Before 1914 a commission had been established to consider a light machine gun suited to the way in which the French Army considered that such guns should be employed. This entailed using the weapon as a form of heavy machine rifle delivering fire during the attack. Several specifications were laid down, including a request for rapid production at minimum cost. The result has been described as the worst machine gun ever devised.

The gun was generally known as the Chauchat after the name of one of the officers on the selection commission. Officially it was the 8mm Fusil Mitrailleur mle 1915 (another name was the CSRG after the initials of all the members of the commission). The list of faults with the Chauchat was a long one. It was badly assembled using rudimentary manufacturing techniques involving low-quality materials. If these were not enough, the Chauchat employed a long recoil mechanism on which everything seemed to move in such a manner as to invite malfunctioning. Added to this was that the design offered several routes for debris and dirt to enter the interior, including via the 'half-moon' curved magazine, liberally perforated to allow the user to see how many rounds remained at any time. Accuracy when firing was problematic as the gun tended to judder on its flimsy bipod.

Overall, the Chauchat was a horror, compounded by suspicions of graft and corruption in the placing of production contracts. As it was all the French possessed during the Great War years the Chauchat had to be endured, with about 225,000 examples being made. Of these 15,918 were sold to the US Army following its arrival in France from late 1917 onwards. The purchase of a further 19,241 Model 1918 Chauchats chambered for American 0.30-06 ammunition only rendered a bad weapon even worse, for the more powerful cartridge simply introduced yet more stoppages to an already weak mechanism.

Some observers have said that the Chauchat was a forerunner of the 'basic' guns that were to follow, such as the Sten and PPD sub-machine guns. In a

A museum example of an 8mm Chauchat mle 1915. Behind it is a battered Lewis Gun.

way it was, for the Chauchat was intended to be manufactured using simple machines and a minimum of components; but that path was followed mainly to improve profits, not functionality. In simple terms, the Chauchat did not operate as a military weapon should.

Once the war was over the US Army immediately disposed of its stocks of Chauchats; but the French Army had to retain the type throughout the inter-war years as there was little else it had of this weapon

Chauchat	
Calibre	8mm; 0.315in
Length	1.143m; 45in
Length of barrel	470mm; 18.5in
Weight	9.2kg; 20lb
Muzzle velocity	700m/s; 2,300ft/s
Feed	20-round magazine
Cyclic rate of fire	250–300rpm

type. It was thus still around when the Germans invaded France – the Germans also encountered Chauchats in Belgian and Greek hands. Those inter-war years had done little to enhance the Chauchat's reputation or reliability and so it was one captured light machine gun that the Germans decided not to adopt.

While the French Army may have been starved of funds for new equipment during the 1920s, what limited small arms development was possible was concentrated on a new light machine gun firing a cartridge better suited to automatic weapons than the old 8 × 50R Lebel dating from 1886. As early as 1920 a 7.5 × 58mm round was under consideration, to be officially adopted during 1924. Also adopted in that same year was a light machine gun named the Fusil Mitrailleur mle 1924. This utilized a gas-operated mechanism based on that of the Browning Automatic Rifle (*see* below), but with oddities such as separate triggers for single-shot or fully automatic fire.

The 7.5mm mle 1924 was a huge improvement over the Chauchat and proved to be a handy and

sturdy weapon. Unfortunately, problems emerged
after the gun had been in service for a while, from
bursting barrels to confusion of the new 7.5mm
cartridge with the similar looking German 7.92mm
cartridge (the French Army made extensive use of
ex-German weaponry for training during the
1920s). In 1928 a decision was taken to reduce
the length of the cartridge case (and thus reduce the
propellant capacity); thus the new cartridge became
7.5 × 54mm. Guns therefore had to be modified for
the shorter cartridge, the new designation being
7.5mm mle 1924/29.

In most respects the mle 1924/29 remained much
as before. The overhead box magazine held twenty-
five rounds and the dual trigger arrangement was
retained. In 1931 a version intended for use in tanks
and fortifications appeared. This had a side-
mounted, hundred-round drum magazine and a

mle 1924/29	
Calibre	7.5mm; 0.295in
Length	1.007m; 39.65in
Length of barrel	500mm; 19.69in
Weight	8.93kg; 19.7lb
Muzzle velocity	820m/s; 2,690ft/s
Feed	25-round box magazine
Cyclic rate of fire	450–600rpm

distinctive curved butt. Some of these mle 1931
guns were later adapted for air defence mounted in
pairs.

Although the mle 1924/29 proved to be a sound
light machine gun, the French armed forces were so

A 7.5mm mle 1924/29 light machine gun. Note the two triggers.

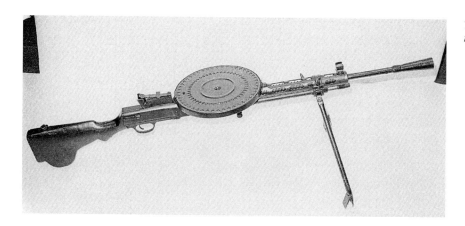

The 7.62mm DP light machine gun.

starved of weapons funding that production at Chatellerault and Saint-Etienne was painfully slow. By 1939 the total manufactured had yet to reach 2,000 (plus an unknown number of mle 1931 guns). This was well below what the French Army really needed and so the mle 1924/29 had little influence on the events of May and June 1940. Captured examples were adopted by the Germans as the 7.5mm leMG 115(f).

Surviving examples of the 7.5mm mle 1924/29 were retained by Free French forces operating in Africa and the Middle East until 1945. The type was retained in service until the late 1950s before being stockpiled for possible reserve use.

THE DP

As far as the Red Army was concerned there was only one light machine gun, the 7.62mm Pulemet Degtyareva Pekhotnii, usually known simply as the DP. It had its origins during the mid 1920s when a programme to replace the new Army's automatic weapons of Tsarist times was initiated. As already mentioned, the Tsarist Army was at one time equipped with Madsen light machine guns but by 1917 there were few, if any, of these left. A need for locally produced replacements was simply ignored as there were other more pressing priorities at the time.

By the time of the 1918–20 Civil War, light

machine gun requirements had to be met by the purchase of light automatic weapons from other countries, so guns such as the Lewis, the Chauchat and the mle 1909 Hotchkiss became familiar to Red and White Army soldiers alike. They were all found wanting in many respects with complexity, poor reliability and lack of robustness high on the list of their shortcomings. It was therefore decided to produce an indigenous light machine gun to meet the Red Army's exacting requirements.

Several design paths were taken. One was to adapt the Fedorov Avtomat (*see* Chapter 3), but that programme did not proceed far. Another approach was to take the well-understood Maxim mechanism (*see* Chapter 6) and lighten it, retaining as many components from the original Maxim mechanism as possible. One result of this was the Maxim-Tokarev (MT); it seemed so promising that in May 1925 it was recommended for adoption. However, once troop trials began the air-cooled MT was found to be too heavy and the belt feed system proved troublesome. Modifications were introduced and the gun actually went into limited production for a while. About 2,450 were made by 1927. Most MTs appear to have been sent to Spain during the Civil War of 1936–38 where they were used by the Republicans.

The MT was considered as only an interim model until something better came along. That duly followed with the selection of a light machine gun designed by Vasiliy Degtyarev, one of the most

A DP in action.

prolific and versatile gun designers of his era. With assistance from other Soviet design luminaries such as Simonov and Fedorov, Degtyarev produced one of the most remarkable light machine guns of all time, the DP.

The DP was a light, reliable and remarkably simple machine gun that exactly met the Army's requirements. In many ways the DP played its part in heralding the way gunmaking was to follow by

being designed from the outset for manufacture with a minimum of machining and components. There were only six moving parts, the locking mechanism relying on a system of flap-like lugs pushed outwards from the bolt by the firing pin at the instant of firing. Standard 7.62 × 54R rounds were fed from a forty-seven-round flat drum magazine over the receiver.

As well as the infantry DP, mounted on a bipod, there was also a tank model, the DT, and aircraft models, the DA and the DA-2, the latter being two DAs mounted side-by-side. The DT had a heavier barrel, a sixty-round drum and could be provided with a bipod for dismounted use.

Production totals for the DP have not been found but they must have been prodigious, for the DP served wherever the Red Army fought. Before 1941, just before the German invasion, so many had been manufactured that production was being run down. Once the Germans attacked that all changed and the DP was kept in production until 1944 to replace the huge losses sustained during 1941 and

DP	
Calibre	7.62mm; 0.30in
Length	1.265m; 49.8in
Length of barrel	605mm; 23.8in
Weight	11.9kg; 26.23lb
Muzzle velocity	844m/s; 2,770ft/s
Feed	47-round drum
Cyclic rate of fire	520–580rpm

The DPM differed from the earlier DP is several ways. Most obvious here are the pistol grip, the protrusion from the rear of the receiver and the revised bipod attachment.

1942. The German Army captured so many DPs that they were reissued widely among German formations as the 7.62mm leMG 120(r).

The DP did have its vices. One concerned the operating spring under the barrel which tended to become hot during prolonged firing due to its proximity to the barrel (there was no single-shot fire mode). The heat distorted the spring, resulting in stoppages. Although this drawback had been recognized many years before, it was not until 1944 that it and a few other weak points were rectified by relocating the operating spring behind the bolt. This resulted in a tubular protrusion from the back of the receiver; thus the usual firing grip around the small of the butt was not practicable. A pistol grip was therefore provided, doing away with the usual DP grip safety at the same time and providing a way of visually differentiating between the DP and the new model, the DPM (*Degtyareva Pekhotnii Modificatsionii*). One further advantage of the pistol grip was that it improved handling steadiness and therefore enhanced accuracy. The DPM also had a more robust bipod relocated further back along the barrel housing to improve its stability during firing. There was a corresponding DTM for tanks.

The DPM went on to have a prolonged post-war career with many Soviet-influenced armed forces.

At one time it was manufactured in China as the Type 53. Many no doubt remain in service in southeast Asia and Africa.

The ultimate replacement for the DPM was the 7.62mm RPD. Design work on this started in late 1943, firing the then-novel reduced-power 7.62 × 39mm M1943 cartridge. However, the first RPDs did not enter service until 1946. Neither did a little-used 7.62mm, belt-fed derivative of the DPM known as the RP-46.

THE LEWIS GUN

One of the machine guns used by both sides during the Russian Civil War was, as mentioned above, the Lewis gun. The Lewis was American in origin but is often regarded as a British gun. In fact it was an international weapon. Despite its name the Lewis Gun was originally designed by an American, Samuel McClean, during the 1900s. The name Lewis came from Colonel Isaac Newton Lewis, another American, who took over the McClean design, promoted it and introduced his own modifications. It was Cololonel Lewis who, from about 1910 onwards, offered the gun to the American government (who remained unimpressed for years after the gun had been adopted by many

A 0.303 Lewis Gun in position as a low-level air defence weapon in 1940.

others) and to other nations such as Belgium and the United Kingdom. It was in the latter that the Lewis was to be perfected by the Birmingham Small Arms Company (BSA). BSA had the Lewis Gun in production in Birmingham by 1914 and was soon overwhelmed by orders.

By 1914 the Lewis Gun had assumed the form it was to retain throughout its service life. It was a gas-operated weapon with clock spring inside a distinctive housing under the receiver to return the mechanism to the firing position once the gas cycle had unlocked the breech, after firing, to eject the spent case and load another round. Loading involved another distinctive feature, the double-stacked, forty-seven-round drum magazine over the

receiver (a ninety-seven-round magazine was a later alternative for aircraft). The mechanism was rather complicated, so regular maintenance was essential to prevent a wide variety of possible malfunctions. To assist barrel cooling it was surrounded with radiator vanes shrouded by a tubular jacket. The jacket also became a recognition feature of the Lewis Gun, although experience was to show that it was not always necessary, especially on aircraft guns when it was often omitted.

A typical land-service Lewis Gun weighed 12.15kg/27lb and was thus no lightweight and handy weapon, especially as the overall length was 1.25m/49.2in, but it could be handled by one soldier.

Chambered for the 0.303 cartridge, the Lewis Gun became a firm favourite with the British infantry. It was adopted by the Royal Flying Corps and also entered the French inventory. It greatly impressed the Germans who utilized as many of them as they could capture.

The Great War consumed Lewis Guns in great numbers. By 1918 the BSA factory at Small Heath had produced no fewer than 145,397 of them, most being sent to France either as land service or aircraft guns.

Only in the USA did the Lewis Gun fail to impress. For various reasons, the US Army did not adopt the Lewis until the USA entered the war in 1917. Before then the gun was in production by the Savage Arms Company of Utica, New York, who had been involved with early models of the gun since 1910. From 1915 onward, Savage produced 0.303 guns to fulfil orders from Britain and Canada. Once the USA entered the war some of their

Lewis	
Calibre	7.7mm; 0.303in
Length	1.25m; 49.2in
Length of barrel	661mm; 26.04in
Weight	12.15kg; 27lb
Muzzle velocity	744m/s; 2,440ft/s
Feed	47-round drum
Cyclic rate of fire	450rpm

capacity was diverted to producing Lewis Guns firing the American 0.30-06 cartridge. None of them reached France before the armistice, leaving American soldiers to grapple with the joys of the French Chauchat at a time when a better weapon was in production at home.

The bulk of 'American' 0.30 Lewis Gun

Air-cooled Lewis Guns still in service for air defence in 1942.

production was intended for aircraft applications; they therefore lacked the cooling jacket and had spade grips. Savage land service production was limited to 2,500 as against 40,303 for aircraft. The US forces retained a stock of 32,000 of the latter after 1918, with more being either handed on to other nations or placed in storage.

Between the wars the Lewis Gun became one of the most widely procured and distributed machine guns of the period. Aircraft and land service models were obtained by many nations, examples being the Baltic States, France, Holland, Portugal and Japan (7.7mm Type 89). The United Kingdom was the source of many of these inter-war weapons, the Lewis being retained by the British armed forces in considerable numbers, although by the late 1930s it had been largely replaced within the Army by the Bren (*see* below).

By the late 1930s the Lewis Gun was widely regarded as, at best, obsolescent, but it was about to obtain a new lease of life. That commenced in 1940 during the post-Dunkirk period when the British armed forces were so desperate for all types of infantry weapon that stockpiled Lewis Guns were hastily reissued for many applications, from the defence of airfields to that of fishing boats and merchant shipping. They were also issued to Regular Army infantry and training units in place of anything better, while more went to the Home Guard.

However, most Home Guard units received Lewis Guns from the USA. After 1918 many American guns were stored against some future contingency, which duly arrived in 1940 when Britain was in a desperate state. A total of 1,157 land service guns and 38,040 aircraft guns were shipped across the Atlantic and hastily issued, still chambered for 0.30-06 ammunition; more were lost when their carrier vessels were sunk in transit. These 0.30 guns received the general name of Savage-Lewis to differentiate them from the 0.303 guns from BSA. As most of the aircraft guns had spade grips, they had to be modified for land use by adding a hastily devised metal butt and revised trigger arrangement. Extra 0.303 guns were assembled from old spare

parts and a programme to recondition worn weapons was put in hand.

By 1943 the numbers of Lewis Guns in British service started to dwindle as they were gradually replaced by more modern weapons, usually Bren Guns. A few aircraft Lewis Guns were still in service in 1945 but few survived after then.

THE BAR

One of the mysteries of the Second World War was why the American armed forces never armed themselves with a viable light machine gun. In almost every other aspect of modern weaponry American industry was able to provide combat personnel with weapons of excellent quality and in the numbers required, but for some reason the American light machine gun never materialized. (It still has not, for the current US Army light machine gun, the 5.56mm M249, is Belgian in origin.) But that is a European opinion. American soldiers saw things differently for they had the Browning Automatic Rifle, the BAR. For the Americans the BAR assumed the role that the light machine gun undertook in other armed forces, even though in operational and design terms it was unsuited to the task.

The BAR was born before the Great War when the French doctrine of attack overcoming all obstacles had been widely adopted by many armies. The French outlook was that massed bayonets, backed by the famous 75mm mle 1897 field gun, would enable waves of soldiers to attack any opposition and overcome it by sheer ferocity and determination. During the attack, fire support could be provided by light automatic weapons, such as the Chauchat. There was even a 'walking fire' drill devised whereby Chauchats would be fired in bursts from the hip every so many paces.

This doctrine of attack permeated as far as the United States, for before 1914 French military philosophy was widely embraced there. It also came to the attention of John Moses Browning, perhaps the most talented and prolific gun designer during

The original 0.30 M1918 Browning Automatic Rifle (BAR).

any period, with a string of pistol, rifle and machine gun designs to his name. He noted the need for light automatic weapons during the expected massed attacks and duly devised a gas-operated mechanism light enough to provide a single soldier with automatic firepower. That was during the early 1900s. At that period interest in such a weapon was non-existent in the USA; the design was therefore duly filed away against some possible future requirement.

That requirement duly arose during 1917 when it became apparent that the USA would, despite all earlier efforts to remain remote, become involved in the war on the European continent. At that time, following years of neglect, the US Army had only 1,100 machine guns and most of those were obsolete or worn out. It was forecast that the planned Army divisions would need 100,000 machine guns, and matching quantities of every other type of weapon as well.

Fortunately, the machine gun requirement could be met fairly directly. That was because the genius of John Browning had already devised two machine guns and in such detail that they were tailored for mass production. One was to become the tripod-mounted, 0.30 Model 1917 (*see* Chapter 6). The other was that light automatic weapon devised a decade before and filed away. During 1917 proto-

types were prepared and demonstrated to high-ranking audiences for possible adoption. The enthusiasm generated by the appearance of an all-American light automatic weapon was such that type classification was almost immediate, with volume production demands following closely. The M1918 BAR had arrived.

The enthusiasm, however, overlooked the fact that the BAR had been devised to meet a tactical situation that no longer applied. The doctrine of the attack overcoming all obstacles had been proved horridly wrong during the 1914 Battle of the Frontiers, when attacking French waves were simply mown down by machine-gun and rifle fire. By 1917 trench warfare prevailed.

The BAR was a heavy machine rifle intended to deliver short bursts of fire from the hip or shoulder to relatively short ranges. The BAR fired the standard American 0.30-06 cartridge, therefore prolonged bursts were not really possible due to the significant recoil forces generated by such a powerful round. As will be described, the fixed, air-cooled barrel could overheat rapidly and there was no bipod or firing support.

Yet the BAR had one prime asset in that it was highly portable and portable firepower was much in demand in 1917. The infantry badly needed automatic firepower under their direct control both for the attack and in defence. The Lewis gun had already indicated how light machine guns could be employed, but the US Army had never adopted the Lewis. In fact, the impetus given to the BAR when it first appeared meant that the ground-based Lewis was never to be deployed by the US Army in France before the war ended.

The rush to get the BAR into immediate volume production brought difficulties in its train. By 1917 most of the American defence infrastructure was already working hard to supply weapons for the British and the French, but capacity was found at the Winchester Repeating Firearms Company and the Marlin-Rockwell Corporation, both of New Haven, Connecticut. At that time most of Browning's patents were held by Colt, but they were already overstretched. Colt's work on the BAR was mainly devoted to preparing working drawings, tools and jigs for others, so their M1918 BAR production was limited.

The same could not be said of the other two contractors. Although the first production examples did not appear until February 1918, the first 1,500

were not considered suitable for front-line issue because there were too many components that could not be readily interchanged between guns. But by July 1918 the number of BARs had already reached 17,000. By the time of the armistice the number accepted by the American government was 52,238; outstanding orders stood at 288,174.

Those particular orders were never completed, for once the armistice was signed there was no longer any need for BARs. The huge army so swiftly formed within the USA was just as rapidly wound down. BAR production continued for a while until about 85,000 had been completed (some sources mention even more – over 100,000). It then ceased, with most of the delivered output remaining in storage cases awaiting some future role. The few BARs that reached France before November 1918 did see action, their first recorded use being during late September. What feedback did emerge from those frantic last days of the Great War was mainly favourable to the BAR, so the seeds of the weapon's future favoured position within the American military were well sown.

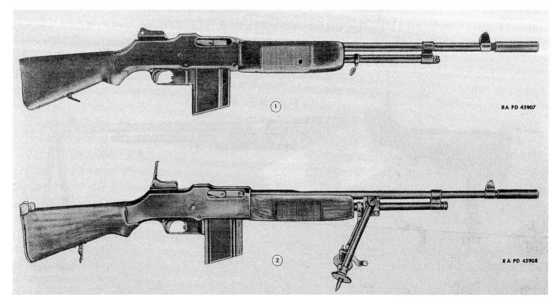

Service manual illustration of the original M1918 (top) and the later M1918A1 (below).

After 1918 Colt launched a campaign to sell the weapon to both home and overseas markets; the US Army already had as many as it was likely to need for years to come. Some home-based sales were made to police and prison authorities while the US Cavalry procured a few hundred examples known as the M1922. Despite the introduction of a bipod to the M1922, it was not considered a success and was later withdrawn. Between the wars BARs were sold to several nations, the most important being Belgium, Poland and Sweden, all of whom obtained local production licences. All three nations introduced their own modifications to the base M1918 BAR in attempts to make it into a more viable light machine gun. The most drastic change involved the Swedish guns being provided with bipods and a barrel-change system.

One little-known aspect of the BAR was that as early as 1922 it was under serious consideration by the British Army. At one stage it was recommended that the BAR should replace the Lewis gun but, thanks largely to a lack of the necessary funding, nothing came of that proposal.

The addition of a bipod to the BAR made it more accurate, for the M1918 was a hand-held weapon. Burst fire from the M1918 was therefore inaccurate as recoil forces soon forced the muzzle away from the target. Prolonged burst fire had two results. One was an overheated barrel. As the barrel was a fixture this had to be avoided by careful fire discipline and short bursts. The second result was an empty maga-

---

BAR M1918A2

Calibre	7.62mm; 0.30in
Length	1.214m; 47.8in
Length of barrel	611mm; 24.07in
Weight	8.73kg; 19.4lb
Muzzle velocity	808m/s; 2,650ft/s
Feed	20-round box magazine
Cyclic rate of fire	500–600 or 300–350rpm

---

zine since it held only twenty rounds, a quantity that soon vanished during combat. These two features limited the utility of the M1918 as a light machine gun, rendering it more of a heavy machine rifle.

Time was to show that these limitations were either overlooked by the US military or simply accepted as such. To offset the recoil and aiming difficulties partially, a programme was undertaken from 1937 to modify in-service M1918s by the installation of a folding bipod, a butt strap and a tubular flash-hider at the muzzle. The result was the M1918A1.

Not all stockpiled M1918s underwent the conversion to the M1918A1. By 1940 there were still thousands of unused M1918s stacked away in the Springfield Armory. They became a godsend to the hard-pressed United Kingdom in the period after Dunkirk. Some 25,000 of them were shipped over

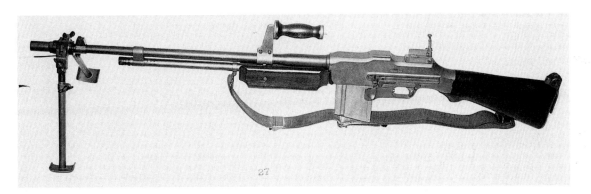

The 0.30 M1918A2, the last production BAR.

to Britain to arm the newly-formed Home Guard (the regular forces did not receive the BAR). This American munificence was later regretted by the donors, for the following year the USA itself became involved in the war and BARs, soon to be demanded by the thousand, were by then in very short supply.

Mass production therefore commenced once again, but this time the BAR involved was the M1918A2. This model had been type classified in 1940 and featured several changes from the earlier models. One was that the fire controls were altered. Single-shot fire was done away with while there were two automatic rates of fire, 300–350 or 500–600rpm. Another change involved a relocation of the bipod to beneath the muzzle, while the return spring was moved from under the barrel to a position inside the butt stock to prevent the distortion caused by barrel heat that could occur on earlier models.

The M1918A2 was manufactured by the New England Small Arms Corporation, a grouping of six engineering concerns which had never before participated in defence production. IBM also became involved with the M1918A2 at one stage but soon switched to other priorities. It took time for the Corporation to prepare and train for the M1918A2, but once the usual initial difficulties were out of the way the production totals soared and eventually met demands – the total M1918A2 production total by 1945 was 188,380, plus the associated spare parts. This total was reached only after some of the usual production short cuts had been introduced. Although Browning had designed the BAR to be mass produced, he was working in a period when the full demands of modern war had not been foreseen and many components on the BAR were time-consuming and expensive to produce. Castings and pressed parts therefore took the place of some items that had previously demanded careful machining.

The BAR was deployed wherever American troops fought between 1941 and 1945. Despite its limitations, it was employed as the standard squad fire-support weapon and American soldiers came to

depend on it and swear by it, for it was rugged, reliable and well understood. They learned that if the M1918A2 fire-control lever were set to the slower rate of fire, single shots could be squeezed off. Once in action, the weight and bulk of the weapon were often considered onerous so it was not unusual for the bipod, butt strap and muzzle attachment to be discarded, reducing the BAR almost back to its M1918 origins.

Gradually, some senior soldiers came to accept that the BAR was not the ideal light machine gun. Front-line soldiers frequently disagreed and were anxious to retain the BAR in any form, ignoring the firepower and performance potential offered by many other contemporary light machine guns. Thus the BAR was still in front-line service during the Korean War (even being placed back into production for a while) and after, remaining with many NATO and other armed forces long after it had passed from American service.

THE M1919A6

One of the main drawbacks of the BAR was its inability to deliver prolonged burst fire. There were many occasions when such a capability was badly missed by the infantry, especially when observers were well aware that other machine guns such as the Bren and the MG34 were churning out the required fire on demand. A request was therefore made for an all-American equivalent. The problem was that the gun had to be portable enough for the infantry to carry and there was nothing in the US inventory suitable for the role at that time, and time was short. The stage was set for a typical example of American wartime improvisation.

A solution emerged in April 1943 with a variant of the 0.30 M1919A4 air-cooled machine gun. Normally a tripod-mounted weapon, the original belt-fed M1919 was an air-cooled version of the M1917 machine gun intended for use on tanks (*see* Chapter 6); but since the tanks concerned were never built the guns were found other ground roles. The M1919A4 was intended to be a multi-role machine gun with variants including a vehicle-mounted gun and the tripod version already mentioned. The M1919A4 gun was used as the basis for what was supposed to be a light machine gun, the 0.30 M1919A6.

The M1919A6 was provided with a lighter barrel, an odd-shaped metal shoulder stock, an awkward-looking bipod, a muzzle-flash cone and a carrying handle. The end result weighed 14.6kg/32.5lb and so it was hardly light, while the retention of the belt feed meant that a second soldier usually had to assist with loading and carrying the ammunition. In theory it was possible to change overheated barrels, but as no provision was made to handle them this was rarely attempted.

All in all, the M1919A6 was something of a clumsy and unsatisfactory weapon, a truth recognized by the US Army by the application of a substitute standard-type classification. Yet the M1919A6 proved reliable in action and robust enough to absorb the many hard knocks it inevitably experienced. An indication of its success can be seen in the final production total of 43,479. Many served on for years after 1945.

THE VB

General Adolphe Berthier has already been encountered in the story of bolt action rifles (Chapter 2). He was also responsible for a series of machine gun

M1919A6	
Calibre	7.62mm; 0.30in
Length	1.346m; 54in
Length of barrel	610mm; 24in
Weight	14.6kg; 32.5lb
Muzzle velocity	853m/s; 2,800ft/s
Feed	250-round belt
Cyclic rate of fire	400–500rpm

designs that were never adopted by the French authorities, due mainly to the vast surpluses retained after 1918, but his salvation was at hand in 1925. During that year the British company Vickers-Armstrong Ltd decided to purchase manufacturing rights to his designs in an attempt to keep their Crayford production lines in Kent in work by the introduction of a modern light machine gun.

The mid-1920s was not a good time for the introduction of new infantry weapons but Vickers-Armstrong persisted. Some sales were made to Baltic and South American nations. Their product, the Vickers-Berthier light machine gun, was a sound, gas-operated, light machine gun outwardly resembling the Bren gun that was later to usurp it, but there were many operating differences.

At one time it seemed as though the Vickers-Berthier would be adopted as the eventual British

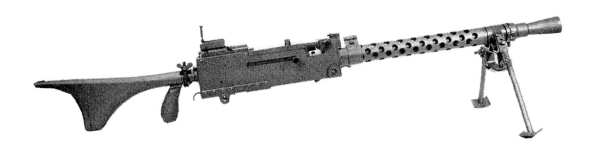

The awkward outline of the 0.30 M1919A6.

Army replacement for the Lewis gun, but, despite extensive testing, the perennial defence funding shortages of the period meant that a decision was constantly postponed. Eventually the Bren was adopted instead.

However, in 1933 the 0.303 Vickers-Berthier Mk 3 was adopted by the Indian government for its army. Licensed production of the gun, soon known locally and elsewhere as the VB, took place at the Ishapore Rifle Factory, although no figures are available. Between September 1939 and December 1943 Vickers at Crayford manufactured 2,767 guns, the majority of which must have gone to India. Before 1939 a contract for 500 had been placed for India and sixty-four for Iraq. The British Army received only forty-six, most of them for trials.

The Indian Army took the VB to war in 1939 and it served throughout the long and difficult campaign in Burma, this being the last campaign of the old Army. The VB served on for some time after 1945 in dwindling numbers as it was gradually replaced by the Bren, more for the purposes of standardization than because of technical obsolescence.

There was one other gun with the Vickers-Berthier title, originally introduced in 1928 as the

---

Vickers-Berthier Mk 3

Calibre	7.7mm; 0.303in
Length	1.156m; 45.5in
Length of barrel	600mm; 23.6in
Weight	10.9kg; 24.4lb
Muzzle velocity	745m/s; 2,450ft/s
Feed	30-round box magazine
Cyclic rate of fire	450–600rpm

Class K aircraft observer's gun. This became the 0.303 Vickers G.O. (gas-operated) gun, based around the Vickers-Berthier gas-operated mechanism but allied with an overhead ninety-six-round drum magazine and a spade grip. The rate of fire was increased to 950–1,000rpm for its expected role. Almost as soon as the Royal Air Force adopted the Vickers G.O. the open cockpits of the 1920s and 1930s biplanes began to give way to monoplanes carrying enclosed turrets within which weapons other than the Vickers G.O. usually proved to be more suitable. Vickers G.O. guns were therefore

This is probably the Mark 3B version of the 0.303 Vickers-Berthier light machine gun.

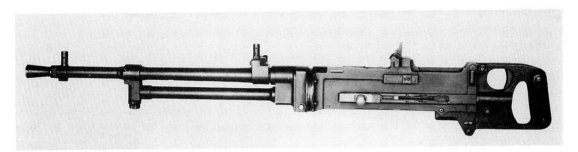

A service manual illustration of the Vickers GO or K gun, originally intended for aircraft use.

gradually withdrawn and stored, although some continued to be employed throughout the war as aircraft-turret guns when space for belt-feed systems was lacking.

Surplus guns were called upon in 1940, when the weapons shortage after Dunkirk meant that anything to hand had to be utilized. The Vickers G.O. therefore acquired a new role as an airfield air-

defence weapon. Many were retained until 1945, some of them still airborne on aircraft such as the Swordfish.

There was also a more colourful role for the G.O. as a vehicle gun. In this case the vehicles were the trucks of units such as the Long Range Desert Group in north Africa and the Jeeps of the embryonic Special Air Service. Single and twin mountings

A Bren Gun on its optional tripod, an illustration taken from a German manual.

could be encountered and there seem to have been few complaints regarding the G.O.'s performance. Vickers produced at least 79,676 G.O. guns between September 1939 and June 1944, although accurate production totals are not available. As with the Vickers-Berthier Mk 3 of the Indian Army, the Vickers G.O. gun was one that never did attain its due share of praise. Both are now almost totally forgotten.

THE BREN

By 1925 the British Army was aware that the Lewis Gun was at best obsolescent owing to its relative complexity, weight and bulk. The Vickers-Berthier was considered a leading contender as the replacement, but at that time funds were short so all that happened was a prolonged series of trials involving several possible gun designs – there seemed to be no great urgency. A General Staff Specification outlining what was required was not issued until

1931. Soon after then the Vickers-Berthier had a serious rival.

This was a Czechoslovak weapon, the 7.92mm ZB vz 27 (vz: *vzor* or model), brought to the notice of the War Office by the British Military Attaché in Prague. The weapon was produced by the Ceskoslovenská Zbrojovká at Brno (hence ZB) as an improved model of the earlier ZB vz 26. Both models were adopted by the Czechoslovaks and many other nations. One example of the ZB vz 27 was purchased by the British government and, once in Britain, was subjected to a series of trials that indicated that the Czechoslovak design, initiated by Vaclav Holek, was by far the best weapon tested to date. Its immediate acceptance was proposed.

There was, however, a snag. The ZB vz 27 fired the 7.92 × 57mm rimless German cartridge, then widely in use throughout central Europe. The gun would have to be modified to fire the British 0.303 cartridge, which was not only rimmed but contained cordite propellant that could foul the weapon's gas-

Bren Guns at the ready.

operated system – the 7.92mm cartridge used a cleaner nitrocellulose propellant.

Thus there began a series of modifications to the Czechoslovak design, carried out both at Brno and at Enfield Lock in Britain, to cater for the British cartridge. They eventually resulted in a light machine gun that still bore some resemblance to the Holek original but much revised in detail. By 1935 the modifications had been successfully tested to the point when a licence agreement was signed between the Brno factory and the British government to manufacture the weapon at Enfield Lock. Brno and Enfield Lock jointly were to give the Bren its name.

The first Bren guns came off the line during September 1937, although full production examples did not appear until the following year. The changes from the ZB vz 27 were marked. Gone were the finned barrel and the straight-sided, overhead box magazine holding thirty rounds. In their place came a shorter, smooth outline barrel and a curved maga-

Bren Mk 1	
Calibre	7.7mm; 0.303in
Length	1.155m; 45.5in
Length of barrel	635mm; 25in
Weight	9.95kg; 22.12lb
Muzzle velocity	744m/s; 2,440ft/s
Feed	29-round box magazine
Cyclic rate of fire	500rpm

zine holding only twenty-nine rounds. The rapid barrel change mechanism was carried over from the original, but the hinged method of gaining access to the interior for maintenance was changed to a rearwards-sliding, bottom receiver configuration. The simple gas-operation mechanism, operating a rising locking breech block, was largely retained but extensively modified to make the action smoother

The Bren Gun carrier. Note the 2in mortar at the rear.

and more forgiving to cordite propellant residues. If fouling did arise the gun could be kept firing by altering the gas-port size, a task that took only seconds.

The cyclic rate of fire was a steady 500rpm, but this was only theoretical since the magazine required frequent changing. All members of a British infantry section carried at least one loaded Bren Gun magazine ready to be passed to the gun, while more were carried by a second soldier forming part of the Bren Gun team. He also carried the spare barrel issued with each gun. To change barrels when they became hot took only an instant and was assisted by a handle that doubled as a carrying handle for the complete gun.

To return to 1938, the supply of Bren Guns from Enfield Lock meant that the Lewis Gun had been supplanted when the British Army returned to

France in 1939. By then tripods convertible into anti-aircraft mountings were available, while mechanized infantry could carry their Bren Guns into battle on a lightly armoured tracked vehicle, the Bren Gun Carrier.

During May and June 1940 things went badly wrong as the British were forced to leave France. As virtually all the available Bren Guns were in France at that time, attempts were made to retrieve as many as possible but the bulk of the British inventory fell into German hands. They welcomed such a useful addition to their armoury so the Bren Gun became the 7.7mm leMG 138(e).

In June 1940 the entire British stock of the guns stood at about 2,300. Bren Gun production thus took on a new importance. The usual short-cuts were introduced to assist production, something made easier by the original guns having some features that

Instruction on the art of using a twin Bren Gun mounting for air defence – note the drum magazines.

came to be regarded as luxuries. One was a complex drum sight at the rear, replaced by a simpler, conventional, leaf sight. Another fire-control feature subsequently eliminated was a bracket for mounting a simple dial sight when the gun was fired from a tripod. Out went the adjustable telescopic bipod legs to be replaced by fixed length components. Another luxury that vanished was the handle under the butt stock intended as a grip for the firer's free hand. It had never been popular in any case and neither had the shoulder strap over the butt plate – that too was another item removed. Many other measures, such as the machined grooves meant to save weight here and there, were omitted.

A Bren Gun with all these changes became the Mk 2, a model that also featured a fixed cocking handle in place of the original one that could be folded. The Mk 2 worked every bit as well as the

Mk 1. The later Mks 3 and 4, intended primarily for airborne and other special forces, had shortened barrels and lightened receivers. Few Mk 4s were made.

Bren Gun production was not easy for it involved numerous machining operations and fine tolerances. For instance, the one-piece receiver was machined from a solid steel billet weighing 17.35kg/38.25lb. The finished component weighed only just over 2kg/4.5lb, and that was but one example of the work involved in making the weapon. The reward for such seeming extravagance came with the high degree of strength and reliability of the end product.

British production of the gun was centred at Enfield Lock. By 1946, when all the war period orders were complete, they had manufactured 214,008 Mk 1 and 2 guns plus a further 57,600

A Bren Gun team in action in Italy, 1943.

examples of the Mk 3. A further manufacturing asset was established by the Monotype Group during 1940. Monotype and May Ltd headed a team of manufacturers who produced mainly components, especially magazines. They also manufactured 83,436 complete Mk 1 and 2 guns.

As early as 1938 the Canadian Army had decided that it would replace its existing light machine guns with the Bren, but to do so it had to establish its own manufacturing facility and no funds were available for such a project. This difficulty was overcome by the Canadian government's offering to act as a sub-contractor for the British, an offer duly accepted. A Bren Gun manufacturing facility was therefore established in the John Inglis Company Ltd factory in Toronto. It also produced anti-tank rifles and pistols (*see* Chapters 9 and 10).

The British duly ordered an initial 5,000 Mk 1 guns, while the Canadian government ordered 7,000. By the time the war was over the final Inglis Mk 1 and 2 total had reached about 122,000, plus a further 3,000 Mk 3s. An undetermined number of these were paid for by the USA under Lend-Lease arrangements.

Inglis also manufactured a Bren Gun variant chambered in the original 'European' 7.92 × 57mm calibre for export to Nationalist China. A total of 42,999 7.92mm guns were manufactured during 1944 and 1945, along with the necessary magazines and spare barrels. A further undetermined (but probably quite limited) number of 7.92mm Brens were produced by Inglis specifically to be supplied to resistance groups operating within Europe.

More Bren Guns were manufactured in Australia at the Small Arms Factory, Lithgow, from 1941 onwards, using locally produced tools and gauges. The total by June 1945 reached 17,335, involving Mk 1 guns, later simplified somewhat but not to full Mk 2 standard. All of them were issued to the Australian armed forces.

As the war progressed a wide array of accessories and mountings were devised for the Bren. A 'high speed' 100-round drum was introduced for air-defence purposes, but it appears to have been little used. Also devised for air defence were mountings such as the Single and Twin Motley mountings and the Lakeland Mount, the latter usually being used for vehicle installations. The early tripod gradually disappeared. Not only was it heavy, expensive and complicated but it was also found to be unnecessary, apart from a few special applications, yet it was still retained as an approved accessory until the 1970s.

The British Bren Gun was one of the finest, if not *the* finest, light machine gun of its era. It proved to be reliable, accurate, sturdy, handy to aim and fire while being adaptable to many situations and circumstances, although it has to be stated that it did not like the sand of the north African deserts. A measure of the gun's quality may be found in the fact that it is with us still during the early 2000s. It remains in production in India, although now rechambered for 7.62 × 51mm NATO ammunition. The British Army retained the Bren well into the 1990s, by then also rechambered for the same ammunition, and it would be unwise to say that it has been totally replaced in British service.

6   Medium Machine Guns

In 1939 all machine guns, other than those classi-fied as light, were known simply as machine guns. By 1945 the introduction of calibres larger than standard rifle calibres meant that more differentia-tion was needed. Rifle-calibre machine guns therefore became *medium machine guns* while the larger calibre weapons became *heavy machine guns*. This chapter deals with the mediums.

Artillery may have dominated the Great War battlefields, but as far as the infantry were concerned the main casualty producer was the machine gun. Every time the troops left the relative shelter of their trenches they had to advance into the hail of bullets generated by machine guns and suffered greatly in the process. During the Second World War the machine gun never quite attained the dominance it had previously held but it remained a potent anti-personnel weapon.

The Great War machine gun was very much the product of one man, Hiram Stevens Maxim (1840–1916), later knighted by the British osten-sibly for his services to the British Empire but in truth for the invention and marketing of his Maxim gun, the first really successful, completely self-powered machine gun. Maxim was an inventive polymath but he exceeded all his other efforts with his machine gun.

The Maxim gun was produced in many forms and calibres, but all models used the same basic, toggle-based mechanism that held the breech locked at the instant the cartridge was fired. The toggle thereafter lost its mechanical advantage as the barrel recoiled and powered the spring-assisted process of ejecting the spent case and reloading a fresh round. The Maxim mechanism could keep on operating as long

as ammunition was belt-fed into the system and the trigger was depressed, so the barrel had to be kept cool within a water-filled jacket. The usual mounting was a heavy tripod since the construction of the Maxim gun was very robust. This ensured not just reliability but a prolonged service-life expectancy. The price for these assets was weight. Maxim gun crews often involved as many as five or six attendants, most of them concerned with the ammunition supply once the gun had been carried into action.

Such was the genius of Maxim that not only was his gun successful but it was designed to be produced on an industrial scale, albeit using the labour-intensive methods and high quality materials characteristic of the 1890s and just after. Maxim also reinforced the supremacy of his design over those of most of his contemporaries by the ruthless enforcement of his numerous patents that, in effect, excluded all other possible machine-gun operating systems from the military market place. If any nation wanted to acquire machine guns they either had to devise a way around Maxim's patents or else purchase Maxim guns or a licence to produce them. Many nations chose the last path. Among them was Tsarist Russia.

THE PM1910

The first Russian Maxim gun was adopted as early as 1895. This 7.62mm gun was not considered as totally satisfactory so gradual development work was undertaken, by way of the first locally produced PM1905 model, as the basis of all

A 7.62mm PM1910 ready to move on its Sokolov mounting.

subsequent Russian/Soviet Maxim guns, the PM1910 (*Pulemat Maksima obr 1910*). On this model the main visual alteration to the gun was the substitution of the original bronze water jacket by a corrugated steel jacket. The other change introduced on the PM1910 was the Sokolov mounting.

The Sokolov mounting was designed to withstand the worst that Russian conscripts could inflict while introducing more mobility to the gun than was achievable using the conventional tripods of the time. In many ways the Sokolov mounting resembled a small artillery carriage, complete with solid

PM1910	
Calibre	7.62mm; 0.30in
Length	1.107m; 43.6in
Length of barrel	720mm; 28.4in
Weight complete	74kg; 152.5lb
Muzzle velocity	863m/s; 2,830ft/s
Feed	250-round belt
Cyclic rate of fire	520–600rpm

steel wheels, a traversing turntable, a short trail for hand towing and even a shield, although the last was sometimes omitted. The carriage was stable and extremely sturdy, but the gun and carriage together weighed 74kg/163lb. With cavalry units the PM1910 was often carried on small 'Tachanka' carts, while under winter conditions sleds were employed. But for most infantry units the only way to transport the PM1910 was either to tow it by hand or, under rough terrain conditions, to carry it manually. (There was also a lighter Koleshnikov wheeled mounting, introduced in 1915, but it was never adopted on the scale of the Sokolov mounting.)

The PM1910 served reliably throughout the Great War and the Russian Civil War, firing the fabric belt-fed 7.62 × 54R cartridge at a steady cyclic rate of 520 to 600rpm. During the 1930s some changes were introduced, mainly concerning ease of production. The sights were simplified, non-ferrous components were replaced by steel and some construction changes were introduced to the receiver. The filling of the water jacket was made easier by the introduction of a tractor radiator cap large enough to allow handfuls of snow or ice to be inserted when necessary. This feature was copied

This 7.62mm PM1910 is without its usual shield.

from the Finns and was introduced on a large scale only in 1943, although some earlier examples were so equipped.

The PM1910 worked well under a wide range of tough conditions but by 1925 it had been decided that it needed to be replaced by something lighter. Development of that was so slow that by the late 1930s the only candidate under consideration was an air-cooled Degtyarev design, the DS-39. Although the development of this gun began in 1930 it was never completely satisfactory and mass production was only just starting when the Germans invaded the Soviet Union in 1941. The only measure open to the Soviet planners was to reintroduce PM1910 mass production just at the time that it was being scaled down in favour of the DS-39, a gun fated to disappear.

By yet another major expansion of weapon production under the most adverse conditions, PM1910 production rose from the 9,691 total for all of 1941 to 55,258 during 1942. Losses and the

expansion of the Soviet armed forces meant that such numbers were far from enough and so for 1944 the annual total reached an estimated (but unverified) 270,000. By 1945 the PM1910 lines were finally being run down. By that time the PM1910 grand production total had been estimated at over 600,000, making the Tsarist/Soviet 7.62mm M1910 the most numerous of all the many types of Maxim gun, and the longest lasting.

Not all PM1910 output was for the Sokolov mounting. Gun and carriage production continued in Leningrad throughout the Great Siege with so many local modifications being introduced that the original carriage became virtually unrecognizable. On the Tokarev mount of 1931, a low-level air-defence mounting that proved highly successful throughout the Great Patriotic War, four PM1910 guns were mounted side-by-side. On this arrangement all four water jackets were joined together by hoses to maintain balanced barrel cooling.

Inevitably, large numbers of PM1910s fell into German hands although they were rarely employed

Riflemen add their bit to the air defence capabilities of a 7.62mm PM1910.

as front-line weapons, no doubt being considered too heavy for modern warfare, even if their Soviet opponents thought otherwise. Most German deployments of the captured 7.62mm sMG 216(r) involved static fortifications such as the Atlantic Wall, although four-gun Tokarev air-defence mountings were maintained along the Eastern Front. After 1945 the PM1910 remained in service with Soviet-allied nations such as Communist China and North Korea for many years. It can no doubt still be encountered in remote parts of the Far East.

THE GORYUNOV GUN

At about the same time as the abortive DS-39 gun was undergoing its final preproduction trials,

An American soldier examining a PM1910 captured from the Germans in 1945.

another design was in the offing. This air-cooled, gas-operated gun was the work of Petr Goryunov, Vasiliy Voronkov and Mikhail Goryunov (Petr's nephew). Their prototype, initially known as the 7.62mm GVG, seemed destined to be overshadowed by the DS-39. However, the difficulties experienced with that gun, coupled with the German invasion, gave the Goryunov design a boost, especially when the urgent need for a machine gun more mobile and easier to manufacture than the PM1910 became apparent during 1941. Field trials with a pre-production batch of Goryunov guns led to necessary changes, so it was not until May 1943 that the design was finally approved for acceptance as the 7.62mm SG-43.

The SG-43 was one of the first Soviet weapons to have rapid manufacturing techniques built into the design from the outset. The heavy barrel could be changed quickly when it became overheated – as usual with Soviet designs the bore was chrome plated. The round fired continued to be the rimmed 7.62 × 54R in 250-round belts. Locking involved a side-locking block that proved to be simple and

extremely reliable. Although lighter than the PM1910, the SG-43 was still on the heavy side at nearly 14kg/30.8lb for the gun alone, while to this could be added 27kg/59.5lb for the mounting. The latter continued to be of the wheeled carriage type and could even accommodate a shield (although this was often left off). When necessary, the mounting could be reversed for air defence, the gun then being secured in an elevated position on the end of the towing trail.

SG-43	
Calibre	7.62mm; 0.30in
Length	1.12m; 44.1in
Length of barrel	719mm; 28.3in
Weight complete	40.7kg; 89.7lb
Muzzle velocity	863 m/s; 2,830ft/s
Feed	50-round belt
Cyclic rate of fire	500–640rpm

Hauling a 7.62mm SG-43 into position the hard way.

Tank- and vehicle-mounted versions of the SG-43 appeared, but owing to the huge numbers of PM1910s in service by 1944 the SG-43 never replaced the Maxim veteran before the war ended – over 74,000 SG-43s had been produced by then. Instead it acted as a most welcome addition to the potential Soviet machine-gun armoury, even if some shortcomings did arise with experience. These were not eliminated until after 1945 when a revised model, the SGM, recognizable by its fluted barrel, was introduced. The SGM remained in use for decades after 1945 and may still be encountered in active service with some countries today. One version is still produced for possible export sales by Egypt.

THE VICKERS

Although the PM1910 was by far the most numerous of the many Maxim guns, outside the former Soviet Union the classic machine gun was the Vickers. To the lay observer the Vickers machine gun and the Maxim looked almost identical. To those involved the differences were many.

The Vickers gun did have its origins in the Maxim. By the early 1900s the Maxim gun had been considerably refined to make it lighter and to make the inner mechanisms, especially the lock, easier to strip for maintenance and repair. The end result was the Vickers Model 1906, a promising marketing venture from which few sales actually resulted, although many Model 1906 features were later employed in the Russian PM1910. By that time Sir Hiram Maxim had retired from the firm of Vickers, Sons & Maxim Ltd (it became Vickers Ltd and later Vickers-Armstrong) and thus had no influence on the following stages of his gun's development.

Following the disappointing sales of the Model 1906 it was decided that a drastic revision of the Maxim design would have to be introduced. Sales prospects were about to become poor, especially as the international machine-gun market had been entered by the excellent Maxim guns then aggressively marketed by Germany. Vickers's initial response was their Model 1908 RC (Rifle Calibre) 'Light Pattern' gun, the forerunner of all the later Vickers machine guns.

Numerous minor changes were introduced on this model. The most important was that the Maxim toggle lock was altered so that it broke upwards. This alteration reduced the height and the internal volume of the receiver, thereby saving raw materials and weight, while making no difference to the reliable functioning of the gun itself. Changes were also introduced to the sights, the ammunition feed and the method of stripping the gun. For the soldier, the changes meant that the gun weight of 12.7kg/28lb was half that of the Maxims then in British Army service, although it would later creep up to 15kg/33lb. A revised and lighter tripod mounting was also introduced.

Vickers machine guns on the ranges.

At first, sales of the new Vickers gun were slow, although Italy ordered 893 before 1914 and another 268 went to Russia. Adoption by the British Army took time. It was not until November 1912 that the Vickers gun was officially accepted by the War Department, chambered for the standard 0.303 rifle cartridge. By then the first application to aircraft had been tested.

Early production of the 0.303 Vickers Mk 1 was at a low rate. The British Army had to undergo a baptism of fire in 1914 before any great enthusiasm for machine guns started to flicker. Thereafter the demand for Vickers guns grew and grew, being expanded still further by its adoption as an air-cooled aircraft gun. As the war progressed the Vickers production facilities at Erith and Crayford, both in Kent, expanded dramatically. The Vickers gun was not easy to manufacture since it was a complex weapon with many hand-finished components – Vickers had to train many of the production line operatives themselves. Between them the two factories produced 75,242 guns between 1912 and

1919. At least twelve subcontractors supplied tripods.

Vickers guns were also produced to fire the French 8mm Lebel cartridge, in response to a French contract. More Vickers guns were chambered for the American 0.30-06 cartridge, but there the story was more involved. By 1915 the demand for Vickers guns was so pressing that the company asked the Colt's Patent Firearms Manufacturing Company of Hartford to supply 6,000 guns. Another order for 10,000 arrived from Russia in 1915, this time chambered for the 7.62 × 54R cartridge (only 3,000 of these actually reached Russia).

Well before then the US Army had expressed an interest in the Vickers gun. In 1915 it had decided to type-classify the gun as the Model 1915, firing the 0.30-06 cartridge. Unfortunately, Colt's soon discovered to their embarrassment that the Vickers gun was more demanding in manufacturing skills and facilities than they had foreseen, far more than they had available at that time. It took many months

A Vickers machine gun team carrying their machine gun into action.

for the company to prepare for Vickers gun production. In addition, by 1917 substantial contracts had been signed with Colt's to re-equip the US Army, then desperate for modern machine guns. Consequently the demands on Colt's were such that the British order was never fulfilled, the only result being the supply of some spare parts. About 2,100 Model 1915 guns reached American troops in France (plus 0.303 Vickers guns on loan from the British Army) before the war ended. By the end of 1918 12,125 0.30 Model 1915s had been manufactured for the US Army. More guns were produced for use on aircraft. The Model 1915 was to have a further part to play after 1940.

To return to the British Vickers: by 1918 the level

of machine gun expertise in the British Army had reached a level seldom matched in later years, although the Army retained a corps of experienced Vickers gun instructors until the weapon was finally withdrawn. From a direct-fire infantry-support weapon, the Vickers gun had evolved into a highly reliable, indirect-fire weapon capable of taking part in area-suppression missions involving hundreds of thousands of rounds being fired over periods of hours or even days. The reliability and performance of the Vickers gun became legendary, the guns continuing to function at a cyclic rate of about 500rpm for as long as ammunition could be fed in 250-round fabric belts and the water in the barrel jacket could be topped up. In practice, rapid fire was delivered in bursts of about twenty-five rounds, with a few seconds' interval between each. Barrels usually had to be changed every 15,000 rounds or so.

Between the wars, production of the Vickers gun continued at a gradual pace to meet orders from around the world, although many end users were supplied direct from the stocks remaining from 1914–18. Australia established a home-based production capability in 1929. This was located at Lithgow, New South Wales, intended to meet local demands from local sources. Initial production was limited to the extent that by the time war began in 1939 only 697 had been manufactured. Thereafter the rate increased until the final 1945 total was 10,170, some of them issued on twin mountings as air-defence guns. The output was not sufficient to

Vickers	
Calibre	7.7mm; 0.303in
Length	1.156m; 45.5in
Length of barrel	721mm; 28.4in
Weight complete	40kg; 88.5lb
Muzzle velocity	744 m/s; 2,440ft/s
Feed	250-round belt
Cyclic rate of fire	450–500rpm

meet all the requirements of the Australian and New Zealand armed forces and so British-produced guns were also issued to both.

By 1939 the number of Vickers machine gun

A 0.303 Vickers machine gun on an armoured train defending the UK in 1944 – the crew are Home Guards.

types had increased. Aircraft guns were no longer in service but 0.303 and 0.50 tank guns were. The Royal Navy had a 0.50 gun on anti-aircraft mountings, some land-based, plus a 40mm version installed on quadruple mountings for ship-board air defence.

In 1939 the Vickers machine gun was back in production at Crayford, from where most other 'British' guns were to be made from then on; there was also a Vickers production facility in Bath. The land-based Mk 1 was still virtually unchanged from its original 1912 design, although numerous types of muzzle-located, recoil booster device were in service, along with other minor changes. The most noticeable alteration after 1939 was to the barrel jacket, originally corrugated but then altered to a smooth outline and made of thicker steel. However, there was no firm rule for the interchangeability of components between guns and therefore old, serviceable parts were often found on new guns. The Vickers land-service gun production total between 1939 and 1945 came to 11,828. Of these, 200 went to Egypt and a further 230 to Iraq. More guns came from refurbished stockpiled weapons dating from before 1918; these were refurbished at Enfield Lock as well as by several other contractors. Just as important as guns were tripods and spare barrels, the production of which extended to Canada,. The former were made by Vickers-Armstrong, Enfield Lock and by several other companies not normally associated with weapons production. During the war the production of tripods, most of them the Mk 4, reached 19,205.

The Vickers gun had become more mobile by 1939. During the Great War some Vickers guns had been carried on motor-cycle sidecars. By 1939 mechanized battalions were carrying their guns on the tracked, lightly armoured Universal Carriers. It should be noted that these were not tank guns, but guns carried on a pintle that permitted firing direct from the carrier vehicle. A tripod and other accessories were carried to allow the dismounted gun to be fired as before.

The losses of the British Army's weapons in

France following the evacuation of June 1940 have been described already. The Vickers guns therefore became German weapons once again, for during the Great War captured examples were frequently turned against their former owners – some were even converted to fire the German 7.92 × 57mm cartridge. The German booty in 1940 became the 7.7mm sMG 230(e) and to the stocks of these were added numbers of 7.7mm sMG 231(h) guns captured earlier from the Dutch Army. (There was also mention of a 7.7mm sMG 230(r) captured from the Soviet-occupied Baltic states in 1941.)

After Dunkirk the British Army had to re-equip with machine guns once again. To ease the situation, the American government decided to sell its remaining 0.30 Model 1915 machine guns to Britain (the US Army had long since concentrated on the Browning 0.30 Model 1917A1 as its standard machine gun). The total that arrived in Britain was 7,071, along with 0.30-06 ammunition to fire from them. As this ammunition was not a standard British issue the Model 1915 guns went to the Home Guard, with red paint bands added around the barrel jacket and feeder to indicate the odd calibre. Later during the war about a thousand Model 1915s were converted by Enfield Lock to fire 0.303 ammunition, but even these remained with the Home Guard.

Not all stockpiled Model 1915s went to Britain. A batch of 500 were sent to the Dutch East Indies where they later fell into Japanese hands. Another batch went to the Philippines for the local auxiliaries; they also ended up in Japanese control. The Japanese were quite familiar with the Vickers gun, having both purchased and manufactured several models under licence between the wars. Air-cooled Vickers guns were carried by many Japanese aircraft.

For the British Army, the main change to the Vickers gun after 1940 was not to the gun itself but to the ammunition. The Mk 8Z 0.303 round was originally produced for the RAF with nitrocellulose propellant taking the place of cordite. Its use spread to the Army, specifically for the Vickers machine gun, as it added an extra 914m/1,000yd of range,

A 0.303 Vickers machine gun mounting on a Universal Carrier.

making the extreme range about 3,290m/3,600yd. Much of the range improvement was due to the boat-tailed base of the bullet that reduced ballistic drag. The range increase enabled the gun to revert to the Great War practice of indirectly fired, area-suppression fire missions where the objective was to deny an area of terrain to enemy movement rather than to strike a specific point target. The Vickers gun was therefore provided with arrangements for on-carriage fire-control equipment such as a dial sight and clinometer (for precise elevation control) and a fire director instrument was added to each machine-gun section. Gun teams learned to fire 'off the map' when it was not possible for an observer to monitor the fall of shot.

By 1945 the general standard of British machine-gun expertise was back to where it had been in 1918, but with extra indirect-fire capabilities. That expertise meant that the Vickers gun served on throughout the Korean War, afterwards being retained in service until 1968. Vickers guns continued to find employment with some other nations after then. One noticeable example was South Africa where Vickers guns were converted to fire 7.62 × 51mm NATO ammunition. They too have now passed from use.

BROWNINGS: WATER-COOLED

The name John Moses Browning was mentioned in the previous chapter. Browning was probably the most prolific and successful gun designer of his or any other period with a string of successful and long-lived guns to his name. Among them were machine guns.

The first Browning machine gun was the Model 1895. When that gun was in the design stage Hiram Maxim's many patents were still in force, so Browning had to somehow find a way of designing a reliable machine-gun operating mechanism that would not infringe them. His Model 1895, manufactured by Colt's, therefore relied on a gas-operated mechanism utilizing a linkage arm that swung down under the gun during firing, giving rise to the nickname of 'Potato Digger'. The Model 1895 was regarded as obsolete by 1914 and so its details need not detain us here, although it was still in production for export orders in 1914 and, eventually, as a training gun for the new US Army after 1917. It was also developed into the Marlin gun (*see* below). In historical terms, the most important influence imposed on later events by the Model 1895 was that it convinced Browning that recoil-operated mechanisms were, at that time, more efficient and reliable than gas systems.

By the early 1900s Browning had therefore prepared the outlines of a novel recoil-operated mechanism that owed nothing to any Maxim influence. It became known as the short-recoil system. In oversimplified terms, as a bullet is fired, the barrel and the breech block recoil accordingly, locked together by a lug. After a short travel, the rearward motion of the barrel is arrested and the locking lug disengages. A mechanical lever device known as an accelerator, together with the mass of the breech block, then thrusts the block to the rear, compressing a spring and ejecting the spent case as it does so. Rearward travel is then halted by a buffer assembly so that the block then moves forward again under compressed spring pressure, loading a fresh cartridge as it travels, until the breech block and barrel lock together once more, ready for firing. If the trigger remains depressed, the cycle will then start again.

Using this short-recoil system, Browning built his Model 1901 and offered it to the American government. There was no interest. They considered that they already had as many Gatling guns

as they needed and saw no reason to replace them. Browning therefore filed away his drawings until such time as they might be needed.

That time came during 1916 when it was apparent that the USA would eventually become actively involved in the European war. At that point the US Army had only some 1,100 machine guns in stock, most of them obsolete or worn out. Planners were already calculating that the US would have to create an armed force of at least one million men, so more than 100,000 machine guns would be needed to equip them. Where those guns were to come from and what type they would be was the cause of considerable debate.

It was time for Browning to make his mark. He invited numerous government officials and the press to a firing demonstration of his gun in February 1917, the same event also involving the first showing of the BAR (*see* the previous chapter). The machine gun involved, a slightly revised version of the water-cooled Model 1901, performed dramatically well, generating a wave of enthusiasm for an all-American gun that could equip the planned expeditionary forces. Further more official testing of the prototype demonstrated the firing of 20,000 0.30-06 rounds without significant problems or malfunctions, and, to add to the promise of Browning's design, it was planned with mass production in mind. The depth of detailed preparation extended to making the gun fairly easy for soldiers to use and maintain. One further asset of the M1917 was that a single example would cost the Treasury $283.52. By contrast a Model 1915 Vickers cost $490.

Browning's gun was soon type classified as the 0.30 Model 1917, later the M1917, and ordered into immediate production. Three production contractors were selected since it was apparent that no single one could generate the quantities needed within the time scale imposed by events in Europe. Once again, and despite their existing workload, Colt's became involved. They were asked to produce 10,000 M1917s and to prepare the necessary tooling and gauges for the other two contractors, Remington (15,000 guns) and Westinghouse (20,000).

A Browning 0.30 Model 1917 seen here as supplied to Poland in 1930.

As matters turned out, Colt's spent more time making the tooling than they did the guns. By the time the armistice was signed, Colt's had managed to manufacture only about 600 M1917s. By contrast, between April 1918 and the end of that year Westinghouse manufactured 30,150, reaching a rate of 500 guns a day. Total M1917 production by the time the initial programme was terminated was 56,608. To these could be added air-cooled versions for aircraft. From a limited base, American industry had created an extensive machine-gun production capability in less than a year.

The first M1917s were in action in France by September 1918, issued as battalion-level fire-support weapons. They were received enthusiastically and performed admirably. At that time few could have realized that the Browning M1917 was only the first of many Browning machine guns that were to remain in service to this day, with no indication they will ever be superseded.

Service experience with the M1917 revealed that some strengthening of the receiver base was needed and from the mid-1930s onwards some small improvements were made to the ammunition feed and in a few other areas. This resulted in the M1917A1, all earlier guns being gradually brought up to the same standard by simply changing the appropriate parts. Thereafter, no further changes to the M1917 mechanism were required, all later Browning machine guns using the same mechanism virtually unchanged. The only external difference was introduced when production restarted during 1942 to meet the demands of another war. The original bronze water jacket was replaced by steel to conserve scarce raw materials.

A complete M1917A1, with tripod, weighed

Members of the Southwick (Sussex) Home Guard crewing a 0.30 Model 1917 they have mounted on a mobile carriage of their own design (1941).

38.5kg/85.75lb, without the cooling water. Ammunition was fed into the gun in 250-round fabric or metal-link belts and fired at a cyclic rate of between 450 and 600rpm.

Although the second round of M1917A1 production did not start until 1942, the gun had already entered the fray during 1940. Between the wars the number of machine gun types in American service had been gradually reduced. Only the M1917 guns were deemed worthy of retention as standard weapons to be used in any future conflict (instead of being disposed of, unwanted guns were stockpiled). Despite this, as part of the post-Dunkirk assistance offered by the USA 10,000 M1917A1s were sold to the British as part of the huge batch of small arms sent across the Atlantic at a time when the USA was not a belligerent. As the M1917A1s were 0.30 weapons, they were assigned as home defence weapons only, most going to the Home Guard. As a result of this assistance, the American government found itself short of machine guns when the country entered the Second World War at the end of 1941. The M1917A1 was therefore placed back in production.

Several contractors were involved in M1917A1

M1917A1	
Calibre	7.62mm; 0.30in
Length	981mm; 38.64in
Length of barrel	607mm; 23.9in
Weight complete	38.5kg; 85.75lb
Muzzle velocity	854 m/s; 2,800ft/s
Feed	250-round belt
Cyclic rate of fire	450–600rpm

production. Colt's was again a contractor as well as the Rock Island Arsenal, while numerous other concerns supplied components. Production peaked in 1943 when 30,724 guns were turned out. Total production by the time the war ended was 53,859.

No records of Lend-Lease M1917A1s can be found, although it is known that the type was used by China. At least some of these may have been purchased commercially between the wars, for Colt's maintained a M1917 production facility to cater for orders from Poland, Norway and some South American states. The models involved in these transactions differed in detail from the standard M1917, as did the several models licence-produced in Belgium by Fabrique Nationale (FN) at Herstal, Liège.

The M1917A1 served the US Army well in every theatre in which it fought, going on after 1945 to serve during the Korean War. It was not finally replaced until the late 1950s.

BROWNINGS: AIR-COOLED

Impressive though the water-cooled M1917/M1917A1 might have been, it was overwhelmed in numerical superiority by the Browning air-cooled variants that began with the M1919 tank machine gun. In almost every respect the M1919 was a M1917 with a heavy, air-cooled barrel. It was thought that, in its intended tank role, the gun would not be called upon to deliver protracted bursts and thus the barrel would remain relatively cool. The short-recoil mechanism was retained virtually unchanged and the round fired continued to be the 0.30-06.

Only a handful of M1919s emerged as the tanks they were meant to arm were never built, their planned construction being cancelled by the armistice. Gradual but slow development of the air-cooled Browning went through several phases during the 1920s and the 1930s, most stages involving water-cooled M1917s being converted for the purpose. Tests with the M1919A3 model

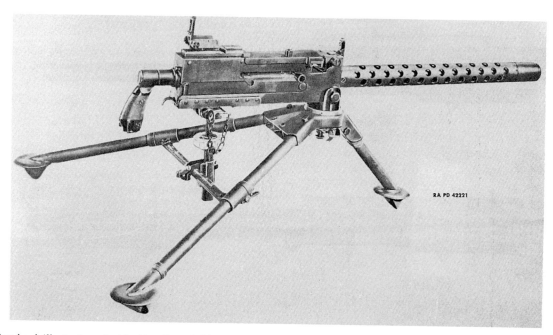

Text book illustration of a Machine Gun, Caliber 0.30, M1919A4.

115

M1919A4

Calibre   7.62mm; 0.30in
Length   1.04m; 41in
Length of barrel   610mm; 24in
Weight complete   19.95kg; 31lb
Muzzle velocity   854 m/s; 2,800ft/s
Feed   250-round belt
Cyclic rate of fire   450–500rpm

indicated that there was potential for an air-cooled Browning machine gun for infantry and also vehicle-mounting applications. The intended gun was to have a 24in/610mm barrel in place of the earlier 18in/457mm one. The result was the 0.30 M1919A4.

The M1919A4 entered production in 1942, and from then onwards the totals became prodigious. No fewer than 389,251 M1919A4 guns for flexible mountings, plus a further 36,292 for fixed installations (mainly tanks), were manufactured. (It was

Training with a 0.30 M1919A4 machine gun.

easy to convert fixed guns for flexible mountings; by 1945 many had been so converted.)

Not all the flexible M1919A4s were destined to be mounted on infantry tripods but a large proportion ended up in that form. They were found to be as reliable and satisfactory as the water-cooled M1917, although the protracted fire rate could never be as great as for the water-cooled weapon. One advantage was that the gun alone weighed only13.95kg/31lb, as opposed to the 14.7kg/32.6lb of the M1917A1 (without water). The M2 tripod was also simpler and lighter.

The M1919A4 featured in the Lend-Lease totals. Other nations received 30,735, including 'British Empire' armed forces (17,631), the Free French (2,272) and the Soviet Union (5,403). However, these totals included the M1919A6 adaptation of the M1919A4 into what was supposed to be a light machine gun (*see* the previous chapter for details).

The M1919A4 remains in service with many nations around the world and many manufacturers still find it worthwhile to make and supply spares. Several nations have rechambered their guns to suit the local ammunition availability, a typical example being South Africa, where their vehicle-mounted MG4 guns now fire 7.62 × 5mm NATO ammunition.

The M1919A5 was a special tank gun produced during 1942 and 1943 and modified post-war into the 0.30 M37 tank machine gun.

It should be emphasized that the M1919A4 and the M1919A6 were only two of the 0.30 Browning air-cooled machine guns produced in the USA during the Second World War. There were also 0.30 M2 series aircraft guns of several sub-types, of which no fewer than 193,556 were manufactured, at

Museum example of a Hotchkiss 8mm mle 1914 machine gun.

least 70,000 of them for the Royal Air Force. However, they are outside the scope of this work. Even so, it should be noted that more than 820,000 0.30 Browning machine guns of all types were manufactured between 1941 and 1945. In Britain, BSA licence-produced 468,098 0.303 aircraft guns for the RAF at their Small Heath facilities.

THE HOTCHKISS

In 1939 the French medium machine gun was the Hotchkiss mle 1914, the latest in a sequence of Hotchkiss models that began with the mle 1897. The mle 1897 was based around a gas-operated system originally devised by the Austrian Adolph von Odkolek and sold to Hotchkiss & Cie of St Denis in 1893. As the original Odkolek system, devised to circumvent the all-enveloping Maxim patents, needed considerable technical development before it could result in a military weapon, the American

Laurence Bénét and his assistant Henri Mercié, both working for Hotchkiss, were largely responsible for the models that followed.

Hotchkiss machine guns were successful enough mechanically, but they did require careful handling, especially with regard to the ammunition feed. Bénét and Mercié decided to adopt a feed system involving 8 × 50R Lebel cartridges carried into the gun on steel (originally brass) strips holding twenty-four or thirty rounds. Visual recognition features of the mle 1897 that came to epitomize the Hotchkiss machine guns were the 'doughnut-ring' fins around the base of the barrel closest to the chamber. These were meant to radiate the heat generated during firing because the air-cooled barrel could not easily be changed if it became hot in action; if it got too hot the rifling was soon destroyed. Despite the fins, usually brass but sometimes steel, barrel overheating remained a potential hazard on Hotchkiss guns throughout their subsequent careers.

Free French soldiers demonstrating a Hotchkiss mle 1914 in the low-level air defence role; note the soldier loading the ammunition strip.

Hotchkiss mle 1914

Calibre 8mm; 0.315in
Length 1.27m; 50in
Length of barrel 775mm; 30.5in
Weight, gun 23.6kg; 52lb
Muzzle velocity 725 m/s; 2,400ft/s
Feed 24- or 30-round strip
Cyclic rate of fire 400–600rpm

The mle 1897 was adopted by the French Army and so were later models such as the mle 1900 and the 1914. It was the mle 1914 that gradually became the standard French machine gun of the Great War and after, and also the one that went to war in 1939.

It seems that there were plans to put the mle 1914 back into production in 1938. In 1917 Hotchkiss mle 1914 guns were among those issued to American troops newly arrived in France.

The mle 1914 had several advantages over previous models, not the least being a tripod mounting that permitted a degree of traverse and elevation (the original mle 1897 had a fixed tripod). There was also an optional ammunition feed with three-round steel strips hinged together to form a 249-round belt. As with the earlier models, the mle 1914 was a serviceable enough weapon but it was heavy (the gun weighed 23.6kg/52lb) and somewhat cumbersome. It was also rather expensive for it made extensive use of high-quality materials and machining operations.

By 1939 Hotchkiss machine guns had spread to almost everywhere French influence could reach.

An unusual illustration of British troops using a Hotchkiss mle 1914, probably in Italy; this photograph has been censored.

German recognition manual illustration of the 8mm Mitrailleuse St Etienne mle 1907, a less than successful French machine gun.

Apart from the French colonies, Hotchkiss guns were used by Belgium, China, Japan (where the base design was modified into the 6.5mm Type 3 and 7.7mm Type 92, the standard Japanese machine guns of 1941 and after), Norway, Poland, Romania and Yugoslavia. After 1940 the mle 1914 became the German 8mm sMG 257(f).

As the Hotchkiss guns were produced commercially, the French defence establishment decided to introduce their own variations on the basic design. The result was the mle 1907 St Etienne. By all accounts the best that could be said of it was that it was not a success. The mle 1907 proved to be highly troublesome since it incorporated oddities such as the gas piston moving forward (the Hotchkiss piston moved to the rear) to unlock the breech and compress a return spring under the barrel. The spring had to be left exposed to the atmosphere as the heat of the barrel would otherwise have drastically reduced its life. The resultant complexity and the likelihood that debris would enter the mechanism meant that the mle 1907 had been relegated to fortress duties by 1917. The survivors of the 39,500 manufactured, apart from those disposed of to unwitting recipients in Romania and Greece,

were still serving in that role in 1939. The mle 1907 was one captured machine gun that the Germans did not adopt and it had little part to play in the events of 1940.

BIT AND PIECES

The account has dealt with the main medium machine gun types used by the infantry between 1939 and 1945, but there were a few others, even if they rarely, if ever, saw combat. Typical of these

Marlin	
Calibre	7.62mm; 0.30in
Length	1.016m; 40in
Length of barrel	711mm; 28in
Weight, gun	10.1kg; 22.5lb
Muzzle velocity	840 m/s; 2,750ft/s
Feed	120- or 250-round belt
Cyclic rate of fire	500–700rpm

One of the US Marlin machine guns supplied to the UK in 1940, this example being a tank model.

was the Marlin, a machine gun developed from the old Colt-Browning Model 1895 'Potato Digger' by the Marlin-Rockwell Corporation of New Haven, Connecticut, between 1916 and 1918.

At the request of the US Navy, the swinging link of the Model 1895 was removed from the design and replaced by a gas piston system. This rendered the gun lighter and more suitable for aircraft use. The resultant air-cooled 0.30 M1916 and M1917 were produced for this role and formed the armament of several American combat aircraft of the period. About 38,000 were manufactured. There was also a 0.30 M1918 variant intended for use on tanks but, as it arrived rather late in the war, only 1,470 of them were made. The M1918 could be ground-mounted on a tripod and had a longitudinal fin radiator assembly to assist barrel cooling.

The Marlin guns proved to be excellent aircraft weapons, but by 1932 they had all been withdrawn and stored. In 1940 15,638 M1917 aircraft guns and 2,602 tank guns were among the large batch of surplus American weapons shipped across the Atlantic to the hard-pressed British, then seemingly in imminent danger of invasion.

The Marlin guns were gratefully received but none of them came with any form of ground mounting, while carrying over the usual problem that the 0.30-06 cartridge was not a standard British issue. The result was that the Marlin was unsuitable for front-line deployment and was therefore diverted to the Home Guard where all manner of improvised mountings were devised for them. The Home Guard was not the only recipient of the Marlin; they were also issued to the Merchant Navy

for low-level air defence, again using hastily improvised mountings incorporating materials not in short supply. They found little employment and so today the World War 2 Marlins are almost forgotten.

Another example of improvisation bought about by the danger of imminent invasion occurred in Australia. By early 1942 an attack on the mainland by Japanese land forces seemed highly likely. The Australian armed forces were desperately short of infantry weapons, especially machine guns, and there seemed no chance that the hard-pressed United Kingdom or the USA would be able to supply any for some time to come. Several measures were introduced, not the least being a boost in Vickers machine gun production at Lithgow. One rather extreme interim measure was to round up all the Great War German machine-gun trophies still held by ex-servicemen's clubs and museums.

Two models were involved, the 7.92mm sMG 08 and the lighter leMG 08/15. These were Maxims that could be converted to fire the readily-available 0.303 ammunition and converted they were, mainly by installing Vickers machine-gun barrels and cannibalizing unusable examples for spare parts. It seems that about 1,500 guns were involved in this programme. The 0.303 Maxims were issued to home defence units only and never left Australia.

There were many other machine guns in the medium category used by the Allies between 1939 and 1945. For instance, the British used 7.92mm Besa machine guns of Czech origin but they were armoured-vehicle guns, not infantry guns.

7   Heavy Machine Guns

The tank was but one instigator of the category of weapons now known as heavy machine guns. Once it became apparent during 1917 that rifle-calibre ammunition was unable to penetrate the armour applied to the early tanks, something heavier was called for. Developments in air warfare were also indicating that heavier-calibre automatic weapons would soon be required, while ground gunners were requesting more effective anti-aircraft weapons.

The French were quick to respond to the new requirements with an 11mm heavy machine gun design from Hotchkiss; but the ammunition proved to be underpowered for the anti-armour role; therefore, despite some early interest from the US Army, that project dwindled away. Yet it had sown the seed of future heavy machine gun developments, not least in the USA.

Infantry weapon par excellence, the air-cooled 0.50/12.7mm M2 heavy machine gun.

BROWNING AGAIN

Once the US Army began to arrive in France in 1917, staff officers made a close study of the weapon types they would need. Among them a large-calibre, automatic weapon featured heavily. Although the credit is usually give to General John J. Pershing, his staff officers drew up a requirement for a machine gun firing a heavy bullet with a muzzle velocity of at least 823m/s (2,700ft/s). Such a performance, it was considered, was the least that would merit long-term adoption. The 11mm Hotchkiss gun was therefore dropped from further consideration.

Back in the USA, John Browning heard of the requirement and promptly scaled up his 0.30 M1917 machine gun to 0.50in/12.7mm, complete with the short-recoil system virtually unchanged apart from calibre-related components. The enlarged gun presented few problems but the proposed ammunition did.

Ammunition development was carried out by the Winchester Repeating Arms Company at New Haven. The 0.50/12.7mm calibre was selected as one resulting in a weapon within the bounds of practicality as regards its weight, bulk and manufacture with existing machinery. However, the initial ammunition performance fell well below that called for in the Pershing specification. That performance was partly limited by the enforced adoption of a 775mm/30.5in barrel, the longest that Winchester could rifle at that time. It was considered that a longer 914mm/36in barrel and a revised propellant charge would provide the necessary performance; thus gun and ammunition development progressed one stage further.

The development of the ammunition was then considerably assisted by the capture of German 13 × 92mm Tank und Flieger (TuF) rounds, developed by Polte of Magdeburg for a future German heavy machine gun with anti-tank and aircraft applications. The development of the gun progressed slowly so the ammunition was used in the world's first anti-tank rifle, the Mauser 13mm Tankgewehr. The cartridge was adapted by

Winchester for a 0.50/12.7mm (12.7 × 99mm) machine-gun cartridge with the result that the Pershing specification was more than met.

It was immediately recommended that an order for 10,000 guns should be placed, even though many soldiers considered that the water-cooled gun, type-classified as the 0.50 Model 1918, was too heavy for general infantry use. Such arguments were set aside by the armistice, following which plans for mass production were immediately reduced to little more than a handful for trials. These were thought necessary to test the suitability of the gun for air-defence and aircraft applications, although the post-1919 dearth of military funding at all levels meant that the trials were sporadic and prolonged.

Development of the 0.50/12.7mm machine gun then passed out of Browning's direct control to Colt's, where continued, low-key development resulted in the Model 1921, a tripod-mounted, water-cooled gun. An indication of the lack of defence funding throughout the 1920s and the early 1930s is that between 1921 and 1934 the US government procured only about a thousand Model 1921 guns. Enthusiasm for the Model 1921, never high because of its weight and handling, diminished still further when the early guns exhibited overheating problems, even when water-cooled. At one point it seemed that the Model 1921 was about to be withdrawn.

Fortunately for the future, Dr S.G. Green, an engineer in the Ordnance Department, considered that the 0.50/12.7mm gun had great potential. His development work on detail gradually produced a common receiver based on the Model 1921 but with a feed system that could accept ammunition belts from either the right or the left. The same receiver could also accommodate either a water- or an air-cooled barrel as well as numerous modifications, each adaptation taking only minutes to introduce without recourse to special tools. In its final form the basic receiver could be adapted for one of seven categories of gun: two water-cooled variants (for Army or Navy installations); an air-cooled gun for ground applications; heavy-barrel, air-cooled guns for armoured vehicles; and fixed, turret and flexible aircraft installations.

In addition, detailed engineering work within the receiver provided many components with greater strength than was once considered necessary. The extra strength permitted the later use of ammunition developing extra power, increasing the muzzle velocity to 858m/s (2,814ft/s), a performance enhanced by the introduction of a 1.1m/45in barrel, although the introduction of this barrel took some time (914mm/36in barrels were retained for aircraft applications). More detailed changes rendered the receiver and mechanisms more suitable for the expected mass production. This development work was completed by 1933, although none of it was immediately applied to in-service models. It was the time of the Great Depression and all military spending was at a minimal level.

Even so, in 1933, and more in hopeful anticipation than anything else, the much-revised gun was type-classified as the Machine Gun, Caliber 0.50 Browning, M2 (the M1 remained a paper exercise). The financial atmosphere of that time meant that there were no funds to carry the project further for the US Army (or the Army Air Force). The better-funded Navy, itself looking for a low-level, automatic, air-defence gun, therefore financed many of the necessary preproduction groundwork stages, such as the preparation of drawings and maintenance procedures, and the funding of 'educational', low-level production sources ready for when more funds might be forthcoming.

A Browning M2 mounted on a Universal Carrier, 1945.

Browning M2

Calibre	12.7mm; 0.50in
Length	1.654m; 65.1in
Length of barrel	1.143m; 45in
Weight, gun	37.8kg; 84lb
Muzzle velocity	884m/s; 2,900ft/s
Feed	110-round belt
Cyclic rate of fire	450–575rpm

By the end of the 1930s defence funding was easier to obtain and M2 production could finally begin on an industrial scale. By the time of the attack on Pearl Harbor in December 1941 about 300,000 M2 guns had been manufactured. Experience demonstrated that the water-cooled guns lacked power as air-defence weapons, the US Navy gradually turning away from the 0.50/12.7mm M2 to 20mm and 40mm guns for ship-borne air defence. Army experience showed that by installing a heavy barrel (HB) the M2 could be a highly versatile, ground-based weapon with many applications, from tripod use to vehicle armament, while remaining effective as low-level, air-defence guns, especially when mounted in pairs or fours on powered Maxson mountings. By 1945 the M2 HB had become the preferred land-use, general-purpose weapon, all water-cooled models gradually being withdrawn to be converted to take air-cooled barrels.

Demand for the basic M2 expanded dramatically from 1942 onwards. At one time nine centres were busy manufacturing the guns as fast as they could. The early development work by Colt's and the attention to detail of Dr Green paid dividends. By the end of the war no fewer than 1,451,842 basic M2 guns had been manufactured for land, sea and air applications. To these could be added a further 429,056 M2 HBs specifically for ground applications, 347,524 of them for use on flexible mountings. The latter term included everything from tripods to vehicle pintles, the remaining M2

HB guns being for fixed and co-axial mountings, both involving remote firing by solenoids.

M2 guns were turned out by Colt's, the High Standard Company, the Savage Arms Corporation, Frigidaire, the Buffalo Arms Corporation, AC Spark Plug, Brown-Lipe-Chappin, the Saginaw Division of General Motors and the Kelsey-Hayes Wheel Company. It will be noted that some of these companies were newcomers to defence production. Even though the M2 was not particularly easy to produce, the design was such that its manufacture was nowhere near as difficult as it might have been, thanks to the genius of John Moses Browning and the early Model 1921 development work carried out at Colt's.

In service the M2 HB soon became a highly popular weapon, although it was something of a load to carry. A complete M2 HB gun weighed 37.2kg/81.8lb and it was 1.65m/5.45ft long. The cyclic rate of fire was between 450 and 555rpm, the exact rate being variable by adjusting the buffer assembly inside the receiver. Bursts usually had to be kept short because the lively recoil was inclined to throw the muzzle away from the target.

Ammunition was fed into the gun by using metal link belts. The standard cartridge was the Ball M2, although the anti-armour origins of the gun were carried over by the armour-piercing AP M2 with a tungsten chrome steel core. The latter gave the M2 HB gun a useful capability against lightly armoured and soft-skin vehicles. Using either cartridge, the M2 HB could deliver fairly accurate fire at ranges of up to about 1,830m/2,000yd. The Ball M2 projectile was a highly effective anti-personnel weapon at any range.

The usual infantry mounting for the M2 HB, the Tripod M3, weighed 20kg/44lb. One alternative was the M63, a high-elevation mounting intended primarily for low-level air defence and weighing 65.3kg/114lb. The M2 HB gun was also a local defence weapon for many half-track carriers, tanks and trucks. Spare barrels were usually carried for a change to be made following prolonged fire.

M2 guns featured in Lend-Lease arrangements; 15,083 M2 HBs were so assigned, the two main recipients being the 'British Empire' (5,233) and the Free French (7,655). Post-war accounts record that only one example was sent to the Soviet Union since it already had heavy machine guns of its own.

The M2 HB is with us still. It was certainly one of the most successful guns of its type between 1941 and 1945 and remains in production to this day, with no sign of passing from favour. In fact, quite the opposite is happening since new applications and customers for the M2 HB seem to appear every year. Browning died in 1926, but he would no doubt have been pleased to see his design's success.

THE DShK

Consideration of a heavy machine gun to equip the Red Army did not start until 1925. Before then, given the Revolution and the subsequent Civil War, the military had other matters of greater importance to consider. To save time, early experiments involving an enlarged variant of a German Dreyse machine gun were carried out with ammunition based on a Vickers 0.50 cartridge intended for the Vickers C Class machine guns. This cartridge proved to be underpowered for the anti-aircraft role, the one that the Soviet planners decided had to be accorded the highest priority.

It was 1930 before a more suitable cartridge was

DShK	
Calibre	12.7mm; 0.50in
Length	1.602m; 62.3in
Length of barrel	1.002m; 39.4in
Weight, gun	33.3kg; 73.5lb
Muzzle velocity	843m/s; 2,765ft/s
Feed	50-round belt
Cyclic rate of fire	550–600rpm

ready. It emerged as a 12.7 × 108mm cartridge with a performance not far removed from that of the Browning 0.50/12.7mm M2. At around that time the first examples of a 12.7mm heavy machine gun designed by Vasiliy Degtyarov were ready for their initial trials. As with many other guns of its type, this was a scaled-up variant of an existing design, in this case the 7.62mm DP light machine gun (*see* Chapter 5) and using a similar side-locking mechanism. Ammunition was fed from a drum magazine. As usual, the wheeled field mounting resembled a miniature artillery carriage, complete with a shield and a small seat for the gunner, the mounting originating from the same Ivan Kolesnikov who had designed an alternative mounting for the 7.62mm PM1910 machine gun before 1917.

12.7mm DShK (Dushka) on its wheeled field mounting.

The 1930 gun was designated the 12.7mm DK. Almost as soon as it was approved for production it was decided that the cyclic rate of fire (360rpm) was too slow for most applications, and rendered far lower in practice by the limited capacity of the drum magazine; therefore almost as soon as production of the gun began it was terminated, with only a few small batches being completed.

To enhance the fire rate of the DK, the talents of Georgiy Shpagin were called upon. He retained the basic mechanism of the DK gun but introduced a rotary ammunition-feed system in which the rounds were taken from a fifty-round metal link belt, to be held on rotating sprockets until they were pushed by the bolt into the chamber. This system was rather complicated but trials held during 1938 showed that it worked, while the cyclic fire rate increased to 550rpm. The Kolesnikov carriage continued to be used, the gun and its carriage having a total weight of a ponderous 155kg/342lb.

The gun was accepted for service in February 1939 as the 12.7mm DShK, also known as the DShK-38. The first production examples were issued in 1940 but its manufacture was not at first given any high priority. In January 1942 there were only 720 examples left in the entire Red Army inventory out of about 2,000 produced before then. Captured examples became the German 12.7mm sMG 268(r).

By January 1944 the numbers in service had reached 8,442. The guns found numerous applications, as they still do since the DShK remains a valued weapon around the world. As well as infantry mountings, the DShK became the main armament of light armoured cars, and air-defence mountings were also introduced.

For this air-defence version of the 12.7mm DShK the usual field mounting has been re-configured.

12.7mm DShK in action in 1945.

In 1946 the ammunition-feed system was drastically modified to accept belt feed from either the left or the right. Production examples thus became the DShKM, or DShK-38/46, but that was a post-war development and the original DShK is still likely to be encountered. After 1945 the DShK and its later variant were still deployed on their field mountings, but more and more were employed as guns for armoured vehicles, mounted over the commander's cupola. The last tank series to carry such guns before they were gradually replaced by the modern 12.7mm NSV family were the T-54/55s, many of which remain in use around the world, still sporting their DShK guns. The later DShKM is still offered for export sales by several nations, including China, Pakistan and Romania.

Something that has altered little over the years is 12.7 × 108mm ammunition. That remains in widespread production, virtually unchanged from the original specification introduced in 1930, although

an armour-piercing incendiary (API) projectile was introduced in 1972.

There remains one further Soviet heavy machine gun calibre to mention and that is the 14.5mm. This was originally introduced as a 14.5 × 114mm anti-tank rifle cartridge (*see* Chapter 9), later transferred to the ultra-simple, KPV heavy machine gun in 1944. These were, and still are, almost exclusively fielded as air-defence or armoured vehicle weapons.

HOTCHKISS AGAIN

Mention was made above of a Hotchkiss 11mm heavy machine gun developed from about 1917 onwards. This gun was often known as the 'balloon gun' since among its intended targets were artillery observation balloons. It was also intended to be deployed as an anti-tank weapon but, as already

Hotchkiss 13.2mm heavy machine gun on its towed field mounting.

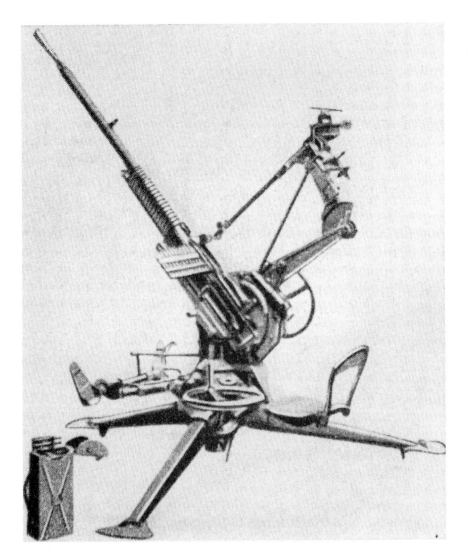

Hotchkiss 13.2mm heavy machine gun on its light anti-aircraft mounting and using strip feed for the ammunition.

Hotchkiss mle 1930

Calibre 13.2mm; 0.52in
Length 2.413m; 95in
Length of barrel 1.651m; 65in
Weight, gun 37.5kg; 87lb
Muzzle velocity N/A
Feed 30-round box magazine
Cyclic rate of fire 450rpm

mentioned, the cartridge (actually 12 × 89mm) lacked performance and the gun/ammunition combination faded away.

The concept of a heavy Hotchkiss machine gun remained and in 1930 a new model was marketed. This mle 1930 fired a 13.2 × 99mm cartridge with more power than the balloon gun and was considered by its makers to have considerable promise. Three basic models were offered. Two of them were horse-towed and fired from a spoked-wheeled carriage, complete with ammunition limbers if required. One was supposed to be for infantry use, the other for cavalry. A tripod could be provided for the infantry version. The third model was a heavy and rather complicated anti-aircraft mounting carrying one or two guns.

Many of the usual gas-operated Hotchkiss features appeared in the mle 1930, including the ammunition strip feed; but an alternative was an overhead, curved, box magazine holding thirty rounds. The cyclic rate of fire was 450rpm and the cartridge provided a muzzle velocity of 800m/s (2,620ft/s).

The mle 1930 was adopted by the French Army, but not as an infantry weapon. It ordered 540 examples as air-defence guns and a further ninety-eight as fortification guns. More were procured to arm some French light armoured vehicles.

Orders for the mle 1930 or its close commercial derivatives were received from several nations,

including Poland, Romania, Greece and the other Balkan states. Some of these were infantry versions. The mle 1930 was also licence-produced in Japan as the 13mm Machine Gun Type 93. Another end user was Germany. It took over as many ex-French mle 1930 guns after June 1940 as the 13.2mm sMG 271(f), deploying them as light anti-aircraft guns.

The 13.2mm mle 1930 must therefore be rated as one of the less successful of the 1939–45 heavy machine guns. The only other one that may be mentioned is the 15mm Besa, a Czech weapon adopted as a tank machine gun by the British Army. Although it was designed to be fired dismounted from its host vehicle it was rarely, if ever, so employed. The total production of this gun by BSA was 3,218. Numbers of the original Czech 15mm ZB vz 60 guns, from which the Besa was derived, were purchased by Greece as light anti-aircraft guns.

8   Mortars

While the mortar may have come to prominence during the Great War, the one devised in 1915 by Wilfred Stokes was a light version of an artillery weapon almost as old as gunpowder itself. What we now know as mortars were first observed in action during the Siege of Port Arthur during the Russo-Japanese war of 1905, although those were usually hastily produced and crude devices.

It took the desperate conditions of trench warfare after 1914 to provide the stimulus that gave rise to the infantry mortar. At that the device was considered as a form of trench artillery capable of delivering high explosive direct into the enemy's trench works, with the projectile concluding its trajectory at a steep angle to fall behind breastworks. Some of the Great War mortars were huge, immobile contraptions, for they were, in effect, siege weapons dedicated to battering the enemy's fortifications. By contrast, the Stokes mortar was portable, handy, simple and cheap and could deliver a high rate of fire (up to 20rpm). These factors gave rise to its introduction as an infantry weapon after 1918.

The Stokes mortar formed the prototype of the modern infantry weapon. A smooth-bored, steel tube is supported at a high angle on a baseplate by a bipod that permits barrel elevation and traverse. A dial sight, usually the most complicated part of the entire weapon, rounds off the equipment. Finned bombs are introduced into the muzzle to fall onto a firing pin that detonates small charges around the bomb tail and propels the bomb from the tube. The bomb climbs at a high angle until the propulsive impetus is lost and the bomb then descends almost vertically onto its target. These infantry

mortar basics have been present in every Stokes-pattern weapon since 1915.

This construction also meant that the infantry mortar could be broken down into sub-assemblies light enough to be carried by a small team of soldiers, providing the infantry with their own locally-controlled fire support. High-explosive bombs were joined by smoke projectiles and illuminating bombs to illuminate targets at night.

Wilfred Stokes had virtually completed the optimum design of his 3in/76.2mm mortar as early as 1918. After that date most of the improvements in performance came from the streamlining of the ammunition and other such measures, rather than in the mortar itself, although gradual developments in the steels and other materials involved could also enhance the performance of the system.

In 1917 Stokes was knighted and financially rewarded for his efforts. The British government thereafter took over what limited mortar development there was in Britain during the 1920s. Being not entirely happy with the remuneration he had received from the government, Sir Wilfred went to France where he joined the company owned by Edgar Brandt.

STOKES-BRANDT

It was in France that what are now considered to be the classic infantry mortars used between 1939 and 1945 were developed. The French Army purchased 81mm Stokes mortars from the British before 1918 (2,100 of them were still in existence in 1939, 680 of them based in France itself). Further development of this model resulted in the 81mm mle 1927, later revised to become the 81mm mle 27/31. It was this that became the forerunner of nearly all other 1939–45 mortars, being copied either directly or closely by manufacturers as diverse as Rheinmetall of Germany and Tampella of Finland. Licence-production agreements were set up with nations as far afield as Japan and the United States. Of all the mortars to be found in 1939, the mle 27/31 and its derivatives were certainly the most numerous. The French armed forces alone had some 5,300 of them in France in May 1940.

French Army 81mm mle 27/31 mortars (the actual calibre was 81.4mm) came in two versions, differing in barrel length. While both used the same bipod and baseplate, one had a barrel 15.6 calibres long and the other 13.7 calibres in length. There was also the choice of a heavy (6.5kg/14.3lb) or light (3.25kg/7.17lb) bomb. The maximum range in firing a light bomb from the long barrel was 2,850m/3,118yd. The weight in action of the long-barrel model was 59.7kg/131.6lb.

Good as the French mle 27/31 was, it could do little by itself to prevent the German victories of May and June 1940, after which surviving French mortars became the 8.1cm GrW 278(f) or 278/1(f), the latter having the short barrel. These mortars

Brandt mle 27/31 L/15.6	
Calibre	81.4mm; 3.2in
Length of barrel	1.267m; 49.9in
Weight in action	59.7kg; 131.6lb
Muzzle velocity	174m/s; 571ft/s
Maximum range	2,850m; 3,120yd
Bomb weight, light	3.25kg; 7.17lb

could fire German ammunition since the standard German 81mm mortar was a direct copy of the French original. More mle 27/31 clones came into German hands from Czechoslovakia, Denmark, Italy, Netherlands, Yugoslavia and Poland.

The 81mm mle 27/31 was employed as a battalion-level support weapon. By the early 1930s it had been decided that the benefits of the infantry mortar could be extended down to company level and so the Brandt 60mm mle 1935 was devised, the first being issued during 1937. This soon became another classic, being little more than a scaled-down version of the 81mm model. Only one barrel length was involved, firing a bomb weighing either 1.3kg/2.87lb or 2.2kg/4.85lb, to 1,700m/1,860yd or

The classic Stokes-Brandt 81mm mortar, the mle 27/31.

Brandt mle 1935	
Calibre	60.5mm; 2.38in
Length of barrel	724mm; 28.5in
Weight in action	17.8kg; 39.25lb
Muzzle velocity	158m/s; 518ft/s
Maximum range	1,700m; 1,860yd
Bomb weight, light	1.3kg; 2.87lb

50mm mle 1937	
Calibre	50mm; 1.97in
Length of barrel	415mm; 16.34in
Weight in action	3.65kg; 8.05lb
Muzzle velocity	70m/s; 230 ft/s
Maximum range	460m; 503yd
Bomb weight	435gm; 0.96lb

950m/1,040yd, respectively. Weight in action was 17.8kg/39.25lb so the usual team was two or three soldiers, one acting as an ammunition carrier.

In May 1940 the French Army had 4,940 mle 1935 mortars, most of them ending up in the German inventory as the 6cm GrW 225(f). The US Army's 60mm Mortar M2 was a licence-manufactured mle 1935.

The success of the 60 and 81mm mortars prompted the Brandt company to extend the series by the introduction of a 120mm mortar. Here the border between an infantry and an artillery weapon becomes blurred, for to this day some armed forces consider 120mm mortars to be infantry weapons, issuing and controlling them accordingly, while others regard them as artillery pieces. As far as the French Army was concerned the division is somewhat academic, for in 1940 the proposed Brandt 120mm mortar was still in the pre-issue stage. It had been intended that two 120mm mortars would

The little 50mm mle 1937, more of a grenade launcher than a true mortar.

replace a section of 81mm mortars in each infantry battalion. The 120mm model did not progress further under French management until after 1945. Another heavy mortar proposal by Chantiers de la Loire, this time of 135mm, did not survive the events of 1940.

There was one other French mortar-type weapon in existence in 1940, although it was even then categorized not as a mortar but as a grenade launcher (lance-grenades). This was the 50mm mle 1937, weighing only 3.5kg/7.7lb. It launched a small, finned grenade weighing only 450gm/1lb to a maximum range of 450m/492yd. The barrel was fixed at an angle of 45 degrees, range variations being introduced by altering the size of a propellant gas vent at the base of the short barrel.

Intended to be a platoon-level launcher, production of the mle 1937 was delayed until after the war started. The programme was afflicted by numerous delays and so few actually reached the troops before the Germans arrived, when all further progress ceased. The programme was revived after 1945 and

the weapon served with French armed forces until 1960.

Although originally intended as a fortification weapon for the Maginot Line, the 50mm mle 1935 did end up in the hands of the infantry, although the users were German. The trigger-fired, 50mm mle 1935 was designed for the close-in defence of the Maginot Line fortifications, mounted in a removable, armoured mantlet at a fixed 45-degrees angle, with variations in range being introduced by the bleeding-off of propellant gases from the chamber to the atmosphere outside the installation. The events of 1940 bypassed much of the Maginot Line so the mle 1935s were then given another role by their transfer to the Atlantic Wall. Once there, they were emplaced, complete with their original mantlets, on pivots in open positions to act as beach-defence weapons. They qualify as infantry weapons only because they were usually manned by locally stationed infantry formations. The 50mm mle 1935 fired a 975gm/2.15lb bomb to a maximum range of just over 1,000m/1,094yd.

The 50mm mle 1935, originally designed for the close-in defence of the Maginot Line forts but removed by the Germans for installation as beach defence weapons for the Atlantic Wall.

BRITISH MORTARS

For many years after 1918 the standard British infantry mortar remained the 3in Mk 1, the Stokes mortar. (The actual calibre was 3.208in/81.48mm.) By 1939 development had reached the Mk 2 stage, although comparisons with the Stokes original were perhaps invidious. On the Mk 2, introduced in 1936, almost every aspect of the mortar had been revised and enhanced, and the ammunition was of an entirely new, streamlined type.

Despite the changes made on the Mk 2, combat experience soon demonstrated that the British mortar was outranged by many of its contemporaries. When first introduced, the Mk 2 had a maximum range of only 1,460m/1,600yd when firing a 4.54kg/10lb bomb. Changes to the propellants and the bomb increased this to 2,515m/2,750yd, although even this remained below the extreme reach of many of the equivalent Italian and German mortars.

Gradual development during the war years led to a number of revised models. A Mk 2 barrel involved some constructional changes, the Mk 3 does not

Details of the British 3in mortar.

Rear view of one of the first 3in mortars to be delivered to the British Army.

appear to have been issued, while the Mk 4 could accommodate a heavier propellant charge, being coupled with a modified baseplate and a new sight. With the Mk 5 barrel, the 3in mortar came to its final form, the barrel being lighter but stronger than before. This model had the firing pin modified to permit the firing of captured German and Italian bombs. The Mk 5 was originally intended for use by airborne forces; about 5,000 were produced. The

3in Mk 2	
Calibre	76.2mm; 3in
Length of barrel	1.295m; 51in
Weight in action	57.2kg; 126lb
Maximum range	2,516m; 2,750yd
Bomb weight	4.54kg; 10lb

The two basic forms of the 2in mortar with (left) the short airborne version and (right) the Universal Carrier configuration.

rectangular baseplates underwent alteration as the war progressed, gradually becoming lighter but stronger with each change.

The combat weight of a Mk 2 3in mortar was 57.2kg/126lb. The three main sub-assemblies plus three-round ammunition packs could be carried in the usual infantry backpack style, although only over limited distances. To carry the mortar and its ammunition it was more usual to employ a suitably modified Universal Carrier or other vehicle that could transport not just the mortar but sufficient bombs, the mortar team and all the fire-control and other accessories. The mortar was not fired from the Carrier but was dismounted before being fired.

A transport alternative, often employed in the Far East, was the pack animal, especially the mule.

During the early 1930s it was decided that a light mortar at infantry company or even platoon level would be a definite asset and a search for a suitable design thus began. By the mid-decade so many hopefuls had appeared that a contest was held to select the most suitable equipment and a 2in/51mm design from Ecia of Spain emerged as the clear winner. Inevitably, some modifications had to be introduced to suit British Army requirements, but by February 1938 the first examples were in production.

The 2in mortar (actual calibre 2.015in/51.18mm)

An early publicity photograph showing a 2in Mark 11*** mortar.

was a light and simple weapon with a firing lever operated by pulling a lanyard. This meant that it was possible to fire bombs horizontally, a definite asset during house-clearing and other close-quarter operations.

Aiming was simple. For direction, a sight was clamped to the barrel. This was later dispensed with as a white line painted on the barrel was found to be just as effective. Elevation could be determined by using a simple clinometer, but frequently even this was done away with, the user simply setting the barrel to what seemed, by experience, to be the appropriate angle and making the necessary corrections as the mission continued. The mortar could be carried by a single soldier, although two usually formed a mortar team.

Two basic versions emerged. One had a rect-

angular baseplate and the other a small spade base which, coupled to a shorter barrel intended for issue to airborne troops, was found to be equally as useful as the more complicated models with the larger baseplate. The larger-baseplate models weighed about 4.1kg/9lb complete, while the shorter,

2in Mk VII*	
Calibre	51.2mm; 2.015in
Length of barrel	481.6mm; 18.96in
Weight	3.32kg; 7.3lb
Maximum range	320m; 350yd
Bomb weight	1.02kg; 2.25lb

The short 2in Mark VII mortar intended for issue to airborne forces.

airborne models with a spade weighed significantly less at 3.3kg/7.3lb. However, the shorter barrel resulted in a shorter range: 456m/500yd, as opposed to 320m/350yd, when firing a standard 1.02kg/2.25lb bomb.

Within mechanized infantry units the 2in mortar was carried on a Universal Carrier. These mortars had the large baseplate with provision for elevation and traverse clamps. The mortar could be dismounted for firing with the baseplate on the ground. Baseplate models were also issued to dismounted infantry, but by the end of the war the

*A 2in mortar team in action, probably with a Mark 11*** mortar.*

spade configuration, allied to a standard length barrel, was the preferred type and the large baseplate models were gradually withdrawn.

The bombs involved were high-explosive, smoke and numerous types of illuminating and signal flare.

The number of types and sub-types of the 2in mortar was considerable. A brief outline of them follows.

Mk 1:   introduced in 1918 and declared obsolete the following year

Mk II: the initial 1938 production version with a large baseplate

Mk II*:   1938 version intended for Universal Carriers

Mk II**:   another Universal Carrier model

Mk II***: for infantry use, with large baseplate

Mk III: a smoke discharger carried by tanks

Mk IV: produced in small numbers only; not adopted

Mk V: not manufactured

Mk VI: not manufactured

Mk VII: for Universal Carriers

Mk VII*:   for airborne forces, having a spade and the barrel shortened to 481mm/18.96in, as opposed to the more usual 665mm/26.2in

Mk VII**:spade baseplate model with long barrel, for infantry

Mk VIIA: Indian Army model

Mk VIII: short barrel, spade model, for airborne troops

Mk VII*:   long barrel, spade model, for infantry.

In all its forms the 2in mortar proved to be a useful little weapon, usually issued one to each infantry

A Bren Gun Carrier armed with a 2in mortar as well as a Bren Gun.

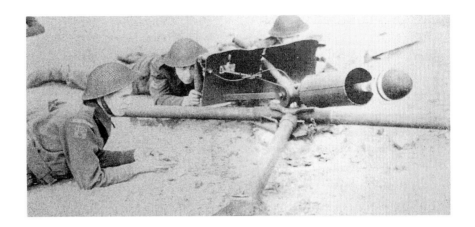

The Blacker Bombard.

platoon, although this was often exceeded. It served with the British Army until well into the 1970s, although after then many continued to be retained to launch illuminating bombs to light up targets for other weapons or serve as airborne training targets themselves. The Mk VIIA is still in production in India and available for export.

The other regular-issue British mortar had a calibre of 4.2in/106.7mm. Introduced in 1941 to deliver chemical agents or smoke, it soon became a high-explosive delivery system and was taken over by the Royal Artillery to expand the versatility of their anti-tank regiments. It was not issued to the infantry.

There remains one further British mortar to mention, although it differed from all the others by being a spigot mortar. With this type of weapon the projectile is placed over a central steel spigot for firing, the propellant charge being in the

projectile tail. The sprung-loaded spigot moved forward to detonate a propelling charge in the bomb tail while acting as a means of guidance. This system was adopted for many Great War mortars since a spigot was much easier and cheaper to manufacture than a barrel, while there was the further advantage that the projectile warhead was not restricted in diameter.

One proponent of the spigot mortar was Lt Col Blacker, to be encountered again in Chapter 9. His Great War experience led him to believe that the spigot mortar had many advantages over the tube mortar, to the extent that during the mid-1930s he devised and promoted a spigot mortar in opposition to the 2in mortar. His device, named the Arbalest, was rejected. Blacker persevered. In 1940 it seemed as though his time had come for after Dunkirk the Army was desperate for all types of weapon. One response came from an unusual War Office department known as MD1, where normal attitudes and procurement procedures were discarded in favour of new ideas and rapidly improvised measures that might plug the many gaps in the Army's inventories.

The Arbalest was therefore revived, modified and then accepted during 1941 as the Mortar, Spigot, 29mm, Mk 1, known almost universally as the Blacker Bombard. The device hurled a 6.35kg/14lb or 9.07kg/20lb high-explosive warhead to a range of about 800m/867yd. The emphasis was on rapid

---

Blacker Bombard

Calibre, spigot	29mm; 1.14in
Length of spigot	177.5mm; 6.99in
Weight in action	156.5kg; 345lb
Maximum range	822m; 900yd
Bomb weight	9.07kg; 20lb

manufacture using low-cost, non-critical raw materials and thus the mounting was a tubular steel quadrupod. The spigot could be traversed around the central junction of the mounting legs, with aiming being of the simplest type, the gunner using bicycle handles for control and relying on luck for successful results. The propellant was black powder and there was no recoil mechanism, all firing stresses being absorbed by the mounting and the

spades at the end of each leg. The complete equipment weighed 156.5kg/345lb.

Unlike many other improvised weapons of the post-Dunkirk period, the Blacker Bombard was an official War Office store and so, by some quirk of Army supply, a few ended up in north Africa to form part of the Tobruk defences. But by far the greatest number were issued for RAF airfield defences or to the Home Guard. With the latter, the Blacker

A typical example of a British Home Guard mortar produced by the troops themselves. This one was a product of the Dorking unit and used black powder as the propellant.

Bombard was supposed to act as an anti-tank weapon as well as a general-purpose, high-explosive delivery system; but it never had the chance to demonstrate its capabilities in action.

Some of the more enterprising Home Guard units went so far as to devise their own mortars. Few of these progressed much further technically than steel tubes, with black powder projecting explosive-filled canisters. Although they no doubt did wonders for local morale the effectiveness of most of these improvisations was, at best, questionable. None were officially adopted.

THE USA

Compared with the range of their weapons, American mortars were unremarkable in design terms. The US Army's battalion mortar, the 81mm Mortar M1, was a licence-produced version of the classic Brandt mortar, virtually unchanged from the original. Where the American version differed from all the others was in the sheer number produced. In June 1940 the total American inventory of 81mm mortars stood at 150, yet between 1940 and 1945 no fewer than 30,254 were produced at a steady pace,

The US Army's 81mm Mortar M1, a licence-manufactured Brandt mle 27/31.

81mm Mortar M1	
Calibre	81.4mm; 3.2in
Length of barrel	1.257m; 49.5in
Weight in action	61.7kg; 136lb
Muzzle velocity	227m/s; 744 ft/s
Maximum range	3,010m; 3,290yd
Bomb weight	3.12kg; 6.87lb

60mm Mortar M2	
Calibre	60.5mm; 2.38in
Length of barrel	726mm; 28.6in
Weight in action	19.07kg; 42lb
Muzzle velocity	158m/s; 518ft/s
Maximum range	1,816m; 1,985yd
Bomb weight	1.36kg; 3lb

originally by Watervliet Arsenal and then by the Pullman-Standard Car Manufacturing Company. To these could be added 850 of a 'lightweight' variant, the T27 'Universal', introduced in 1944 for issue to forces operating in the Pacific theatre. This featured a shorter barrel, firing the same ammunition as the M1.

American ammunition was developed for these mortars. The high-explosive M43A1 bomb was based on a French design and weighed 3.12kg/6.87lb, fired to a maximum range of 3,010m/3,290yd.

The customary manual method of moving the 81mm M1 was on the Hand Cart M6A1. Mechanized infantry battalions carried their M1 mortars in either the M4 Mortar Carrier, based on the M2 half-track, or the later M4, M4A1 and M21 Mortar Carriers, based on the M3 half-track. The mortars could be fired from on board the carrier. Other vehicles were employed from time to time and special mule harnesses were available. Special 'paracrates' were developed for dropping these mortars by parachute. Many of the M1 mortars sent to the Soviet Union on Lend-Lease terms (2,540, out of a total Lend-Lease allocation to all-comers of 5,273) were mounted on half-tracks. What the Red Army did with them is now unclear.

The US Army was rather late in deciding to obtain company-level mortars, owing mainly to the funding restrictions and higher priorities that existed until the mid-1930s. It was 1938 before anything was done to rectify the situation; at first

this was confined to the purchase of eight 60mm mle 1935 mortars from the French Brandt company. These eight were immediately adopted as the 60mm Mortar M1 and plans were made to place the model into licensed production virtually unchanged, apart from measures introduced to suit American manufacturing techniques. Watervliet Arsenal prepared the drawings for what then became the 60mm Mortar M2.

American industry was involved in 60mm M2 production from the outset, the first concern obtaining a contract being the Read Machinery Company of York, Pennsylvania. That was in January 1940. By the end of the year the total finished had reached 786, not enough to meet the forecast requirements so further contracts were placed with the Kennedy-Van Saun Engineering and Manufacturing Company of Danville, Pennsylvania. Production proceeded at a good pace until September 1942 when supplies of the seamless steel tubing used for the barrels were diverted to meet more the more pressing needs of the US Army Air Force. Production had to cease for about a month.

After that, matters settled down again, with production apparently tailing off during early 1944. The war in Europe then boosted demand once more so the two existing manufacturers were asked to increase production dramatically. In addition, the Firestone Tire and Rubber Company were called upon to rapidly manufacture a further 24,250. Demand was met to the extent that during the first eight months of 1945 no fewer than 30,152

The American 60mm Mortar M2 was identical to the French Brandt 60mm mle 1935 as it was copied direct for licensed production.

60mm M2 mortars were made. When the war ended the production total had reached 67,561.

The 60mm Mortar M2 proved to be a popular weapon. Firing M49A2 high-explosive bombs weighing 1.36kg/3lb, it had a maximum range of 1,816m/1,985yd. The weight in action was 19.07kg/42lb and a team of at least two was required.

A total of 6,337 M2s were set aside for Lend-Lease, by far the majority of them (4,183) being sent to China. The Chinese armed forces were suffi-

ciently impressed by the M2 for them to copy the design post-war as their 60mm Type 31.

One variant of the M2 followed much the same lines as the British airborne 2in mortars. This was the 60mm Mortar T18E6, redesignated the M19 after 1945. The usual baseplate and bipod of the M2 were discarded in favour of a spade base, the resulting weapon weighing 9kg/20lb. As only one charge could be used (compared with the five of the M2) the maximum possible range was reduced to 747m/816yd and, as the barrel was hand-held, accuracy tended to suffer accordingly. The T18E6 was introduced to meet the requirements of the Pacific campaign. Production began in 1944, the final total being 6,145.

An indication of the significance of the American 60mm and 81mm mortar is the quantity of the ammunition they necessitated: from July 1940 until the end of August 1945 the 81mm mortar ammunition production total came to 37,043,000 bombs. For the 60mm mortars it was 51,756,000.

The US Army also fielded a 4.2in Chemical Mortar. As its name implies, this was originally developed (during the 1920s) to deliver chemical warfare agents to an enemy by saturating large target areas rapidly, using a Stokes 4in mortar as the basis of the weapon. The role required a heavier bomb than could be delivered by 81mm mortars and therefore 4.2in/107mm was selected as the calibre as early as 1924. To increase the range and accuracy of the mortar the barrel was rifled and the bombs resembled conventional artillery projectiles, but with a gas check plate at the base. The bombs were still muzzle-loaded.

The US Army Chemical Warfare Service had the responsibility for these mortars and the chemical agent and smoke bombs that they fired. The Service expended considerable resources on making them easier to handle in the field. It was found more convenient to change the original bipod support to a single, tubular strut, connected to the forged steel baseplate by rods to prevent the recoil from forcing the support and baseplate apart. The mortar sub-assemblies could be carried on a hand cart pulled by two or four soldiers, although mule packs were developed. Attempts to develop self-propelled 4.2in mortars involving half-tracked or other chassis all came to naught before 1945.

When the war started, the Chemical Warfare Service still retained what had become the M1A1 mortar. During 1942 it became apparent that chemical warfare was unlikely in the foreseeable future; it was thus proposed that the mortars should be used to deliver high-explosive projectiles. There was no technical reason why not (trials involving high-explosive bombs had been undertaken from

4.2in Chemical Mortar	
Calibre	107mm; 4.2in
Length of barrel	1.019m; 40.1in
Weight in action	149.8kg; 330lb
Maximum range	4,025m; 4,400yd
Bomb weight	14.5kg; 32lb

1934 onward), but the M1A1 had been designed to deliver chemical payloads to, at most, 2,195m/2,400yd. This was considered insufficient for effective front-line fire support. Trials demonstrated that a stronger barrel would be needed to accommodate the stresses generated by a more powerful propellant charge and so a new 4.2in Mortar M2 emerged. In time, this produced a range extending to 4,025m/4,400yd with a bomb weighing 14.5kg/32lb.

Production of the 4.2in mortars was centred on the Bell Machine Company of Oshkosh, Wisconsin after 1941. Totals had reached 5,425 by the end of 1944. Of these, 327 were sent to China on Lend-Lease terms.

The 4.2in mortar was first used in action in Sicily during 1943, still crewed by Chemical Warfare Service teams since chemical munitions continued to be held ready for possible use and the ability to generate smokescreens was still necessary. The mortars were used in support of infantry operations. Their employment gradually extended to providing artillery-level fire support during the period immediately after an amphibious landing and before conventional artillery could be brought ashore. Provisions were also introduced to fire the mortars from landing-craft decks during the run-in phase of amphibious attacks. By 1945 the 4.2in M2 had been assigned to some infantry formations as a general-purpose fire-support weapon delivering a very effective explosive payload.

After 1945 the Service lost control of its mortars. Development continued after 1945 to result in the 107mm Mortar M30, a model still in widespread service around the world; the last US National Guard examples were withdrawn during the mid-1990s. Several nations, including Greece and Turkey, continue to find it worthwhile to manufacture the ammunition.

The extension of the 4.2in mortar's capabilities meant that two planned heavy mortars were procured in small quantities only. They were the 105mm Mortar T13 and the 155mm Mortar T25. Their T designations denote that neither mortar was fully type-classified. The limited numbers manufactured were deployed to the Pacific where, despite their weight and bulk, they were fired from locations that conventional artillery could not reach. Some 500 examples of the 105mm/4.14in T13 were manufactured and 244 of the 155mm/6.1in T25, both during 1944–45. Once the war was over both models were withdrawn. As far as can be determined, neither of these mortars was issued to infantry units.

SOVIET SIMPLICITY

Soviet military planners were somewhat late in the introduction of infantry mortars. Throughout the 1920s and the early 1930s they had other more urgent priorities but once they started they adopted the mortar with enthusiasm. They recognized the firepower advantages that the mortar could provide for the infantry while noting that mortar manufacture was relatively inexpensive and required only limited raw materials and resources when compared with other weapon types, such as artillery. Steel, the main ingredient for mortars, was something that Soviet industry could provide in abundance by the mid-1930s.

Once battalion mortars had been accepted as a requirement there was no prolonged further development. The classic Brandt 81mm mortar was simply copied direct and placed in series production, although the calibre was enlarged marginally to 82mm/3.228in. Exactly why this change was introduced is not certain, but the slight difference entailed that captured 82mm bombs could not be

82-PM 37	
Calibre	82mm; 3.228in
Length of barrel	1.32m; 51.97in
Weight in action	57.34kg; 126.3lb
Muzzle velocity	202m/s; 663 ft/s
Maximum range	3,100m; 3,390yd
Bomb weight	3.35kg; 7.4lb

safely fired from 81mm mortars, while 81mm bombs could be fired from 82mm mortars, although with a reduction in accuracy and range.

The first Soviet 82mm mortar to be produced in quantity was introduced in 1936 as the 82-PM 36. It differed little from the French original apart from the baseplates being rendered more complex than usual by the provision of three alternative sockets for the barrel base nut. The range attained firing a 3.35kg/7.4lb bomb extended to 3,000m/3,280yd, and the complete equipment weighed 62kg/137lb in action.

The Red Army had taken to the mortar enthusiastically; but it was not completely happy with the 82-PM 36. During training exercises it was required to deliver prolonged fire missions but during these recoil forces tended to shift the barrel and so frequent relaying was necessary. A spring buffer assembly was therefore interposed between the barrel and the bipod assembly to isolate most of the firing stresses from the bipod and maintain steadiness. At the same time the traversing controls were altered but the main change was to the baseplate. This became circular, instead of rectangular, and only one socket location was provided. The circular baseplate became a Soviet mortar feature from then onwards, allowing large traverse changes to be made without the need to embed the baseplate every time. In addition, a baseplate could be manufactured as a one-piece steel forging. The revised model became the 82-PM 37.

Both the 82-PM 36 and the 37 required a crew to carry them, unless some form of transport vehicle or

The interim 50-PM 41 was produced for only a short while before production of the 50-PM 40 could recommence.

animal was available. In some formations the mortar was carried on a motor-cycle sidecar. By 1941 it had been acknowledged that suitable transport was likely to remain in short supply and therefore, to increase the mobility of the 82mm mortar, the usual bipod mounting was considerably altered to become a central strut with an extension on either side at the base. Wheels were added on each end of the extensions, the intention being that the mortar, with baseplate and mounting strut still attached, could then be hand-towed. To assist in towing, a handle assembly could be attached over the barrel muzzle. This model became the 82-PM 41.

The 82-PM 41 provided to be much easier to manufacture that the two earlier models and thus became the main Soviet 82mm mortar until after 1945. In 1943 it was joined by the 82-PM 43, on which the wheeled arrangement was altered for the wheels to become a fixture; on the 82-PM 41 they had to be removed before firing. The expediencies of war meant that the 82-PM 41 and the 43 had to be maintained in production until the war ended, although neither was completely satisfactory, both tending to be unstable during firing. After 1945 the 82-PM 37 was placed back in production, but that is another story.

Realizing that heavy mortars could form a useful adjunct to conventional artillery, Soviet designers simply enlarged the 82-PM 37 to 120mm to producer the 120-HM 38. This was destined to become one of the most efficient of all the mortars

82-PM 41	
Calibre	82mm; 3.228in
Length of barrel	1.32m; 51.97in
Weight in action	45kg; 99.2lb
Muzzle velocity	202m/s; 663ft/s
Maximum range	3,100m; 3,390yd
Bomb weight	3.35kg; 7.4lb

120-HM 38

Calibre	120mm; 4.72in
Length of barrel	1.862m; 73.3in
Weight in action	280.1kg; 617lb
Muzzle velocity	272m/s; 892ft/s
Maximum range	6,000m; 6,564yd
Bomb weight	16kg; 35.3lb

of 1939–45 as it combined firepower and mobility with a good range. The firepower involved a 16kg/35.3lb bomb fired to 6,000m/6,565yd. Mobility was considerably enhanced by the introduction of an ingenious, two-wheeled, tubular steel limber on to which the entire mortar, bipod and baseplate, weighing 280kg/617lb in action, could be lifted for towing behind a small ammunition cart. The towing vehicle could be of the Jeep type, but horses or mules were widely employed.

At first the 120-HM 38 was issued as an artillery

weapon, but after 1941 more and more were issued to infantry divisions in place of infantry guns. By 1945 the 120-HM 38 was one of the most common of all Soviet mortars. It so impressed the Germans that not only did they use as many as they could capture, as the 12cm GrW 378(r), but they even copied and manufactured the design and its ammunition direct as their 12cm GrW 42. In 1943 the basic design was changed slightly by having a single-spring buffer cylinder between the barrel and the bipod in place of the original two. This became the 120-HM 43, a design that remains in use in eastern Europe service to this day and one that is still offered for export by China.

Another model, the 107-PBHM 38, was essentially similar to the 120-HM 38 but was scaled down to 107mm/4.2in calibre to meet the requirements of mountain artillery units. As far as can be determined it was not issued to infantry units.

To move from the largest mortars down to the smallest, Soviet planners had decided by 1935 that

A 120-HM 38 on its towing carriage.

50-PM 38, one of the first Soviet attempts to produce a light infantry mortar.

149

50-PM 40	
Calibre	50mm; 1.97in
Length of barrel	630mm; 21in
Weight in action	9.3kg; 20.5lb
Muzzle velocity	96m/s; 315ft/s
Maximum range	800m; 875yd
Bomb weight	850gm; 1.875lb

Soviet stalwart – the 50-PM 40.

the company-level mortar calibre was to be 50mm/1.97in. Unlike the 82mm development programme, that for the 50mm mortar was prolonged over a period of years yet the end result proved not to be exactly what was wanted. This was the 50-PM 38.

The 50-PM 38 was a complex little weapon, expensive to manufacture. The barrel could be clamped at just two elevation angles, 45 or 75 degrees. Interim range adjustments at either angle involved uncovering a series of gas ports around the base of the barrel to bleed off propellant gases

The mysterious 37mm Spade Mortar shown here in its firing position.

as appropriate. This feature proved to be too demanding to manufacture in quantity or at reasonable cost and so something more conventional was requested, the result being the 50-PM 39. The same ammunition was retained but the fixed elevations and gas ports were replaced by a normal barrel and a variable-angle bipod. This could fire a 0.85kg/1.875lb bomb to a maximum of 800m/875yd. The weight was 17kg/37.4lb.

Almost as soon as the 50-PM 39 was being issued on any scale it was realized that, for its utility and performance, it was still too involved and costly to manufacture in quantity. A much revised design therefore emerged. The main feature of the resulting 50-PM 40 was the extensive use of steel stampings throughout. While the barrel remained a carefully finished component, the baseplate and the bipod were formed from steel stampings. The bipod was kept simple by a provision for only two elevation angles (again 45 and 75 degrees), with the 50-PM 38 gas-venting system reintroduced in a simpler form. The performance remained as for the earlier models, although the combat weight was considerably reduced to 9.3kg/20.5lb, enabling it to be carried in a single load by one man, with others carrying the ammunition in satchels.

The 50-PM 40 was probably the most numerous of the 1941–45 Soviet light mortars, but it was not the only one. There was also a 50-PM 41 that originated from the shift of Soviet industry to beyond the Urals after the German invasion. On the 50-PM 41 the barrel remained as before, complete with gas-vent ports, but the barrel was supported in a yoke connected to an enlarged baseplate. The yoke incorporated the traverse controls and provision to clamp the barrel at the usual two elevation angles. A special backpack was devised to allow its carrying by a single soldier. It now appears that the 50-PM 41 was manufactured as an expedient model

only, priority reverting to the 50-PM 40 when the situation was less desperate.

Production totals regarding the Soviet mortars have yet to be found, but they must have been measured in the tens of thousands, with ammunition tallies to match. There are still several unknowns regarding Soviet mortars, including anything regarding a 37mm Spade Mortar. Data relating to this weapon appear in several sources but it remains unknown whether it was produced in any quantity or even issued as a serious weapon. The name denotes its main feature in that it normally resembled a trench spade. By removing a cap and rod from the top of the steel handle the 37mm/1.45in muzzle was revealed and the rod became a rudimentary monopod support for the barrel. Releasing a hinge converted the spade into a baseplate. The user then had a light mortar firing a 680gm/1.5lb bomb to about 300m/328yd. With hindsight, it now appears that the 37mm Spade Mortar was more of a design exercise than a viable weapon.

For all that surmise, the mortar appeared in German identification lists. The Germans adopted as many Soviet mortars as they could capture, the example of the 120-HM 38 having been already mentioned. A check list of captured Soviet mortars employed by the German armed forces shows the following:

Soviet	German
50-PM 38	5cm GrW 205/1(r)
50-PM 39	5cm GrW 205/2(r)
50-PM 40	5cm GrW 205/3(r)
82-PM 36	8.2cm GrW 274/1(r)
82-PM 37	8.2cm GrW 274/2(r)
82-PM 41	8.2cm GrW 274/3(r)
107-PBHM 38	10.7cm GebGrW 328(r)
120-HM 38	12cm GrW 378(r)

9 Anti-tank Weapons

Soon after the first tanks struggled across the Somme battlefields in 1916 the rudiments of anti-tank warfare were established. Tank-killer squads were formed, field artillery was redeployed and the first tank obstacles were prepared. By the time of the armistice specialized anti-tank weapons had arrived, including the only one to see action, the German 13mm Tankgewehr anti-tank rifle.

Much of the limited development of weapons that did take place between the wars was devoted to anti-tank warfare. The need to provide the infantry with some measure of defence against tanks was generally regarded as a priority but, due to the perennial shortages of funds plus an often endemic lack of urgency in many countries, any anti-tank developments were sporadic and often spread over periods of years. As far as the Allies of 1939–45 were concerned, very little development began until well into the 1930s.

Infantry anti-tank weapons had to be portable while requiring only a minimum of personnel to crew them. It was considered that any diversion of trained men to crew these weapons would result in an erosion of the number of rifles that could be deployed operationally, especially as novel weapons, such as mortars, and equipments such as radios, were already appearing to absorb soldiers. As a result, anti-tank guns were usually allocated as artillery, as in the British Army, for instance. While such an arrangement formed clear demarcations, the need for the infantry to have some form of defence under their own control remained. For many armies this meant anti-tank rifles, but not every nation followed this route. One that did not was France.

FRENCH STOP-GAPS

When the first tanks appeared, the French 37mm/1.46in mle 1916 TR trench guns assumed an extra role. In 1917 these little guns were effective enough against the early tanks, despite their short range and the lack of any really effective armour-piercing ammunition. While it may have been a reasonably effective infantry gun, it was of little use as an anti-tank weapon by 1940, even if a somewhat optimistic armour-piercing round had been introduced during 1935. But such was the lack of urgency regarding the need for anti-tank weapons before 1939 that the mle 1916 TR was still in wide-spread service when the Germans invaded France in 1940. (*See also* Chapter 13.)

For some reason, the French planners declined to pursue the anti-tank rifle. Instead they spent what limited funds were available on a light anti-tank gun specifically for the infantry, the 25mm/0.98in mle 1934 Hotchkiss. By 1940 about 4,500 had been manufactured. Unfortunately, the mle 1934 was to prove itself virtually useless in its intended role.

25mm mle 1934	
Calibre	25mm; 0.98in
Length of barrel	1.8m; 70.87in
Weight in action	496kg; 1,093lb
Muzzle velocity	918m/s; 3,010ft/s
Maximum combat range	900m; 985yd
Projectile weight	320gm; 0.7lb

A Hotchkiss 25mm mle 1934 on tow behind a light tracked carrier and trailer/limber.

One result of measures intended to limit the weight to about 496kg/1,094lb in action was that the split-trail carriage emerged as too light for hard knocks, while the ammunition proved to be lacking in punch against anything but the lightest tanks.

French Army mle 1934 guns were towed by horse teams, although in the few mechanized infantry formations they were carried on half-tracks. By 1940 the mle 1934 had also been issued to the British Army which considered them so flimsy that they carried them portée fashion on light trucks, dismounting them for firing. The British received the guns as part of a demonstration of Allied co-operation, the French receiving Boys anti-tank rifles in exchange.

Light as the mle 1934 may have been, it was considered that an even lighter gun would be an advantage. Designers at the Puteaux arsenal therefore devised what turned out to be much the

25mm mle 1937	
Calibre	25mm; 0.98in
Length of barrel	1.925m; 75.8in
Weight in action	310kg; 683lb
Muzzle velocity	900m/s; 2,952ft/s
Maximum combat range	900m; 985yd
Projectile weight	320gm; 0.7lb

Free French troops serving in Palestine in 1941, still with their 25mm mle 1934 guns.

Waiting for the Germans. British troops with a 25 mle 1934 in France 1940 – the character on the right seems to have caught the mood of the moment.

same 25mm ordnance as the mle 1934 but on an even lighter horse-drawn carriage, reducing the weight in action to 310kg/684lb. This became the 25mm mle 1937 Puteaux, rushed into production during 1938 so that by 1940 the French infantry had about 1,600 guns. It fared no better than the mle 1934 in that it lacked penetrative power against the tanks of 1940.

Captured French infantry anti-tank guns were little used by the Germans, apart from some installed as beach-defence guns in the Atlantic Wall.

BRITISH METHODS

The British infantry of 1939 placed their faith in the Boys anti-tank rifle, one of the most unloved things they ever had to carry. The development of what was to become the Rifle, Anti-tank, 0.55in Boys

The light 25mm mle 1937.

The long lines of the 0.55 Boys anti-tank rifle. This is a Canadian version manufactured at the Inglis plant and is minus its bipod – note the late pattern muzzle brake.

Mk 1, began in 1934, although such a rifle had been proposed in 1925. The original name for the programme was the Stanchion Gun. It was changed after the officer in charge of the project, Captain H.C. Boys, died just before the gun was accepted in late 1937.

The Boys rifle fired a powerful 0.55in (13.97 × 99mm) round with a steel-cored bullet that could penetrate 21mm of armour at 300m/330yd. It was long (1.614m/64in overall) and heavy (16.56kg/36lb empty), with an overhead five-round box magazine. By 1940 the rifle's performance had already been overtaken by increases in tank armour and thus it proved of limited value thereafter and

The armourer's den with a Boys anti-tank rifle being attended to. Note also the No.1 Mark III rifles and the Bren Gun.

Boys Mk 1

Calibre	13.97mm; 0.55in
Length	1.614m; 63.5in
Length of barrel	915mm; 36in
Weight	16.56kg; 36.5lb
Muzzle velocity	990m/s; 3,245ft/s
Feed	5-round box magazine

had been withdrawn by 1943. Many old soldiers remember the Boys rifle mainly for its ferocious recoil.

The Boys was a bolt action rifle. In its original form it was fired from a monopod support, but this, along with several other refinements, was eliminated after 1940 to speed production. The revised model was the Mk 1*, recognizable by its bipod and a modified muzzle brake. A tungsten-cored bullet was introduced in late 1940 but was little used as the rifle had by then fallen so far from favour that further efforts to improve it were deemed counterproductive. This did not prevent the development of a shortened Mk II model for airborne forces (it was not adopted) nor the continued practice of using the Boys rifle as the main armament of Universal Carriers. For dismounted use the Boys rifle was an awkward load, increasingly resented after 1940 but retained in lieu of anything better for use against tanks.

The main producer of the Boys rifle was BSA at Small Heath and Mansfield. Total production by BSA came to 68,847, the last contract being completed during 1943. Production also took place at the John Inglis plant in Toronto, Canada. Canadian production reached 44,553, of which 6,129 went to China, paid for by American Lend-Lease. Most of the rest of the Canadian output crossed the Atlantic for the British and Commonwealth armies, but a handful got to the Philippines to serve with the American forces units during late 1941 and early 1942.

Other Boys rifle users included France, in exchange for 25mm mle 1934 anti-tank guns; the quantity was described as 'several hundred'. Finland was another 1940 recipient, although of how many and how they fared is not known. Resistance forces throughout Europe also received the Boys rifle.

The British infantry of 1940 had other weapons too for local anti-tank defence. Thus they had the No.73 'Thermos Grenade' that relied on blast alone for anti-armour effects; it was therefore of little utility against well-armoured vehicles and so was more often used as a demolition charge. The No.75 Hawkins Grenade could be used either as a heavy (1.02kg/2.25lb) hand grenade or it could be emplaced as an anti-tank mine to damage tank tracks. Then there was the No.68 grenade launched from a cup attached to the muzzle of a standard rifle. It proved to be so ineffective against anything but the lightest armour that it had been withdrawn from front-line service by 1942.

The period after the evacuation from France was a desperate time for the British Army. Not only had

The No.75 Hawkins anti-tank grenade that could be either thrown, or emplaced as an anti-tank mine.

The odd appearance of the Northover Projector.

the bulk of its weapons holdings been left behind but the nation's industrial capacity was largely unprepared to manufacture replacements on the necessary scale and at such short notice. It was a period of expedients of all kinds, one being the Northover Projector.

The Northover Projector was a simple pipe gun using black-powder charges to propel grenades to an effective range of little more than 91m/100yd. The barrel swivelled in a hand-directed cradle on a four-legged steel tube frame held in position by spades and the weapon was aimed using very basic sights. There was no recoil mechanism. Standard grenades could be fired, including the No.68, although the Northover is perhaps best remembered for its ability to launch the No.76 grenade, a glass bottle filled with a smoke/incendiary mixture of phosphorus, latex rubber and benzene. The intention was that the bottle would shatter on contact with a target and the smoke would blind the occupants; there was also an incendiary effect, with the latex helping the mixture to adhere to the target. More often than not, the bottle shattered while still in the barrel. Such a weapon could have little effect

on most tanks, but it had the advantage that it was something that could be manufactured rapidly and cheaply using non-critical raw materials. At least 21,000 were hastily made during 1940 and 1941 by the Bisley Clay Target and Selection Manufacturing companies.

The main recipients were the Home Guard, although there are records of Northovers being issued to Regular troops under training. The Northover Projector never became an officially accepted War Office store.

A further oddity from this period was the No.74 (ST) grenade, another product emanating via the unorthodox government MD1 'think tank'. Usually known as the 'Sticky Bomb', the No.74 (ST) was produced in considerable numbers for issue to Regular as well as Home Guard units but it was never a popular weapon. It was a stick-pattern grenade with the bulbous glass warhead contained within two thin metal covers. Before being thrown, the covers were removed to reveal a layer of thin fabric covered with a powerful adhesive. The intention was that the adhesive would hold the grenade against a target vehicle until the 5-second

Throwing a No.74 Sticky Bomb.

delay igniter detonated the explosive contents. As the grenade had a tendency to stick to anything, including the thrower, it was not well received. In addition, as the No.74 (ST) relied on blast alone its anti-armour effects were limited. When the first American troops landed in Northern Ireland they were issued with the No.74, but not for long.

The Blacker Bombard (*see* the previous chapter) was another MD1 product. The designer, Lt Col Blacker, took his spigot mortar ideas one stage further with a smaller design capable of being carried and fired by a single soldier. He christened his brainchild the 'Baby Bombard', but almost as soon as he began work on the design he was posted away from MD1 to other duties. His project passed to Major Jefferis who developed the weapon into the Jefferis Shoulder Gun firing high-explosive projectiles. The War Office was not impressed since they wanted a portable anti-tank device and the warhead launched by the Jefferis device could make little impression on tank armour. By early 1942 the Jefferis Shoulder Gun was meeting with more favour for, by replacing the high-explosive warhead with a shaped charge (*see* below), the anti-armour

A PIAT, complete with its hollow charge bomb.

PIAT

Length overall   990mm; 39in
Weight   14.4kg; 31.7lb
Muzzle velocity   137m/s; 450ft/s
Maximum combat range   100m; 109yd
Projectile weight   1.35kg; 3lb

performance could be much enhanced. At the same time, the gun could also launch warheads other than anti-armour, thus providing the infantry with a versatile fire-support weapon system.

War Office approval was finally bestowed in late 1942 and during 1943 the infantry began to receive the Projector, Infantry, Anti-Tank, or PIAT. It was an unlikely-looking device about 990mm/38.9in long and weighing 14.4kg/31.7lb, the weight being supported by a monopod assembly during firing. The steel body was cylindrical, housing a powerful

spring to drive the spigot. At the business end an open trough was provided to take a 1.35kg/3lb, drum-finned bomb. Pressing a large trigger, with the padded shoulder piece held firmly against the shoulder, released the spigot to detonate a cartridge in the tail of the bomb and propel the bomb from the open trough. The recoil re-cocked the weapon ready for the next firing.

The effective range against tanks was about 100m/110yd, although the bomb could be used against structures up to 320m/350yd away.

The PIAT worked but it was never liked. Its weight and shape made it awkward for one soldier to carry, while another had to carry the ammunition. Then there was the matter of cocking the mechanism. To prepare the PIAT for firing, or if a firing failed to re-cock the weapon, called for strength and an acquired skill as the substantial power of the spigot spring had to be overcome. This could be accomplished readily enough in the standing position, but to carry out the procedure when prone in a trench required acrobatics, great effort and time.

Despite this, the PIAT became the standard

Left-hand side view of a PIAT showing the sighting arrangements.

The 2-pounder anti-tank gunner's office showing the sight bracket and ready-use ammunition lockers.

British infantry anti-tank weapon down to platoon level, although, due to its development never being fully completed, it never did become a comprehensive fire-support weapon system. Its was carried over to the Korean War period but replaced thereafter.

The PIAT formed part of the armament of Universal Carriers and light armoured cars and was parachuted into occupied Europe to arm resistance forces. Production was mainly by ICI Ltd who produced at least 115,000 by 1945.

By 1945 the infantry had acquired more anti-tank weapons in the form of anti-tank guns. Despite early fears that guns would divert troops from their basic infantry function, by late 1942 some battalions (but not all) began to be issued with 2-pounder anti-tank guns.

The infantry obtained guns as a side effect of the constant battle between armour and anti-tank guns that began in earnest in 1940 and continues to this day. The anti-tank guns of 1940 were rendered obsolete by increases in tank armour, so more powerful and larger-calibre guns had to be developed and produced. That took time and hence the

The 6-pounder anti-tank gun. This is the airborne version, as used at Arnhem, with trail legs that could be split into two halves to save space in aircraft and gliders.

2-pounder, the standard gun of the Royal Artillery's anti-tank batteries in 1940, had to be maintained in production even though it was already recognized as obsolete – there was no other option available at that time. The 40mm/1.575in 2-pounder's replacement, the 57mm/2.244in 6-pounder was not ready for service until late 1941; thus by late 1942 there were plenty of 2-pounders to pass to the infantry. Most of the infantry battalions involved were sent to the Far East where the 2-pounder could still be effective against the lightly armoured Japanese tanks. They remained in action there until 1945.

By 1945 the 2-pounder was being joined by the 6-pounder within infantry battalions, and by late 1943 the 6-pounder too was outclassed by increases in tank armour and therefore it, in its turn, was gradually replaced within Royal Artillery batteries by the 76.2mm/3in 17-pounder. Thus 6-pounders were then available for the infantry to assume into their ranks. Airborne units were given a special carriage with reduced width and trail legs in two halves bolted together. They were used at Arnhem in Operation *Market Garden*.

SOVIET MEASURES

When one considers the emphasis that the Red Army (it became the Soviet Army in 1941) placed upon massed tank operations during the 1930s, the corresponding significance of anti-tank weapons was somewhat neglected. The usual philosophy was that if tanks were encountered, every soldier and weapon was to be turned against them, from artillery to infantry hurling grenades. If grenades were not to hand there was always the weapon that epitomized the Soviet approach to warfare, the 'Molotov cocktail'.

First employed on any scale during the Spanish Civil War (1936–38), the Molotov cocktail was a bottle filled with petrol (or some similar combustible fluid) with a rag around the neck to be lit as a fuze. When the bottle shattered against a tank the contents ignited, supposedly for the resulting flames to seep into the tank. The results were usually more spectacular than effective, but as fear of fire is one of the most basic of human emotions the morale effects could be considerable against

Molotov cocktails were not the prerogative of the Soviets. Here a line of British troops practice throwing the things on a training range .

tank crews. Molotov cocktails remained a central part of the Soviet Army's anti-tank inventory throughout the war years, as well as with the partisans, the British Home Guard (their No.76 grenade supposedly had a more effective filling) and numerous resistance forces. As the cocktail is easy to prepare, with only a minimum of readily available ingredients, they continue to appear whenever civil unrest arises.

A more formal anti-tank grenade was introduced in 1940, the RPG-40. It was thrown by using a short handle, but, as it relied on blast alone, it was

Molotov cocktails in use on the Eastern Front.

Hasty training for Partisans on the RPG-40 grenade.

not very successful, being replaced by the RPG from 1943 onwards. This had a hollow charge warhead. To keep the charge pointing towards the intended target the handle, once thrown, came away from the warhead to reveal two fabric strips that acted as a drogue. The throwing range was short but the RPG could be effective against lightly armoured vehicles.

Soviet infantry battalions did have anti-tank guns, although they were termed regimental guns to denote that they were supposed to act as fire-support as well as anti-tank weapons. They therefore had to deliver high-explosive as well as anti-armour projectiles. The guns concerned were based on a German Rheinmetall 37mm gun that eventually became the Wehrmacht's 3.7cm Pak 35/36. As it was small, light and handy, this gun seemed to suit the Red Army admirably, and so in 1930 it procured a batch along with a licence to manufacture the design. The gun became the 37mm Model 1930 (1-K); about 500 were built.

Experience soon demonstrated that the German design was too light and fragile to meet the Soviet needs and within just over a year a drastic revision appeared, this time in 45mm calibre to enable the gun to deliver a more useful high-explosive payload. The carriage was considerably strengthened and the wire spoke wheels introduced on the Model 1930 carriage were carried over to what became the 45mm Model 1932. This was produced in some numbers before it was supplanted by the 45mm Model 1937 (53-K), having all the numerous carriage detail improvements introduced by Rheinmetall in the final form of their 3.7cm Pak 35/36.

The 45mm Model 1932 and Model 1937 were the mainstays of the Soviet infantry's regimental gun holdings when the Germans invaded. Over 12,000 of both guns were destroyed or lost to the Germans during 1941 and 1942 (out of the 14,900 held in June 1941), so a stop-gap was hastily improvised to provide something for the hard-pressed troops in the field. The 45mm Model 1938 was a tank variant of the towed Model 1937 ordnance, which was in the process of being withdrawn from production in favour of 76.2mm tank guns just as the Germans invaded. These tank guns were hurriedly placed on makeshift field mountings made from whatever steel was to hand and rushed to the fronts. This gun was so much of an improvisation that no designation appears to have survived.

This makeshift gun was not in production for

Recognition illustration from a German manual relating to the 45mm Model 1932 regimental gun.

long. Once the Soviet defence infrastructure had been relocated east of the Urals, work started on a more powerful gun. To avoid the weight and size problems that would arise if the more usual course of adopting a larger calibre were adopted, the barrel was lengthened from 46 to 68.6 calibres, a revised semi-automatic breech was added and some carriage changes were introduced, including the reintroduction of steel-disc wheels. These changes provided an improvement in anti-armour capability while allowing what was still supposed to be an infantry regimental gun to retain a high-explosive capability. The lengthened gun became the 45mm Model 1942 (M-42). It was still in production in 1945 and remained an important gun within many armed forces for decades after then. By the time production ceased, no fewer than 48,537 had been manufactured at ordnance factories around Perm.

The Soviet Army did have infantry anti-tank rifles. They arose from a 1936 specification asking for a penetration of 25mm/1in of armour at 500m/547yd. That required the development of a suitable cartridge, the 14.5 × 114mm, which was not accepted until July 1941. By then the Soviet Union was being overrun by the Germans. This delay, coupled with the development of three rifles that all proved unsatisfactory for one reason or another, meant that front-line soldiers had virtually nothing other than thinly spread and not very effective regimental guns to defend themselves with against German tanks. In part, this situation had been

compounded by staff planners approaching the need for anti-tank rifles at a leisurely pace. They expected that the armour increases on their next generation of tanks would be matched by similar increases by the Germans. As anti-tank rifles would have little effect against tanks such as the T-34/76, they decided to downgrade their anti-tank rifle programme.

When the Germans did invade it was discovered that they were a long way behind the Soviets in tank development and were still fielding light vehicles that should have been replaced but for the relatively slow output of the German tank factories. Anti-tank rifles of the type originally specified would therefore remain viable weapons, but none were to hand.

Fortunately, two designs were available from the Degtyarov and the Simonov design bureau, both meeting the 1936 specifications. Of the two, the Degtyarov PTRD-41 was the simpler and so was immediately ordered into mass production. As a back-up to meet the urgent requests pouring in from the fronts, the Simonov design, the PTRS-41, was also ordered at the same time and on the same priority basis.

The Degtyarev 14.5mm PTRD-41 had been designed with mass production in mind. Every component, nearly all of them tubular, could be manufactured with basic machine lathes. It was a single-shot, bolt action rifle over 2m/6.56ft long and weighing 17.3kg/38lb; thus it was a hefty load that in action required a team of two. The considerable

The 14.5mm TRD-41 anti-tank rifle, a simple and easy to produce weapon.

recoil was reduced by a muzzle brake and a padded butt. Recoil never seems to have been a perceived drawback with the 14.5mm rifles as it was with many other contemporary designs.

An indication of the ease of manufacture of the pipe-like PTRD-41 can be judged from the fact that by the end of 1941 the production total had already reached 17,668, compared with just seventy-seven PTRS-41 rifles. Thereafter production continued at a rate of around 20,000 rifles every month, until by January 1944 the Army had a stock of 142,861 of both models. Each infantry regiment had an establishment of fifty-four. Production ended in January 1945.

The Simonov PTRS-41 was a more complicated design than the PTRD-41. Using a semi-automatic, gas-operated action fed from a five-round box magazine, it had much the same anti-armour performance as the PTRD-41 and was handier to carry as it could be broken down into two loads. This was just as well for it weighed nearly 21kg/46lb.

Both rifles were obsolete as anti-tank weapons by the end of 1942, but both soldiered on until well after 1945. The Soviet infantry learned to employ them as general purpose weapons, capable of knocking out targets such as trucks, artillery pieces and any lightly armoured vehicles. They proved invaluable during urban warfare and were even pointed at aircraft on occasion. Some cropped up during the Korean War.

PTRD-41	
Calibre	14.5mm; 0.57in
Length overall	2.02m; 79.5in
Length of barrel	1.35m; 53.15in
Weight	17.3kg; 38.14lb
Muzzle velocity	1,012m/s; 3,320ft/s
Feed	single-shot

PTRS-41	
Calibre	14.5mm; 0.57in
Length overall	2.108m; 83in
Length of barrel	1.216m; 47.875in
Weight	20.9kg; 46lb
Muzzle velocity	1,012m/s; 3,320ft/s
Feed	5-round box magazine

SHAPED CHARGES

Shaped charges have been mentioned already. The term relates to a characteristic of high explosives demonstrated when a concave depression in the surface of an explosive is brought into contact with a hard material such as rock or metal. The blast waves inside the depression cause extremely high temperatures to occur within the space between the explosive and the hard substance. This, coupled with the blast produced by the explosive, creates a high-temperature jet that rapidly burns its way through any material in its path.

This phenomenon was first noted by an American chemist Charles Munroe during the 1880s, but there seemed to be no practical applications for what became known as the Munroe Effect at that time. Further examination of the effect during the 1920s revealed that, if the concave depression in the explosive was conical and thinly lined with metal, the velocity and penetration performance of the resulting high-temperature jet were considerably enhanced. From this came the shaped (or hollow) charge that was to have a considerable influence on the future of anti-tank warfare.

This finding was initially seized upon by the German defence industry and liberally applied to artillery projectiles of all calibres. The results were not as good as expected. It was discovered that projectile spin disrupted the jet and degraded its on-target results. Only if the shaped charge were delivered without spin could the full penetrative effects be obtained. From this finding sprang the two types of shaped warhead (now known as High Explosive Anti-Tank or HEAT) delivery system that are still used in today's infantry weapons: namely, the German recoilless Panzerfaust and the American Bazooka rocket launcher.

These two systems were the prototypes of the many anti-tank systems carried by the infantry of today. Between them they provided the ordinary foot soldier with the ability to defeat any tank he was likely to encounter, considerably altering the nature and scope of anti-tank warfare as soon as they appeared.

As shaped charges involve what is in effect chemical energy rather than the brute force, kinetic energy of high-velocity solid projectiles (as with anti-tank rifles, shaped charges could thus remain effective at extreme ranges as well as short. While early applications were largely confined to anti-armour operations, experience soon demonstrated that the shaped charge was also highly effective against field fortifications and structures. The foot soldier had thus acquired a new and versatile weapon. For the US Army, the new weapon was the Bazooka.

THE BAZOOKA

The Bazooka came about by way of the US Army's adoption of shaped-charge rifle grenades. These went to the USA via Switzerland, where one Henri Mohaupt attempted to interest potential customers with a secret armour-piercing high explosive. It was soon discovered that Mohaupt was applying the shaped-charge principle but, in the event, the US Army brought the rights to two grenades. These were type-classified as the M9A1 launched from rifle muzzles, and the M10, intended to be launched from M2 0.50/12.7mm machine-gun muzzles.

The M9A1 provided the US infantry with an effective anti-armour weapon capable of penetrating about 100mm/3.9in of armour. Employing the rifle grenade involved the fitting of a launcher extension to the muzzle and loading a special blank cartridge to provide the propulsion. The resulting stresses on the rifle proved considerable and so, although the rifle grenade was tolerated in this respect (the British No.85 grenade of 1945 was a close copy), the machine gun-launched M10 was not adopted, despite its type-classification.

The M10 grenade warhead was to have a totally different career. A Captain Skinner placed one of these warheads on the end of a solid rocket motor. Another officer, Lieutenant Uhl of the US Navy, who had been given a directive for rocket investigation similar to that of Captain Skinner, co-operated by devising a steel tube launcher to

Bazooka M1

Calibre   60mm; 2.34in
Length of barrel   1.37m; 53.94in
Weight   5.9kg; 13lb
Muzzle velocity   83m/s; 272ft/s
Rocket weight   1.54kg; 3.4lb

deliver the rocket/warhead combination. Together with a team of civilian scientists, these officers were ready to demonstrate their innovative weapon system in May 1942. It was an immediate success, being ordered into immediate mass production with a high priority.

The name Bazooka arose from a quip that the launcher tube resembled an outsize example of one of the comedian Bob Burns's stage props, an outsize cigar. In time virtually every similar rocket-delivery system came to be dubbed as a Bazooka but the original, the Launcher, Rocket, AT, 2.36in, M1, was a 1.37m/54in steel tube supported over the right shoulder for firing. A 1.53kg/3.4lb rocket was

loaded into the rear of the tube and connected to a battery-powered circuit for launching. Using rudimentary sights, the launcher was aimed at targets up to about 150m/164yd away (the maximum possible range was 640m/700yd) and launched by depressing a trigger. The launch resulted in a sheet of flame and debris from the rocket exhaust so users were advised to keep clear of the rear of the launcher tube and wear protective goggles.

As the HEAT warhead of the 2.36in/60mm M6 rocket could penetrate 120mm/4.7in of armour it meant that virtually any tank was capable of being destroyed by a portable weapon brought into action by a team of two, the launcher and a loader who also carried extra rockets. The Bazooka was a nasty shock for the Germans during the launcher's combat debut in Tunisia in 1943. They were so impressed that they adopted the Bazooka principle directly for their 8.8cm Racketenpanzerbüchse 43 (Panzerschreck) series.

The 1943 debut was the result of yet another feat of American industrial prowess, considerably assisted by the Bazooka's presenting few production problems, being little more than a steel tube with a few controls and a shoulder rest attached. In

The US Army infantry's anti-armour arsenal in mid-1943 showing M1 Bazookas and Springfield rifles with muzzle attachments to launch M9A1 grenades. The soldier is holding a No.74 Sticky Bomb.

*2.36in M1 Bazooka
showing a M6A1 rocket
(top) with a M6A5 rocket
(below).*

addition, few production problems occurred with the rockets. An immediate contract placed with General Electric of Bridgeport, Connecticut, called for 5,000 launchers to be delivered in thirty days. From a complete zero capability basis, General Electric completed that contract with 89 minutes to spare. More orders followed to equip all US Army infantry units with the Bazooka; the total for 1944 alone reached 215,177.

By 1944 the base Launcher M1 had been modified by introducing a stronger steel for the tube and adding wire coils around the rear of the launcher in case of in-bore rocket-motor detonations. The launcher then became the M1A1. The rockets were gradually modified to improve their safety and performance, the original pointed nose of the early versions being replaced by a dome outline from the M6A3 onwards, together with the replacement of the original tail fins by a drum fin assembly.

A more involved change came with the Launcher M9. As the original one-piece tube was something of a lengthy load to carry, even if it did weigh only 5.9kg/13lb, it was not long before someone devised

a method of dividing the tube into two halves to be joined by a bayonet fitting. This became the Launcher M9 (the M9A1 involved alterations to the junction hardware). On the M9 series the firing circuit was modified to become magneto-powered and so the earlier troublesome batteries were no longer required.

There was also an aluminium M18 launcher, intended for airborne troops. About 500 had been manufactured by the Cheney Bigelow Wire Works of Springfield before the war ended.

When this happened the final production total for all types of launcher had reached 475,628, plus 15,603,000 rockets. The Bazooka was one of the few American weapons not supplied on Lend-Lease.

The advent of the Bazooka came at a fortunate time for the American infantry for, apart from grenades, they had no other anti-tank weapons of their own, other than 0.50/12.7mm M2 machine guns (considered to have an anti-armour capability), when they entered the war. The only other weapon was held at battalion level and by 1941 it was already obsolete. This was the 37mm Antitank Gun M3A1, a light, towed gun with affinities to the Rheinmetall 3.7cm Pak 35/36. When first proposed, the M3A1 was as sound a design as any in its category, but by 1941 it was ineffective against anything other than the lightest armoured vehicles. But since ordnance planners had not foreseen the rapid increases in tank armour in progress by 1940, the 37mm M3A1 was all there was to equip the anti-tank units within the infantry battalions. Production began in 1940 and finished during 1943. In 1940

Bazooka M9

Calibre	60mm; 2.34in
Length of barrel	1.55m; 61in
Weight	5.96kg; 13.14lb
Muzzle velocity	83m/s; 272ft/s
Rocket weight	1.54kg; 3.4lb

The little 37mm M3A1 anti-tank gun, obsolete when first issued in 1940 but still around in 1945.

each infantry battalion had six truck-towed 37mm M3A1 guns, increased to eight in 1942.

The total number made was 18,702. To this significant total could be added a further 47,235 closely allied 37mm M5 and M6 guns for tank, half-track and armoured-car mountings. Lend-Lease totals for the M3A1 came to 2,359, the largest proportion going to China (1,669). The M3A1 continued to crop up in south-east Asia as late as the 1980s.

Production was originally confined to government establishments such as the Watervliet and Rock Island Arsenals. As the demand increased, American industry was called upon to participate. The companies involved had little experience of defence production since they included the United Shoe Machinery Corporation, the York Safe and Lock Company, the National Pneumatic Company, the Muncie Gear Works and the Duplex Printing Press Company. How they managed to convert from the demands of peace to those of war formed a saga in itself.

If proof were needed, combat use in Tunisia in 1943 pressed home the obsolescence of the M3A1 and from then on most were diverted to the Pacific

theatre where they could still have an effect on any Japanese tanks that might appear. Its gradual diversion to become an infantry-support weapon was expanded by the introduction of high-explosive projectiles and anti-personnel canister rounds.

Although the first issues were made during 1942, infantry battalions operating in Europe from 1944 onwards were issued with the 57mm Antitank Gun M1, the American version of the British 6-pounder. Each infantry battalion had four towed 57mm guns. The M1 guns were not exactly popular weapons as they were generally regarded as inadequate for their task, while their recoil was regarded as too lively for crew comfort. Even so, they provided each battalion with an anti-tank asset capable of destroying all but the heaviest of German tanks.

Production of the 57mm M1, and the later M1A1 with a free-traverse cradle, was almost as prolific as for the 37mm M3A1. Between 1942 and 1945 16,037 were manufactured. Of these, 5,342 were assigned as Lend-Lease, most (4,242) going to the British and Commonwealth forces. For some reason the Soviet Union received 400 M1 guns. Most of these were on T48 self-propelled half-track carriages.

10 Pistols

The pistol is not really an infantry weapon. Traditionally, it is an officer's weapon carried more as a badge of authority and rank than as a serious combat arm. Apart from when it is handled by highly skilled practitioners, the pistol is rarely of much use as a combat weapon at ranges beyond arm's length and it is as likely to harm friends as enemies in careless or anxious hands.

Yet in 1939 the issuing of pistols to military police and personnel other than officers was a widespread fact, although a pistol remained as much part of an officer's kit as his rank badges. Within any armed force, including the infantry, there are always specialists whose tasks require the use of both hands or who are already laden with equipment such as radios. For such men a rifle or a carbine is of limited utility, whereas a pistol is a mild encumbrance while remaining better than no weapon at all. After 1939 the number of potential pistol carriers grew rapidly as more and more specialists appeared to operate or look after new equipments. More pistols were needed to arm resistance organizations for whom the pistol was the ideal concealed weapon.

When considering the pistols carried by the Allies between 1939 and 1945 it has to be stressed that only the most important models can be mentioned here. The array of types likely to be encountered was considerable, ranging from non-standard personal purchases by officers to trophies adopted by their finders. In addition, the ages of the pistols involved varied from the antique to the most modern. They cannot all be dealt with here but an indication of their range can be provided.

Compared with the Axis forces, wholehearted advocates of the automatic, the Allies' choice between automatic (or self-loading) pistols and revolvers had never been completely decided between one or the other. Allied armies tended to use both, with some, for example the British, conservatively retaining the trusted revolver. Yet by 1945 the automatic was the preferred combat pistol. This will be demonstrated by outlining how the British equipped themselves.

BRITISH AND COMMONWEALTH

For many British and Commonwealth soldiers there was only one pistol, the Webley revolver. Webley & Scott of Birmingham had been manufacturing military revolvers since 1887 and in 1939 there were still many serviceable Webley veterans of considerable age to be found, due to the excellent, solid construction of their break-open frames. Many dated to the Great War years, chambered for the 0.455in Webley cartridge (nominally 11.2 × 19mm, as the true calibre was 0.441in). This had a heavy and highly effective 'man-stopper' bullet that by

---

Webley 0.455

Calibre	11.2mm; 0.441in
Length	286mm; 11.25in
Length of barrel	152mm; 6in
Weight	1.09kg; 2.4lb
Muzzle velocity	189m/s; 620ft/s
Feed	6-round cylinder

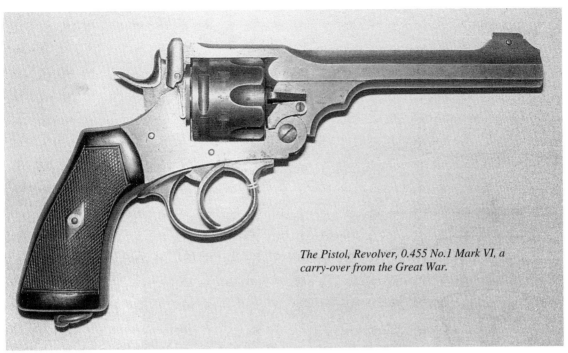

The Pistol, Revolver, 0.455 No.1 Mark VI, a carry-over from the Great War.

1939 had settled down from a series of propellant loadings and bullets into the jacketed Mk VI pattern issued during the war years.

Although many elderly marks of Webley 0.455 pistol were still available in 1939, the main service model between then and 1945 was the Pistol, Revolver, No.1, previously known as the Mk VI. This was something of a handful for it weighed 1.09kg/2.4lb and was 286mm/11.25in long overall. The revolving cylinder held six rounds and the construction was so solid that it could also be used as an effective trench club. Action was either double or single, but in either mode the trigger operation was often stiff and took time and training to master. Consequently, few users could obtain any degree of accuracy at anything other than very close quarters, although the pistol was inherently accurate to considerable ranges.

Great War experience indicated that good and powerful as the 0.455in revolvers might have been, something lighter was desirable for semi-trained or occasional users. Thus there was no large-scale manufacture of 0.455 pistols after 1939 other than clear-up orders for about 26,000 relating to pre-war

contracts. Repair and refurbishment contracts relating to stockpiled pistols were carried out during 1940 by Webley & Scott and the Royal Small Arms Factory at Enfield Lock.

Webley 0.455 revolvers were carried throughout the war years, being finally declared obsolete in 1946. They still crop up in many countries where British influence once held sway and 0.455 Webley ammunition remains commercially available.

The 'something lighter' pistol mentioned above evolved during the 1920s, chambered for a 0.380 (9.6 × 31R) cartridge. The pistol was originally a 1923 Webley police model, a scaled-down version of the 0.455 design and just as solidly made as the original. In 1926 the Royal Small Arms Factory took over the design, introducing so many of their own modifications that the resulting pistol was renamed the Enfield, although the official designation was Pistol, Revolver, No.2 and it remained identifiable as a Webley revolver. Low-rate production commenced in 1930 although official adoption was delayed until 1932.

The intention was that the lighter cartridge would make the 0.380 pistol easier to handle and fire than

More often known as the Enfield, this is the 0.38 Pistol Revolver No.2 Mark 1.

the cumbersome 0.455. The original 0.380 Mk 1 model featured the same single- or double-action mechanism as the 0.455 revolver. As early as 1938 the hammer spur was found to be undesirable as it tended to snag on clothing or equipment, so whenever Mk 1 pistols were returned for repair the hammer spur was machined off and the trigger action lightened. This converted the Enfield pistol

Enfield	
Calibre	9.65mm; 0.38in
Length	260mm; 10.25in
Length of barrel	127mm; 5in
Weight	766gm; 1.68lb
Muzzle velocity	183m/s; 600ft/s
Feed	6-round cylinder

to the double-action only Mk 1* standard. Production was centred at Enfield Lock, with about 150,000 made by mid 1945. In 1940 a further production line was established at Albion Motors, Glasgow, where another 42,516 were manufactured. Components were supplied by numerous sub-contractors.

These totals included the Mk 1**, an expedient model intended to hasten production by omitting the hammer safety stop and a few other details. These pistols proved potentially dangerous for they were prone to fire if they were dropped or knocked. Consequently they were modified back to Mk 1* status after 1945.

Such were the demands for more and more pistols after 1940 that recourse was made to the Webley 0.380 1923 model that gave rise to the Enfield pistol. In 1940 this model was ordered 'as is' and thereafter supplemented the numbers of Enfield pistols in service. The Webley pistol, the Mk IV, resembled the Enfield externally, although the original hammer spur was retained and any general

The Webley 0.38 Mark IV, introduced to supplement the Enfield pistols.

interchange of parts between the two was not possible. Total production was over 100,000, the last contract not being completed until after the war had ended.

British pistol production could not keep pace with demand from 1940 onwards and so once again application was made to the USA. The array of models, calibres and types that resulted was alarmingly large to the point of becoming a quarter-master's nightmare. It seemed that whatever was offered, commercial or military model alike, was purchased to a total of over 400,000 items. But mention must be made of one particular model that, although American in design and manufacturing origin, was so tailored to British requirements that it may be regarded as a British pistol.

This was the Pistol, Revolver, 0.380in, Smith & Wesson No.2. It was originally a police model produced by the Smith & Wesson Arms Company of Springfield, Massachusetts. Small modifications to the swing-out cylinder allowed the loading of six British standard 0.380 cartridges with 200gr/11.53gm jacketed bullets (the same as for the Enfield and the Webley 0.380 pistol), so that these pistols were often known as the 0.38/200. As a design, the 0.38/200 was entirely conventional and sound, with both single- and double-action operation. The barrel length could be 4in/107mm, 5in/127mm or 6in/152mm and the finishes varied as the war continued. The original 1941 production examples had a high-quality, blued finish. This was later omitted to speed supply, while basic wooden butt grips replaced the earlier chequered walnut.

Between 1941 and the end of the war the Smith & Wesson 0.38/200 production total reached 889,203, a large proportion (666,231) being supplied to Britain and Canada under Lend-Lease arrangements (the balance, from early orders, was

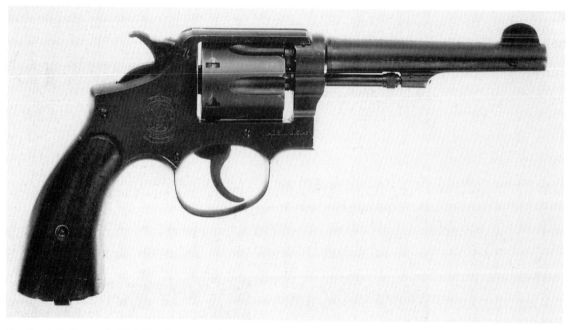

The Smith & Wesson 0.380/200, officially known as the Pistol, Revolver, 0.38, Smith & Wesson No.2.

paid for by Britain). Many pistols sent to Britain ended up with resistance forces all over Europe. The 0.38/200 pistols served on for many years after 1945 and may still be encountered in military service with some nations.

Another non-British pistol used by the British armed forces before 1945 may be dealt with in this section. It was of Belgian origin, another highly successful design from John Moses Browning. He had formed an association with the Belgian

company Fabrique Nationale (FN) at Herstal, Liège, well before the Great War. In 1925 he devised an improved version of his swinging-link locking system for yet another automatic pistol that entered production in 1935 as the 9mm/0.354in Modèle à Grande Puissance (GP), generally known as the GP35. Numerous sub-variants existed, one with a wooden holster that could be clipped to the butt to serve as a shoulder stock. Also available were models with optimistic tangent sights for long-range aiming.

The GP35 remains one of the finest and most widely distributed automatic pistols of all time. Exactly how many have been made is unknown as it is still widely manufactured today in both licensed and plagiarised forms. Well over ten million have been manufactured and there seems to be no end to the type.

As far as pre-1939 sales were concerned, FN soon obtained GP35 orders from all over Europe, only to have them interrupted by the German invasion of Belgium in 1940. The design and production draw-

0.38/200	
Calibre	9.65mm; 0.38in
Length	257mm; 10.125in
Length of barrel	127mm; 5in
Weight	820gm; 1.81lb
Muzzle velocity	198m/s; 650ft/s
Feed	6-round cylinder

A Canadian Sergeant loading his Smith & Wesson 0.380/200 pistol.

ings were spirited away to Britain as the Germans approached Liège. Those drawings were sent to Canada where the John Inglis plant at Toronto manufactured the GP35 in large numbers for delivery to China and the Canadian and the British armed forces under the general name of the Browning High Power. Canadian production omitted all the pre-war accessories such as the shoulder stock/holster.

All who fired the High Power came to appreciate its reliability, good handing qualities and ability to withstand hard use. They also came to appreciate its magazine capacity of thirteen 9 × 19mm Parabellum rounds, a definite asset under combat conditions. The attractions of the High Power led to its acquisition for British commando and special forces with whom it saw out the war. It gradually replaced all the British in-service revolvers over the next two decades. The British thus finally adopted the automatic pistol, even if revolvers did serve on for many years after 1945.

One completely British pistol remains to be

The 9mm Browning High Power automatic. This example was manufactured in Canada by John Inglis.

mentioned, one of a very special nature. This was the Welrod, intended from the outset to be a silent assassination pistol. It was designed by Colonel Dolphin of the Special Operations Executive (SOE) at Aston House, Welwyn, chambered for the 7.65 × 17SR (0.32 ACP) pistol cartridge that proved amenable for firing through sound suppressors while retaining lethal on-target effects at short ranges.

The Welrod was a single-shot pistol with the barrel totally enclosed in a tubular suppressor housing resulting in a virtually soundless firing signature and no muzzle flash. Up to seven cartridges could be stored within the butt, although each had to be individually hand-loaded, the bolt being manually cocked for every shot. The trigger mechanism was very elementary and the overall impression left by the Welrod was that it was not intended to have a long service life.

Few operational details of the Welrod seem to

High-Power	
Calibre	9mm; 0.354in
Length	197mm; 7.75in
Length of barrel	118mm; 4.65in
Weight	1.01kg; 2.44lb
Muzzle velocity	354m/s; 1,150ft/s
Feed	13-round box magazine

*Silent special – the
7.65mm Welrod pistol.*

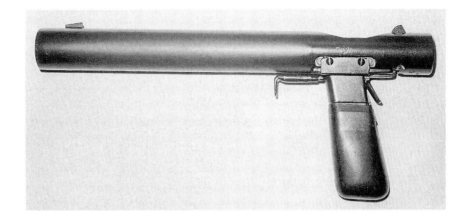

have survived. Only relatively few were ever made by BSA to be sent into occupied Europe from late 1943 onwards. The survivors were nearly all destroyed after 1945 to prevent their possible misuse. Only a few museum examples remain.

AMERICAN ABUNDANCE

The close association between American society and the hand gun was to prove invaluable to the Allies between 1939 and 1945. Thanks to the ever-present market for firearms, especially pistols, in the USA, it took little reorganization for the small arms industry to turn out pistols on a massive scale when they were needed for war. The example of the Smith & Wesson 0.38/200 revolver has already been discussed, but it was far from being the only example of its kind.

To start with the standard American service pistol: this was the Colt M1911 automatic and its later variant the M1911A1. Throughout its life the M1911/M1911A1 proved time and again to be one of the strongest automatic pistols ever devised. As with so many other American small arms, the original M1911 was based on a Browning design chambered for the 0.45 ACP (11.43mm) cartridge, a powerful 'man-stopper' intended for one hit, one neutralization performance against the most deter-

mined human targets. The cartridge can still produce this level of performance and so remains a firm favourite with many pistol users. Not all continue to favour the 0.45 ACP as it produces considerable muzzle blast and to fire any M1911 can be a daunting experience for the recruit. The M1911 and the 0.45 ACP cartridge combination requires training and experience to take full advantage of its considerable capabilities, although once mastered the M1911 can become a devastating and accurate weapon at close ranges.

The M1911 pistol was one of the few American weapons the US Army was able to take to France in 1917. In 1926 the M1911A1 appeared with a revised grip safety, shortened trigger, revised grip contour and some other changes. Thereafter the M1911A1 was the only production model, but the M1911 was retained unchanged and may still be encountered to this day, most of them rebuilt several times over using spare parts.

The US Army entered the Great War with about 75,000 M1911 pistols. By December 1918 Colt had managed to produce 425,000, with another 13,152 coming from the Remington Arms-Union Metallic Cartridge Company. As a result, there were still significant stocks of the M1911 and the M1911A1 still to be found in 1940. British purchases and other sales meant that as soon as the USA entered the war in December 1941 there were once again not enough pistols to equip the rapidly expanding

This text book comparison shows the 0.45 M1911 (top) and the M1911A1 (below).

American forces. Demands for pistols came in from all sides while at the same time every one of America's allies was calling for yet more. Despite all these demands, pistol production was never accorded a high priority for there were always more pressing calls on industrial resources. It also has to be remembered that the M1 Carbine (*see* Chapter 3) was supposed to assume many of the self-defence roles formerly carried out by the pistol, but that never greatly affected the perceived needs for more and more pistols, with the M1911A1 always being the preferred choice.

M1911A1 production by Colt's had never really ceased between the wars. A steady series of minor

export orders from nations such as Argentina and Norway (both of whom eventually negotiated licence-production agreements with Colt's), plus sales to individuals and police forces, kept production ticking over until 1940. Home-based military orders then started to grow. The total for 1941 reached 35,256, compared with 4,693 for the whole of 1940. After 1941 production soared. Colt's were joined by Remington-Rand, the Union Switch & Signal Company, and the Ithaca Gun Company. Barrels were made by the Springfield Armory, the High Standard Manufacturing Company and the Flannery Bolt Company. Numerous other sub-contractors contributed components.

The results were considerable. By the time the war ended, wartime M1911A1 production had reached 1,877,069, production peaking in 1944 with 754,436 delivered. Of this total only a comparatively small number (78,625) were assigned to Lend-Lease, half (39,592) going to the 'British Empire'. Once in Britain some Lend-Lease pistols were modified to fire 0.455 Webley ammunition to ease the local supply situation.

Even with all these huge numbers of M1911A1 pistols being produced, the demand was never entirely met. This repeated the experience of

M1911A1	
Calibre	11.43mm; 0.45in
Length	218mm; 8.6in
Length of barrel	127.7mm; 5.03in
Weight	1.1kg; 2.44lb
Muzzle velocity	262m/s; 860ft/s
Feed	7-round box magazine

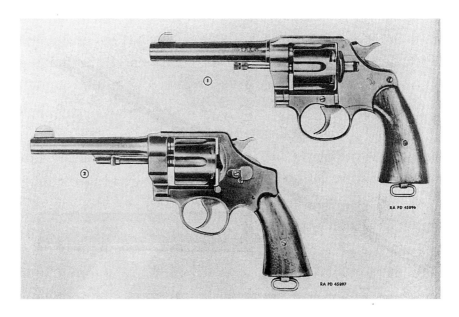

Another comparison, this time between the US 0.45 M1917 revolvers with the Colt model (top) and the Smith & Wesson model (below).

1917–18, when a rapid expansion of M1911 production was planned but took time to get going. Two revolvers were adopted to make up numbers, both chambered for 0.45 ACP and both type-classified as M1917. One came from Smith & Wesson, the other from Colt.

The two were basically similar and both had to be adapted to utilize the 0.45 ACP round. As this is rimless, the rounds had to be held in three-round clips for loading and spent-case ejection. Both revolvers were based on existing designs, the Smith & Wesson being already in production in 1917 for a British order placed in 1915–16, chambered for

the 0.455 Webley cartridge. The change to 0.45 ACP required a change of barrel, cylinder and the clip-loading feature. The Colt M1917 revolver was the 'New Service' model of 1897, already well established in production and chambered for numerous cartridges, including (again) 0.455 Webley.

By the end of 1918, 151,700 Colt M1917 pistols had been delivered to the US Army along with 153,311 Smith & Wesson M1917s. With the war over, these revolvers were withdrawn from service in favour of the M1911/M1911A1, apart from those retained by military police and other security personnel. Batches were disposed of commercially between the wars. In 1940 the remaining stocks were purchased by the British government among the 400,000 US pistols of all kinds procured at that time. Once in Britain the M1917 pistols, being non-standard apart from the surviving 0.455 Webley chambered examples, were issued to home defence and Home Guard units.

The array of pistols purchased from the USA during 1940 and after was enormous. Most were police or paramilitary models produced by Colt's, with others coming from Smith & Wesson. The two

---

Colt Model 1917

Calibre	11.43mm; 0.45in
Length	274mm; 10.8in
Length of barrel	140mm; 5.5in
Weight	1.135kg; 2.5lb
Muzzle velocity	253m/s; 830ft/s
Feed	6-round cylinder

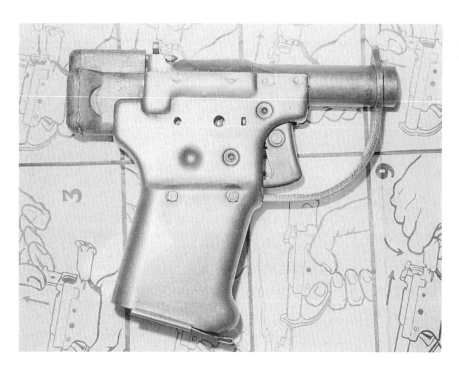

The Liberator pistol, a cheap and basic assassination pistol.

main calibres were 0.38 Smith & Wesson and 0.45 ACP, but there were others. The British purchases must have emptied the commercial stocks of Colts and Smith & Wesson. When the USA entered the war its armed forces suffered accordingly from the consequent supply shortage. Home-based American soldiers therefore often found themselves being issued with some definitely non-type-classified pistols. There were too many to be mentioned here.

Liberator	
Calibre	11.43mm; 0.45in
Length	141mm; 5.55in
Length of barrel	101mm; 3.97in
Weight	454gm; 1lb
Muzzle velocity	ca 250m/s; ca 820ft/s
Feed	single-shot

But mention must be made of one American weapon of the 1941–45 period, the Pistol M1942 Liberator. This was most definitely an odd, non-standard design for it was a cheap, single-shot pistol intended to be issued or para-dropped into enemy occupied areas for aggressively-minded locals to use against their occupiers. The Liberator was promoted by the Office of Strategic Services (OSS) in an attempt to arm resistance forces. For political purposes it was sometimes referred to as the 0.45 Flare Projector or Flare Pistol to disguise its true intent.

The Liberator was truly cheap – each one delivered cost just $2.10. It used steel stampings throughout and the barrel, firing the 0.45 ACP cartridge, was a smooth-bored steel tube. Press fits, pins and rivets kept the pistol together. A trap in the butt held five cartridges for individual loading, with the cocking system and trigger being simple to the point of crudity. There was no extractor so each spent case was ejected by pushing a wooden rod into the muzzle. Each example was delivered as a kit in a sealed, transparent, plastic bag containing the pistol, ten rounds and an illustrated instruction sheet capable of being understood by the illiterate.

Many details relating to the Liberator are still not public. It is known that about one million were made by the Guide Lamp Division of Detroit, Michigan, between June and August 1942, using drawings supplied by the Inland Manufacturing Division; both companies were Divisions of General Motors. It seems that some were used as assassination weapons in parts of the Pacific theatre but precise operational details were, perhaps understandably, not disclosed. Of the total made, only a small proportion appear to have been distributed as intended. It no doubt became apparent that to provide all and sundry with such a weapon could perhaps have its drawbacks. Consequently, most Liberator pistols were later destroyed.

SOVIET DUO

Compared with the myriad pistol models that other Allied armed forces adopted, the Soviet Army of 1941–45 had but two, a revolver and an automatic.

The revolver dated from 1895. The Revolver Nagant obrazets 1895G was originally a Belgian design from the gunsmith Léon Nagant. When the Nagant revolver was adopted by the Tsarist Army the first examples were manufactured in Belgium. A production line was soon established at Tula and from then on the M1895 was regarded as a Russian pistol.

The M1895 fired a unique cartridge. Nagant went to extreme lengths to reduce the leaking of propellant gas from the small gap between the front end of the revolving cylinder and the start of the barrel. As the hammer moved forward for firing, the cylinder was pushed forward towards the barrel until the gap was minimal. Further sealing came from the special cartridge, a 7.62 × 38R round with the flat-nosed bullet entirely located inside the case. The front of the case tapered slightly so, as the cylinder moved forward, the case mouth entered the barrel to form a gas-tight seal when the gun was fired. As the

M1895	
Calibre	7.62mm; 0.30in
Length	230mm; 9.055in
Length of barrel	110mm; 4.35in
Weight	795gm; 1.75lb
Muzzle velocity	272m/s; 892ft/s
Feed	7-round cylinder

trigger was released the cylinder and the case moved back from the barrel for indexing to the next chamber. With hindsight, it became apparent that the complications involved in providing such a tight seal were hardly worth all the effort, but once the M1895 was adopted the gas-seal feature remained, as did the cartridge. Nagant revolvers of the M1895 pattern were also adopted by Greece and Poland.

After the Revolution the Red Army retained the M1895. It remained in production, with a few gaps, until 1942. How many were made is now uncertain but it was in the hundreds of thousands – the total for 1941 alone was 118,453. There were two main models. The so-called Officer's Model was single- and double-action. Intended as issue for NCOs and enlisted users, the Trooper's Model was double-action only, and that double-action was usually stiff and awkward, so accuracy was usually minimal other than at close ranges. The standard of finish for both pistols was usually rather poor, but the M1895 proved itself sturdy and reliable.

By the end of the 1920s the Red Army was investigating the possible adoption of an automatic pistol to replace the M1895 revolver. The round selected for the change was the 7.63 × 25mm Mauser cartridge with slight tolerance changes introduced to become the 7.62mm/0.30in Tokarev or Type P, thereafter the standard Soviet pistol and sub-machine gun cartridge for many years. After numerous competitive trials, the selection finally fell on a Tokarev design adopted in 1930 as the TT-30 (*Tula-Tokareva* M1930). The TT-30 underwent further development to simplify mass

The 7.62mm M1895 revolver, robust and dependable.

7.62mm TT-33, a pistol still likely to be encountered today.

production before series production began at Tula in 1933; thus the full production model became the TT-33.

The 7.62mm TT-33 was based on the well-tried Colt-Browning designs with some variations all its own, such as the hammer mechanism. Once in production it became apparent that the design still had its faults, therefore plans to end production of the M1895 revolver were repeatedly put back, even if it did stop during 1934 only to restart the following year. The main faults of the TT-33 were a tendency for the eight-round box magazine to fall out of the butt unexpectedly and a short service life before the main operating spring fractured. These problems had been eliminated by 1941. Thereafter the TT-33 proved to be a reliable and sturdy weapon.

How many TT-33s were manufactured is also uncertain, but the numbers were substantial. The last available annual production figures were for 1942, when 161,485 were delivered. TT-33 production in the Soviet Union ceased in 1954, but continued for some while after then in other nations. One was China where it is known as the 7.62mm Type 54.

Variants of the 7.62mm TT-33 were the Models R-3 and R-4, both 0.22 training models.

FRENCH PISTOLS

It is always unwise to make definitive statements regarding small arms, but of the pistols in service in 1939 the distinction of being the oldest design must surely go to the French. The pistol in question was a revolver, the 11mm mle 1873, together with its close counterpart, the 11mm mle 1874, the model numbers denoting the year of acceptance.

The mle 1873 was intended for use by the rank and file and so it was issued without an attractive final finish for the metal surfaces. By contrast, the mle 1874 was intended for officers and so had a blued finish, with further recognition features coming from the flutes on the cylinder. The mle

TT-33	
Calibre	7.62mm; 0.30in
Length	195mm; 7.68mm
Length of barrel	116mm; 4.57in
Weight	854gm; 1.88lb
Muzzle velocity	420m/s; 1,378ft/s
Feed	8-round box magazine

1874 was also marginally lighter and shorter than the mle 1873. Both weapons fired an 11 × 17.5mm (nominal) cartridge, originally containing black powder but altered to a smokeless propellant in 1890, a change that pushed the strength of the pistol frame to its limits.

Production for the military, at the Manufacture d'armes de Saint-Etienne (MAS), was completed by 1886, although both models were also manufactured for commercial sales. No fewer than 438,005 military examples were made and thus the revolvers were carried throughout the Great War with many surviving to 1939 to experience yet another war. By then most of these revolvers were issued to colonial troops, although some remained in mainland France. Mention can be found of these revolvers being used by resistance units, some apparently bored out to fire 0.45 ACP ammunition,

mle 1874	
Calibre	11mm; 0.433in
Length	235mm; 9.25in
Length of barrel	112mm; 4.4in
Weight	1.01kg; 2.22lb
Muzzle velocity	190m/s; 623ft/s
Feed	6-round cylinder

a procedure to be adopted only under extreme circumstances and with great caution, considering the age and stress limits of the frame.

The 11mm revolvers were something of a heavy handful and therefore in 1892 a new revolver firing a 8 × 27R cartridge was introduced. (The choice of

Two of the oldest revolver models likely to be encountered in 1939, the French 11mm mle 1873 (top) and mle 1874 (below).

mle 1892	
Calibre	8mm; 0.315in
Length	235mm; 9.25in
Length of barrel	118.5mm; 4.665in
Weight	792gm; 1.75lb
Muzzle velocity	225m/s; 738ft/s
Feed	6-round cylinder

The French 7.65mm mle 1935A.

8mm was apparently made so that the barrels could be manufactured using 8mm mle 1886 Lebel rifle machinery.) The revolver was the 8mm mle 1892, also known as the Modèle d'Ordonnance or the Lebel, a sturdy and well-made weapon with no rank-related distinctions for its users. The mle 1892 was considered an advanced design for its day. It was the first European revolver to have a swing-out cylinder for loading and case ejection, even if the cylinder did swing out to the right rather than to the more convenient left.

For some reason, military production of the mle 1892 ceased in 1915, just at a time when the demand for pistols was about to expand enormously. The reliable mle 1892 continued to remain the standard French military revolver throughout the Great War and in 1939 it still held that distinction, later being used to equip Free French units. Many survived the war to remain in French service for years after 1945.

The extreme demands for pistols arising from the Great War were largely met by the purchase of pistols from Spain and the USA. One of the Spanish purchases was a direct copy of a standard Smith & Wesson revolver chambered for the French 8mm cartridge. About 500,000 of these were purchased to become known as the 8mm mle 1892 dit 'du commerce' to differentiate them from the French mle 1892 revolver. Many of these were still to be found in 1939.

Also still in existence were two models of a 7.65mm automatic, also purchased from Spain. They were known simply as the Star and the Ruby,

both standard commercial pistols that proved to be perfectly serviceable for military use, even if they were considered as rather underpowered for trench combat and their long-term durability was suspect. About one million examples of the Star and the Ruby had been acquired by 1918. Of the two the Ruby fared better than the Star in wear terms so only a limited number of Stars remained in 1939, whereas the Ruby was still a standard issue. Their cartridge was the 7.65mm ACP (7.65 × 17SR) and so these pistols required a non-standard ammunition supply by 1939.

This was because in 1935 the French Army had decided to adopt an entirely new pistol cartridge for the standard automatic pistol intended to replace all existing models then in service. The pistol was the 7.65mm M1935A, later replaced in production by the M1935S. The cartridge was the 7.65 × 19.5mm,

mle 1935S	
Calibre	8mm; 0.315in
Length	188mm; 7.4in
Length of barrel	104mm; 4.1in
Weight	795gm; 1.75lb
Muzzle velocity	345m/s; 1,132ft/s
Feed	8-round box magazine

The French 7.65mm mle 1935S.

usually known as the 7.65mm Longue, which was also used by the 7.65mm mle 1938 MAS sub-machine gun (*see* Chapter 4). Neither the pistol nor its cartridge was destined to be adopted by any country outside French territory (other than the German occupation forces). Designed by Charles Petter of the Société Alsacienne de Construction Méchanique (SACM), the original model, the M1935A, was little more than a modified variant of the Colt/Browning M1911. The main production variant, the M1935S, had some slight construction alterations to assist in production at several government arsenals, the butt was reshaped to make the grip more comfortable and it was slightly shorter overall.

The full number of M1935A and M1935S pistols produced has not been found recorded. It is known that production proceeded with no apparent sense of urgency. SACM delivered only 1,900 between 1938 and 1940, while MAS had produced only 1,404. Other lines were established or planned at Chatelleraut (MAC), Tulle (MAT) and the Société d'Applications Electrique et Méchaniques (SAGEM). The pistols could therefore have had little influence on the events of 1940, the lack of numbers being accompanied by the poor on-target effects delivered by the underpowered cartridge. Yet these pistols were still around in 1945, having been issued to some Free French units, with some production even restarting to ensure that the M1935S remained a military police pistol for many years.

11 Hand Grenades

The hand grenade fell out of favour during the decades following the Napoleonic Wars. It had a brief resurrection during the American Civil War, but the first indications of its modern revival came during the Russo-Japanese War of 1905. It took the Great War to bring the grenade to its current level of favour as an established infantry weapon.

Grenades developed for anti-tank warfare were mentioned in Chapter 9. The less specialized high-explosive hand grenade had by 1939 divided into two main types, offensive and defensive. The offensive grenade was, and still is, intended for throwing during an attack, creating blast, noise and flash to distract and disorientate an enemy. This has to be accomplished with the minimum of risk to the attacker who will want to follow-up rapidly and exploit the created effects. By contrast, the defensive grenade generates lethal fragments as well as blast and noise to disable the enemy. With defensive grenades users have to take cover to avoid becoming casualties themselves. Most defensive grenades had, and can still have, a lethal radius greater than the usual throwing range of about 30m or 33yd.

In 1939 all but a few of the hand grenades fielded by the Allies were of the defensive type. They were all similar, having small explosive charges inside ovoid, cast-steel or iron bodies to be detonated by a

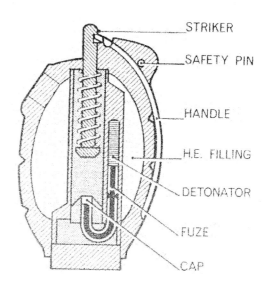

STRIKER

SAFETY PIN

HANDLE

H.E. FILLING

DETONATOR

FUZE

CAP

The No.36M Mills Bomb, with a cutaway section on the right.

short-delay igniter. The body walls were serrated on the outside, supposedly to assist the formation of lethal fragments. Research and experience later showed that to control the fragment size any serrations have to be inside the body. All too often 'pineapple' pattern grenades simply fragment haphazardly into oversize lumps and dust, no matter where and how the external serrations are notched. Little was done to correct this until after 1945 so the soldiers of 1939–45 could at least use the serrations as positive grip surfaces for sweaty or wet hands.

Offensive grenades are supposed to create a minimum of fragments but a maximum of blast, flash and sound. Their explosive charges are held in thin metal casings or, in some instances, plastic, fibre or fabric containers.

Rifle grenades of the type much employed during Great War trench warfare were hardly used by the Allies after 1940. The French retained a few veterans from before 1918 (such as the Vivien

Bessière grenade) but to little effect. The main reason for the neglect of this grenade was that firing most of the types available between 1939 and 1945 inflicted damaging stresses on the rifles involved. Wrecking rifles to deliver small amounts of high explosive over limited ranges was not cost-effective. Using rifles to launch anti-tank grenades was another matter – they were frequently all the infantry had with which to counter tanks.

As most hand grenades were similar in essentials, they will be dealt with by type.

DEFENSIVE GRENADES

The archetype of the World War 2 defensive grenade was the British No.36M, the Mills bomb. Developed during the Great War from the earlier No.5 and No.23, the No.36M utilized the widely adopted 'mousetrap' arming mechanism that

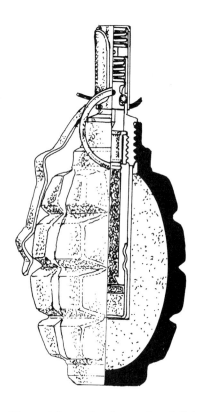

One of the most famous hand grenades of all time, the Russian/Soviet F-1.

required the removing of a safety pin while a side-mounted lever was held closed. Throwing the grenade released the spring-loaded, fly-off lever to initiate a 4 to 7sec delay before the grenade detonated. As the No.36M weighed 773gr/1.7lb it could be thrown about 25m/27yd, a range achievable by many other similar grenades. The No.36M was widely used by British and associated forces, including resistance units, throughout World War 2 and was not replaced by a more modern design until long after 1945. It remained in production in India and Pakistan until the end of the 1990s and remains a service store with many nations. The No.36M was certainly one of the most successful hand grenade designs of all time.

The main rival for such an accolade could be the Soviet F-1. Although it originated during the early 1940s, the F-1 appeared to be a somewhat dated design. Often of crude and unfinished appearance, it became an evocative symbol of Soviet opposition to the German invasion. After 1945 it repeated the process by becoming a further symbol, this time of Marxist 'freedom fighters' and social insurgents. The F-1 has been produced in millions and is still in production in Bulgaria, Poland and Romania, although now with updated fuzes.

The US Army's Mk 2A1 was similar in appearance to the Soviet F-1, which is not really surprising since both were modelled on the French mle 1916 grenade, also known as the Grenade DF. This Great War design was still used by the French Army in 1939–40. The mle 1916 did not survive for long after 1945 as it had been scheduled for replacement from 1937 onwards. In the event, few of the mle 1937 grenades, which were lighter than the mle 1916 type and contained more explosive in a non-serrated, cast-iron body, were manufactured in time for 1940. The type was not issued on a large scale until after 1945.

The US Mk 2A1 could be converted to a rifle grenade by attaching to it a tail unit that allowed it to be launched from the muzzle launcher unit for the M9A1 anti-tank grenade (*see* Chapter 9). Still retained and produced in Taiwan, Turkey and a few other nations, the Mk 2A1 was manufactured in huge quantities. Between July 1940 and August 1945 American industry managed to manufacture no fewer than 87,320,000 grenades. This massive total included all types of grenade in American service; but the largest proportion must have been the Mk 2A1. It has not been possible to discover the corresponding grenade output totals for the other Allies.

One of the few stick-pattern grenades used by any Allied nation between 1939 and 1945 was the Soviet RGD-33, introduced in 1933. The RGD-33 had a TNT warhead and an igniter delay of only 3.6sec. One feature of this grenade was that the cylindrical warhead was surrounded by a serrated steel sleeve. This could be removed if the grenade were thrown as an offensive weapon.

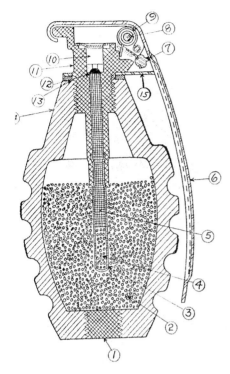

*Cross section the American Mark 2A1 grenade,
usually known as the Pineapple Grenade.*

OFFENSIVE GRENADES

In common with the other Allied nations, the British
Army entered the Second World War without an
offensive grenade. One was not introduced until late
1940 when the No.69 pattern was approved for
service. This differed from other contemporary
grenades in several respects, for it had a Bakelite
plastic body and an all-ways percussion fuze. The
fuze was armed by unscrewing a cap to reveal a
length of fabric tape; this was grasped as the grenade
was thrown. The act of throwing pulled a safety pin
from the fuze, leaving it free to detonate when it
landed.

The No.82 grenade, introduced in mid-1943 and
intended for issue to airborne forces, was also
known as the Gammon grenade. It used the same
percussion fuze as the No.69 type and when issued
it contained no explosive. As airborne troops went
into action carrying a small amount of plastic
explosive for demolitions, the idea was that a piece
could be inserted into the No.82's fabric container
and sealed there by an elastic band enclosure. The
grenade could then be thrown as with the No.69.
The advantage of this arrangement was that users
could vary the amount of plastic explosive to suit
the tactical situation. A small charge would produce
little more than noise and flash, while a large one
could bring down structures.

*The British No.69 grenade had an 'all-ways'
impact fuze.*

The Soviet offensive grenade was the RG-42, with the same fly-off fuze as the F-1. The cylindrical body contained pressed TNT inside a tin-plate cover. The RG-42 is still produced in Poland and Romania and remains in service with several countries formerly under Soviet influence, as well as China.

The American offensive grenades were the Mk 3A1 and the Mk 3A2. The cylindrical Mk 3A2 unusually had a pressed-fibre body, although the earlier model involved cardboard. They used a similar type of fuze to that on the Mk 2A1 grenade.

The French Army of 1940 employed the mle OF as its offensive grenade. It was ovoid in shape and had a light aluminium body. The same design was also used to contain smoke or incendiary mixtures. All the wartime Allies employed smoke and incendiary hand grenades, but there were too many types for it to be practicable to mention them all here.

The Soviet RG-42 offensive grenade is still marketed to this day.

French soldier about to throw an OF offensive grenade.

12 Portable Flamethrowers

Flamethrowers are not usually issued to the infantry. They are customarily employed by combat engineers; but, since many infantry battalions contain personnel trained to carry out routine combat engineer duties, they often handled flamethrowers. No soldier likes the flamethrower in any form. As mentioned elsewhere, the fear of fire is a basic emotion so that the appearance of flame as an offensive weapon is never welcomed. On the other side of the coin, many flamethrowers were as likely to harm their users as the enemy. The very appearance of a flamethrower was usually met with countermeasures, including the turning of every available weapon against the user.

Between 1939 and 1945 the flamethrower was converted from the limited performance, unreliable systems left over from the Great War, to much more compact, dependable and efficient weapons. They proved devastating against the defensive bunkers and field fortifications prepared by the Japanese throughout the Pacific theatre. Flamethrowers were often the only weapons that could persuade Japanese defenders to leave their positions. Elsewhere, flamethrowers proved their worth time and again.

This chapter will deal only with portable flamethrowers; other types included self-propelled systems carried by armoured vehicles. Systems such as those were not usually issued to the infantry, although within the British Army the Universal Carrier equipped with a flamethrower (the Wasp) was included within mechanized infantry battalions by 1945.

The functioning of all flamethrowers in use between 1939 and 1945 remained much as it had done when they were first used in combat by the German Army in 1914. Fuel in one tank was propelled by gas under pressure from another. The fuel was directed via a hose to a nozzle where it was ignited by electrical or other means. The resultant flame was then carried on a jet of burning fuel to the target. This simply described technique was sometimes varied by the use of slow-burning explosives to provide the operating pressure.

FRENCH AND SOVIET SYSTEMS

As far as can be determined, the French infantry did not possess flamethrowers in 1939 and 1940 and there is little to be found regarding any being deployed elsewhere in the French Army during May and June 1940. The only French portable flamethrower recorded was the P4, a backpack unit with a single cylinder containing the fuel and pressure tanks. It was a weapon with a very short range, only 10–12m/11–13yd, and contained fuel sufficient for only a few short flame bursts.

Equally little is known of Soviet Army portable flamethrowers either. Mention can be found of two models, the ROKS-2 and the ROKS-3. The two models differed in their backpack components. The ROKS-2 carried the fuel oil in a rectangular container apparently configured to make it look like an ordinary regulation backpack. On the ROKS-3 the fuel container was an undisguised cylinder. On both models the flame gun resembled a rifle, complete with shoulder stock.

The Soviet ROKS-2 portable flamethrower with its pressure tanks disguised as a backpack.

ROKS-2	
Weight	22.7kg; 50lb
Fuel capacity	9l; 2gall
Range	36.5–45m; 40–50yd
Duration of fire	6–8sec

Both systems were rather heavy at about 22.7kg/50lb and could project flame for about 8sec. The maximum possible range was of the order of 36 to 45m (40 to 50yd).

AMERICAN FLAMES

Perhaps the most complete account of flamethrowers deployed between 1939 and 1945 is the American one, thanks mainly to their thorough and open account keeping. As late as 1940 the US Army did not have any flamethrowers, a result of their experiences of the weapon during 1917 and 1918, when the few crude systems then available were regarded as failures. A change of priorities during

1940 meant that their first experimental example, the E1, was produced for the Chemical Warfare Service by a non-governmental concern, the Kincaid Company of New York.

The E1 had a heavy (31.75kg/70lb) backpack arrangement with an unreliable, battery-powered ignition system. Further development by the Kincaid Company resulted in the E1R1. Despite still being unsatisfactory in many ways, the E1R1 was produced in limited numbers for training and familiarization purposes, a few seeing limited action in New Guinea during 1942. Continued development of the E1R1, considered as too delicate, awkward to operate and unreliable, resulted in the improved Portable Flame-Thrower M1. The M1 was first used in combat on Guadalcanal in January 1943. Although it could work well, the ignition system remained unreliable and the range was limited.

The invention of the thickened petroleum mixture known as napalm converted the M1 into a much more reliable and efficient flame weapon. The addition of aluminium-based substances known as soaps to petroleum enabled flamethrowers to project a much denser flame jet to a longer range

M1A1	
Weight	31.8kg; 70lb
Fuel capacity	18.2l; 4gall
Range	41–45m; 45–50yds
Duration of fire	8–10sec

A US Marine Corps M1A1 in action on Saipan, June 1944.

*M1A1 portable
flamethrower in action,
New Georgia, 1943.*

193

M2-2

Weight   30.9–32.7kg; 62–72lb
Fuel capacity   18.2l; 4gall
Range   23–36.5m; 25–40yd
Duration of fire   8–9sec

(46m/50yd). There was also the added advantage that the fuel would adhere to a target for the flame to do its work with greater efficiency. Converting the M1 to utilize the new fuel resulted in the M1A1.

Some 14,000 M1A1s were produced from mid-1943 onwards, but the old battery-powered ignition problems remained. They were not eliminated until the M2-2 was introduced in July 1944. The M2-2 differed by having the electrical circuit replaced by six pyrotechnic cartridges held in a revolver-pattern device situated close to the flame-gun jet-nozzle. As the operator pressed the flame-gun trigger, a cartridge produced a shower of sparks to ignite the fuel jet. Six cartridges could thus produce six flame jets – usually sufficient to empty the fuel tank contents – with a high degree of certitude.

No fewer than 25,000 M2-2 flamethrowers were manufactured, the first seeing action on Guam in July 1944, although M1A1s were still to be found when the war ended. M2-2s were used wherever the US Army fought during World War 2, but even that was regarded as not entirely satisfactory. It was considered to be too heavy and uncomfortable to carry, and the fuel content was too limited for many combat situations. But it was almost certainly one of the best of its kind in use anywhere before 1945.

The planned replacement for the M2-2 did not appear until after the war ended. A development programme involving a simple, lightweight, one-shot, disposable flamethrower was carried out on a low priority basis from the start of 1943. Progress was so slow that the project had not reached the troop-trial phase by the time the war ended and the entire project was then dropped.

BRITISH EQUIPMENTS

As with the US Army, and for much the same reasons, it was 1940 before the British Army decided to adopt the flamethrower. Their first attempt at one was not over-inspired since it consisted of no fewer than four fuel tanks and one pressure cylinder on a metal-frame backpack, all connected to a flame gun configured like a rifle. This was the Flame-Thrower, Portable, No.1, Mk 1, generally known as the Marsden. It proved to be unreliable during troop trials and it also emerged as too heavy at 38kg/84lb. The range was limited to 18 to 23m/20 to 25yd under ideal conditions. Consequently the Marsden did not proceed very far.

The next attempt was much more successful and was no doubt influenced by examination of captured examples of the German Flammenwerfer 40. This design involved a doughnut-shaped fuel tank, one selected because it offered the maximum possible volume within a pressurized container. The British approach improved on the German layout by locating a spherical gas pressure tank in the well of the fuel tank, making the whole equipment compact and fairly comfortable to carry, even if the ready-for-use weight, complete with a lightweight flame gun, was 29kg/64lb.

Known universally as the 'Lifebuoy' from its shape, the Flame-Thrower, Portable, No.2 was ordered into production in 1942. Unfortunately, trials of the production version revealed defects which meant that the first batch, the Mk 1, had to be relegated to training duties only. It was early 1944 before the fully approved version, the Mk 2, was in series production, only for it to be terminated in July

---

Lifebuoy

Weight   29kg; 64lb
Fuel capacity   18.2l; 4gall
Range   27.4–36.5m; 30–40yd
Duration of fire   10sec

Flame-Thrower,
Portable, No.2, Mark 1
– the Lifebuoy.

of that year. The Lifebuoy was used in action in Europe and the Far East and was considered effective, but after 1945 it was not retained for long.

Mention must also be made here of one of the 'emergency' flame devices rushed into use following Dunkirk when the invasion of the United Kingdom seemed imminent. Measures ranged from placing fuel tanks behind walls along roads likely to be used by the invader (the fuel was simply allowed to pour into the road before it was ignited), to the more official Flame-Thrower, Transportable, No.1, or Harvey.

Even if it was an official equipment, the Harvey was crude and simple. Apparently modelled on the Great War *Flammenwerfer* introduced by the Germans in 1914, it consisted of a cylindrical fuel tank and a commercial gas-pressure cylinder

mounted together on an upright, wheeled frame to be pushed along in the same manner as a porter's barrow. The two large cylinders were connected to a flexible hose 10m/11yd long on the end of which was a pipe nozzle. Exactly how the fuel was ignited is uncertain, but it appears that a flame was applied when the fuel first appeared from the nozzle, or perhaps the target was sprayed with fuel which was then ignited. The maximum range of the Harvey was supposed to be 46–55m/50–60yd and the device contained enough fuel for a 12sec burst.

The Harvey was issued to the Home Guard who no doubt regarded it with suspicion. Thankfully it was never called upon to be used in earnest. It was discovered that it could be modified for smoke-screen production so some were later sent to the Middle East for this purpose.

195

13   Infantry Artillery

Infantry guns grew out of the trench warfare of 1914–18, providing the infantry with artillery assets under their own control. This enabled them to have a more flexible method of providing fire support where and when needed and, if the opportunity arose, providing an ability to depart from the rigid artillery barrages that accompanied most trench battles. The mortar was one outcome of this adoption of infantry artillery, but many European armies continued to employ infantry guns and howitzers. This often meant the diversion of mountain guns, already light and compact, to the trenches, but more specialized artillery pieces were developed specifically for the infantry.

Infantry guns had to be reasonably small and light to provide them with the mobility and ease of handling that infantry actions demanded. Ranges did not need to be extensive since most firing was direct, using open sights. The usual allotment was between two and four to a battalion.

Despite the attractions of integrated artillery for the infantry not every nation adopted such a policy. Adding artillery to the infantry battalion or brigade took away personnel from other functions. By 1918 infantry battalions had altered considerably from being a collection of rifle companies. Riflemen had been joined by signallers, machine gunners, mortarmen, chemical warfare specialists, combat engineers, anti-tank teams, drivers for numerous vehicles and others. Battalion strengths were rarely adjusted to meet this diversification of effort away from the rifle companies and so the addition of artillery was usually resisted.

The British Army was one that decided to adopt mortars rather than artillery although, as will be related, they nearly succumbed to the lure of the infantry gun. By the end of the war a degree of compromise between mortars and artillery had been reached with the advent of recoilless artillery, enabling the foot soldier to carry a highly portable and effective weapon system without any great diversion of men to look after and fire the weapons.

FRENCH GUN

As already mentioned in Chapter 9, the French 37mm/1.46in mle 1916 TR trench gun assumed an extra role against the early tanks, despite the gun's short range and lack of any really effective armour-piercing ammunition. The mle 1916 TR was, in effect, a half-scale version of the famous 75mm mle 1897 field gun with the barrel cut back to 22 calibres (814mm/32in) so that the maximum range was limited to 2,400m/2,615yd, quite sufficient for trench warfare. On tow, the mle 1916 was carried on wheels that were removed as the gun was emplaced. If required, the gun could be broken down into three loads for pack transport – the total weight was 108kg/238lb.

The mle 1916 was retained as an infantry weapon after 1918, despite the adoption of the infantry mortar. The main reason was that the gun was supposed to provide anti-tank defence as well as fire support. Consequently the mle 1916 was still in widespread service when the Germans invaded France in 1940; the total French inventory was then 1,036. They were swept away during the events that followed and thereafter were never heard of again.

Peacetime training with a 37mm mle 1916 TRP trench gun, still in service in 1940.

A 37mm mle 1916 TRP gun on its wheeled carriage – it was more common for the mle 1916 to be manually carried into action.

BRITISH ATTEMPTS

By 1940 the British Army was painfully aware that its German and Italian opponents were using infantry guns to good effect, so, despite the established policy of making do with mortars, the call was to supply the infantry with similar weapons. That call was resisted until early 1942, in the aftermath of a programme to develop a 3.7in/94mm gun for use in tanks and a self-propelled mounting. To save time and resources, it was decided to adopt a cut-down section of barrel from the production of 3.7in anti-aircraft guns and ally it with the breech from a 25-pounder gun-howitzer. The combination was supposed to fit into 6-pounder tank-gun mantlets and fire existing 3.7in mountain-howitzer ammunition.

This dog's dinner of an approach proved to be ineffective as tank armament, but, as there was still a degree of interest in the infantry gun, it was

197

An example of the ill-fated British 95mm Infantry Howitzer on a testing range.

decided to adapt the design to become a towed infantry weapon. The ordnance remained much as for the abortive tank project but was now allied to a modified 6-pounder anti-tank gun-recoil system. A box trail and shield were added, the result being named the 95mm Infantry Howitzer to avoid confusion with other weapons.

As the existing gun production facilities had quite enough to do already, the prototype was produced by Thornycroft of Basingstoke during 1942. Extensive trials followed, revealing that all was not well with the piece. There seems to have been a rush into production before the trials were completed, which was unfortunate. The 95mm

The 3in Smith Gun, one of the more unusual of the British emergency guns of 1940 and after.

Infantry Howitzer revealed a host of shortcomings. The carriage was prone to turn over when on tow behind its proposed tracked carrier and the recoil system gave constant trouble. During 1944 an extensive redesign was proposed, but by then there was no longer any pressing need for infantry artillery while the personnel necessary to serve and maintain such a gun were still in short supply. By late 1944 the entire project had been quietly terminated.

There was one other British artillery piece that could be regarded as an infantry gun. It was the Smith Gun introduced in late 1940, yet another of the several 'pipe guns' hastily produced after Dunkirk to make up the lack of many forms of weapon; the Blacker Bombard and Northover Projector have been mentioned elsewhere. Despite being an extemporized weapon, the Smith Gun

provides a remarkable design study, especially with regard to its configuration in action.

The 80.9mm/3.185in smooth-bored barrel (nominally described as 3in) could be moved in one arc only, but since the weapon was turned on to its right-hand metal disc wheel for firing, this movement catered for the elevation. Traverse was introduced by pushing the barrel around on the wheel hub. There was a shield and the upper wheel added further protection for the crew. The gun was manufactured by using readily available, commercial steel components bolted together. Gun and limber were towed behind a light van or saloon car, using a lunette attached to the muzzle.

The Smith Gun was supposed to act as an anti-tank gun as well as firing high explosive. Both types of breech-loaded projectile were based on existing mortar bombs, with the propellant charges in small

76.2mm Infantry Gun Model 1927 (76-27), as much a German infantry gun by 1945 as it was for the Soviet Army.

tinplate containers. The maximum combat range firing high explosive was 458m/500yd with reasonable accuracy; the anti-tank range was less than half that. There was provision on the gun to carry ten rounds ready to fire while another forty could be carried on a limber.

When it was first presented to a somewhat incredulous Ordnance Board, the Smith Gun was condemned as unsatisfactory on several counts. Yet it was adopted, probably because it was the Smith gun or nothing. The Home Guard were the main recipients, with whom it was retained it until 1945.

SOVIET STALWART

The pre-1941 Red Army remained an ardent advocate of infantry artillery, despite the introduction of the infantry mortar. There were two classes of gun involved, one being the series of 37 and 45mm regimental guns that also served as anti-tank weapons (*see* Chapter 9). The second was a 76.2mm/3in gun introduced in 1927 and destined to be one of the most widely produced and used infantry guns ever.

The 76.2mm gun was the Model 1927 (76-27). It was the latest in a series of specialized infantry guns that began with the stubby little 37mm/1.456in Model 1915R. Then there was a 76.2mm Model 10P

produced by Putilov. Both of these Great War veterans were retained for some years after the Civil War but by 1941 they were rarities, assuming that any survived until then as other than reserve weapons. Both were very basic designs, built more for durability than ballistic finesse.

The 76-27 followed much the same durable lines, but considerable thought went into the design details. To save on production costs the ordnance did not have a conventional breech. The breech block had threads that simply engaged into corresponding threads inside the barrel – there was no breech ring. A shield and large steel disc wheels provided protection for the crew and the gun itself. The overall design was sound and sturdy. The performance was also very acceptable. The 16.5 calibre barrel could deliver a 6.21kg/13.7lb high-explosive projectile to 8,555m/9,350yd. The weight in action was 780kg/1,720lb.

Exactly how many were manufactured is now uncertain but there must have been thousands. This can be deduced from the total impressed by the Germans after July 1941. By the end of 1943 there were 1,815 in service with German infantry battalions serving on all fronts. The 76-27, known to the Germans as the 7.62cm IKH 290(r), became an established German infantry weapon. They modified the fire controls to accommodate German sights and even went to the length of manufacturing

A 76-27 emplaced somewhere along the Central Front, early 1944.

their own ammunition for the type; during 1943 no fewer than 1,219,000 projectiles were manufactured for the 76-27.

The 76-27 was still in Soviet Army service when the war ended and the type served on for a few more years

AMERICAN INNOVATION

When the US Army arrived in France in 1917 it was issued with the French 37mm mle 1916 trench gun mentioned above. The troops do not appear to have been particularly impressed with the little gun as it was soon withdrawn from service once the war was over. The concept of a highly portable gun was met by weapons such as the 75mm/2.95in Pack Howitzer M1A1, designed for use by mountain artillery and other special units but organized as part of the artillery.

However, when the US Army landed in north Africa in 1943, it had Infantry Cannon Companies specially tasked with the close forward support of infantry units. They were equipped with a short 105mm/4.134in howitzer originally intended for airborne units. This was the 105mm Howitzer M3 with the ordnance being a shortened (16 calibres) version of that on the 105mm M2 field howitzer. The split-trail carriage had several advanced features, one being stub axles that could be reversed and raised to allow the carriage to rest on a firing pedestal for firing stability. The Howitzer M3 had an extreme range of 6,633m/7,250yd firing a standard HE M1 projectile. The weight was 1,133 kg/2,495lb.

Almost as soon as the Infantry Cannon Companies had been formed and deployed the US Army had second thoughts. By the end of 1943 the companies had been disbanded, their personnel and howitzers being allocated to other priorities.

The 105mm Howitzer M3, a short-lived attempt to provide infantry units with close support, that passed to other duties after 1943.

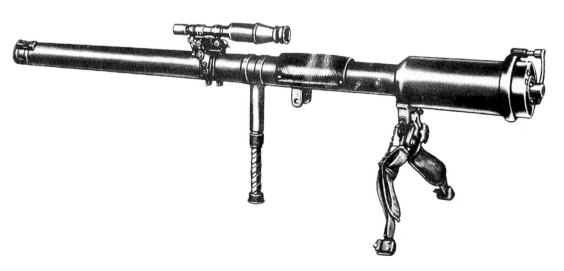

57mm Recoilless Rifle M18 introduced into US Army service in late 1944.

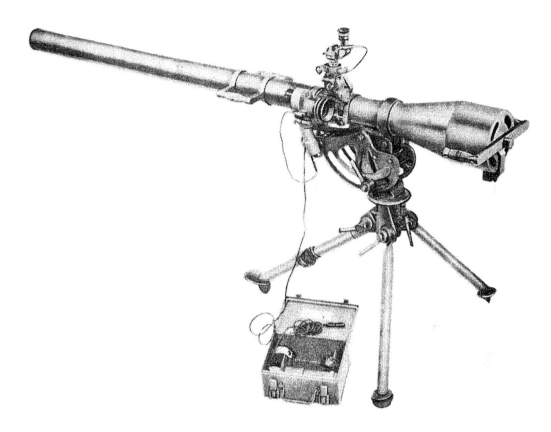

75mm Recoilless Rifle M20, first produced in September 1944.

Production of the Howitzer M3 continued until 1945, the final total being 2,580. None were allocated for the Lend-Lease programme.

US infantry units therefore went without their own integrated artillery until they encountered the German recoilless guns. It was immediately appreciated that the scope for such weapons within infantry formations would be considerable. The Small Arms Branch at Frankford Arsenal was charged with investigating such a possibility. Two recoilless guns emerged, their main designers being William J. Kroeger and C. Walton Musser.

One gun had a calibre of 57mm/2.244in and the other 75mm/2.95in. Both were termed as Rifles to denote their infantry function. Their development

took time so it was late 1944 before firm orders for a thousand of each were placed and production was planned. It could not start quickly as two factors became apparent. One was that full preproduction development work had to be completed. By the time that was finished, to find the production capacity presented something of a problem, so the lighter weapon, the 57mm Recoilless Rifle M18, was produced in Canada by the Dominion Engineering Works at Quebec. The 75mm Recoilless Rifle M20 was manufactured by the Miller Printing Machine Company of Pittsburgh.

Both guns were deployed operationally. About a hundred guns were sent direct to Europe in March 1945, just in time for some combat experience to be

A 75mm Recoilless Rifle M20 in action .

gained. More went to the Pacific theatre to take part in the Okinawa campaign. In both theatres the light weight and hitting power of the two guns were much appreciated. The 57mm M18 was light enough at 18.33kg/40.4lb to be carried by one soldier and fired from the shoulder. The heavier 75mm M20 (46.75kg/103lb) was best fired from a machine-gun tripod. The two were really direct-fire weapons, but the 75mm M20, with a range of 6,504m/7,000yd, could be adapted for indirect laying.

For infantry fire missions both weapons could fire high-explosive and anti-personnel canister projectiles. For anti-tank defence HEAT ammunition was available. Both proved highly effective as bunker-busters.

The guns arrived too late to have much effect on the course of World War 2. The production total of the 57mm M18 was 951 and of the 75mm M20 was 1,238; more were produced after the war ended. While the 75mm M20 faded out of service after the Korean War, the 57mm M18 remains in widespread service around the world, Brazil maintaining the weapon and its ammunition in production until at least the late 1990s.

Index